Network Reliability

Scrivener Publishing
100 Cummings Center, Suite 541J
Beverly, MA 01915-6106

Performability Engineering Series
Series Editors: Krishna B. Misra (kbmisra@gmail.com)
and John Andrews (John.Andrews@nottingham.ac.uk)

Scope: A true performance of a product, or system, or service must be judged over the entire life cycle activities connected with design, manufacture, use and disposal in relation to the economics of maximization of dependability, and minimizing its impact on the environment. The concept of performability allows us to take a holistic assessment of performance and provides an aggregate attribute that reflects an entire engineering effort of a product, system, or service designer in achieving dependability and sustainability. Performance should not just be indicative of achieving quality, reliability, maintainability and safety for a product, system, or service, but achieving sustainability as well. The conventional perspective of dependability ignores the environmental impact considerations that accompany the development of products, systems, and services. However, any industrial activity in creating a product, system, or service is always associated with certain environmental impacts that follow at each phase of development. These considerations have become all the more necessary in the 21st century as the world resources continue to become scarce and the cost of materials and energy keep rising. It is not difficult to visualize that by employing the strategy of dematerialization, minimum energy and minimum waste, while maximizing the yield and developing economically viable and safe processes (clean production and clean technologies), we will create minimal adverse effect on the environment during production and disposal at the end of the life. This is basically the goal of performability engineering.

It may be observed that the above-mentioned performance attributes are interrelated and should not be considered in isolation for optimization of performance. Each book in the series should endeavor to include most, if not all, of the attributes of this web of interrelationship and have the objective to help create optimal and sustainable products, systems, and services.

Publishers at Scrivener
Martin Scrivener (martin@scrivenerpublishing.com)
Phillip Carmical (pcarmical@scrivenerpublishing.com)

Network Reliability

Measures and Evaluation

Sanjay K. Chaturvedi

Scrivener
Publishing

WILEY

Co-published by John Wiley & Sons, Inc. Hoboken, New Jersey, and Scrivener Publishing LLC, Salem, Massachusetts.
Published simultaneously in Canada.

For general information on our other products and services or for technical support, please contact our Customer Care Department within the United States at (800) 762-2974, outside the United States at (317) 572-3993 or fax (317) 572-4002.

Wiley also publishes its books in a variety of electronic formats. Some content that appears in print may not be available in electronic formats. For more information about Wiley products, visit our web site at www.wiley.com.

For more information about Scrivener products please visit www.scrivenerpublishing.com.

Cover design by Russell Richardson

Library of Congress Cataloging-in-Publication Data:

ISBN 978-1-119-22356-6

Printed in the United States of America

10 9 8 7 6 5 4 3 2 1

गुरु गोबिन्द दोउ खड़े काके लागूँ पाँय ।
बलिहारी गुरु आपने गोबिन्द दियो बताय ॥
- संत कबीर

कबीर ने गुरु की महिमा का वर्णन करने के लिए इस कविता को लिखा था, जिसकी मदद के बिना, कोई भी इस सांसारिक सागर को पार नहीं कर सकता | उन्होने कहा की "अगर गुरु और भगवन दोनों गोविन्द के रूप में दरवाज़े पर प्रकट हो जाएँ तो मैं किसके चरण पहले स्पर्श करूँ?" उन्होने उत्तर दिया "पहले गुरु के चरणों को स्पर्श करो क्योंकि उनके बिना मैं भगवान को कैसे पहचानता?"

(Saint Kabir wrote this verse to sing the glory of Guru, without whose help, one cannot cross this ocean of worldly life. He asks, "If both, Guru and God in form of Govind were to appear at the door, whose feet will I worship first?" He answers, "It has to be the Guru's feet first, because without him, how would I have recognized (known) God?")

Fondly dedicated to
Prof. Krishna B. Misra (My Guru)- Veena (Guru Maa)

And my very own small world
Sanjekta(Daughter), Shaurya(Son), Ekta(Wife) and Uma-(late) Aditya (parents)

Contents

Preface

The growth of reliability has assumed a new dimension in the recent years primarily because of the consequential impact(s) of failures of present day's complex systems that may lead to day-to-day annoyance to the operational efficiency and uneconomical maintenance, and even to the extent of endangering life to our planet where a compromise with quality and reliability might be disastrous.

Although several books have been published in the area of reliability theory and practice, no book has been published on the topics covered in this book as the information presented in this book has either been confined to journals or given some space as a part of a chapter in a book. The topics covered in this book will interest not only the reliability community but also the teachers/educators and students of electrical, computer science, electronics, communication engineering with their allied areas. The text of this book is envisioned to be useful and can also serve as a one-semester course to senior undergraduate, graduate or postgraduate students in engineering. For researchers, practising engineers, managers, and designers, it would serve as a valuable reference and primer in the area of network reliability.

A very concerted effort has been made to keep the book ideally suitable for first course or even for a novice stepping into the area of network reliability. The mathematical treatment is kept as minimally as possible with an assumption on the readers' side that they have basic knowledge in graph theory, probabilities laws, Boolean laws and set theory. A number of solved examples have been provided to make the topics pellucid with some exercises given at the end of chapters for readers to voluntarily test themselves and to have a better command of the material. The references provided at the end of each chapter are no way complete as no book of this size can claim to give a comprehensive survey of the subject spanning over a several decades. But they indeed serve as a platform and guiding factor for further research in this area.

In engineering theory and applications, we think and operate in terms of logics and models with some acceptable and reasonable assumptions. Reliability theory is not an exception where a rather popular model for studying and analysing computer/ communication/ transportation/ water/ electrical networks is as a probabilistic graph with a characteristic of edges and/or nodes subject to failures. The network reliability modelling and analysis is an important issue in system design, manufacture and maintenance, wherein the performance of a network depends upon the probability of a specified set of nodes being communicable or not being communicable. The popular measures of network reliability in vogue are 2-terminal reliability with or without capacity constraint on links, k-terminal and all-terminal reliability. The publications of hundreds of research papers in the last few decades on the assessment of such measures indicate the importance of this area.

Among the several approaches of network reliability evaluation, the multiple-variable-inversion sum-of-disjoint product (MVI-SDP) approach finds a well-deserved niche as it provides the reliability expression in a most efficient and compact manner. However, it does require an efficiently enumerated minimal inputs (minimal path, spanning tree, minimal k-trees, minimal cut, minimal global-cut, minimal k-cut) depending on the desired reliability. The present book is a maiden endeavour by the author to cover these two aspects in detail through the application of various techniques devised by the 'reliability fraternity' and could be its *USP*.

The author does not claim to be an ace programmer, and has provided very efficient and user friendly Matlab® programs which can be downloaded at www.scrivenerpublishing.com However, they are amenable to such modifications for the readers who love to do programming. The book is organized as follows.

Chapter 1 introduces the basic definitions, terminology, common assumptions with a broad category of techniques to tackle and evaluate network reliability problems. Chapter 2 succinctly provides the commonly employed hazard models and basic building blocks of a reliability block diagram. It describes a flexible Misra Matrix Method to solve a General series-parallel system reliability model consisting of various types of redundancies.

Chapter 3 pertains to the notion of network connectivity with respect to a specified set of nodes of the network graph termed as *Minimal Path Sets*, in general or 2-terminal, k-terminal and all-terminal minimal path sets, in particular. It describes several methods of enumeration to such requirement for measuring network reliability metrics. The chosen methods are simple enough for classroom teaching but become powerful once implemented on a computer using a suitable programming language.

Chapter 4 deals with the dis-connectivity criteria of a network reliability graph under a specified set of nodes termed as *Minimal Cut Sets,* in general or 2-terminal, k-terminal and all-terminal minimal cut sets, in particular. It also provides a general algorithm developed by the author to enumerate them. It also explains various sub-problems encountered in enumerations and their solutions thereof.

Chapter 5 discusses and describes *Sum-of-Disjoint-Product* based MVI approaches such as KDH88, CAREL, HM-1 and HM-2 to obtain and evaluate 2-terminal, k-terminal and all-terminal network reliability/unreliability measures.

Chapter 6 puts network reliability methodology and measures discussed in earlier chapters under a unified framework and extend 2-terminal reliability measure to link's capacity-based reliability measure-CRR and describe a methodology to obtain the measure under such scenario.

In the last Chapter 7, the author has provided two case studies to show the approaches in action.

The author has tried his level best to make the text complete with logical flow and free of omissions. Nevertheless, as a student of reliability engineering, the author realises that 'failures are inevitable and can never ever be predicted in advance, and cannot be eliminated' but they and their consequences can definitely be minimized and mitigated. The author takes full responsibility for all those that still remain and shall be grateful if any such shortcomings or suggestions be brought to his notice.

Comments and suggestions regarding the book are most welcome and can be sent to skcrec@hijli.iitkgp.ernet.in.

Kharagpur, India   **Sanjay K. Chaturvedi**

March, 2016

Acknowledgements

The author would like to express his gratitude to the people who have motivated or helped at various stages of writing this book. Although, the skeleton of the text was drawn in the author's mind long back, the impetus to bring it to fruition was provided by Professor Krishna B. Misra - a 'Guru' of eminence who had shown the research path to the author and to many others as well.

Admittedly, it would not have been possible to complete this task without painstaking secretarial assistance provided by my student-friend, Lt Col Rajvinder Singh for proof-reading, incorporating numerous corrections on several drafts, and formatting. My research scholars, notably Mr. Gaurav Khanna (for collating the references and executing the software codes on several examples); Mr. Rajarajan, Mr. Tauheed Ahamed and Ms. Shabnam Samima deserve special thanks for providing assistance as and when it was needed.

The author also owes special thanks to his colleagues Prof. V. N. A. Naikan (Head of our Centre) and Prof. Neeraj Goyal for their helpful comments and suggestions at the early stages of this task.

Finally, the author would like to express his sincere thanks to the authority of his institution, Indian Institute of Technology, Kharagpur, India, for providing the necessary facility, aura and environment to undertake this project.

1

Introduction

As the systems grow in size and complexity, they become more prone to failures and it becomes essential to ensure their performance by carrying out reliability analysis. Here, the word system connotes any assemblage of functional units and may be used to denote a complete installation or equipment. A system may be quite gigantic such as computer communication networks or it could be as small as an integrated circuitry.

The problem of determining the reliability of systems, whose components can have one or more failure modes, often arises in variety of applications, ranging from telecommunication, transportation, power systems, and mechanical systems to integrated circuits and computer communication systems or large software structure. Therefore, all such systems can naturally be expressed as in the form of a network, arising from the interconnections of various system subdivisions. For instance, a telecommunication or a computer communication network may have vertices representing the physical locations of computers or transmitters/ receivers and may have several edges representing the communication links between different sites. Depending on whether vertices or edges work or fail, the network itself can be considered to be either working or failed.

For the applications cited above, continued availability of communication between specified vertices of a network is an important requirement. With the widespread use of and dependence upon such networks, it becomes imperative for these networks to be highly reliable. Hence the networks are often designed with the criteria of having several communication paths between any two vertices.

Ideally, if completely diverse path between every pair of vertices were available, the probability of existing at least one communication path between any two vertices at a given time would be very high. However, cost of designing and maintaining such networks inhibit this solution. As a compromise, networks are designed in such a way that any two vertices connected through a few *disjoint* path sets; additional path sets that have common links are also made available.

A major problem in this area lies with the task of determining reliability of such a network and it is desirable to have some quantitative measure of a given network's performance.

1.1   Graph Theory: A Tool for Reliability Evaluation

Graph theory has drawn increased interest of scientists and engineers in the last several decades. The main reason for this accelerated interest in graph theory is in its demonstrated ability to solve problems from a wide variety of areas. Because of their intuitive diagrammatic representation, graphs have been found extremely useful in modelling systems arising in physical science, engineering, social sciences and economic problems and reliability engineering has not been an exception.

The application of graph theory to reliability studies received little attention till 1970. Ever since the application of the graph theory for network reliability evaluation was suggested by (Misra & Rao, 1970), a large number of studies have appeared in the literature. To quote (Singh & Proctor, 1976): "*Until 1970, the subject received little attention with the exception of* (Shooman, 1968) *popular text Probabilistic Reliability, published in 1968. Nevertheless, he did little more than mention the topic. However* (Misra & Rao, 1970), *developed signal flow graphs- a development recognized as a significant step forward in the evaluation of network reliability*". After this a number of algorithms, techniques and approaches have been suggested in the literature. In fact today, the use of graph theory has become inseparable from network reliability evaluation.

In performing the reliability analysis of large and complex systems, it is almost impossible to treat system in its entirety. The logical approach is to decompose the system into its smaller functional entities composed of units, subsystems or components. Even a unit can be quite a sizeable subsystem. A unit can further be broken into elements each of which can only be a circuit or a part. In general, the hierarchical order is: system, subsystems, units, equipment, parts and components. The operational relationship amongst its constituent entities is provided through the logical relationship of system failure (or success) with the failure (or success) of its parts. These relationships are depicted through what is commonly known as the *reliability logic diagram* (RLD). Based on the functional interaction that subsystems or elements of a subsystem can have, the entities may fall in either of these categories viz., *series, parallel, series-parallel* (SP) *or parallel-series* (PS). However, certain design considerations or complex failure mode may produce a system in which its representation by pure parallel or series or their combination may not be possible or appropriate. In general, almost all practical systems fall in this category and are better known as *non-series-parallel systems* (NSP).

The reliability analysis and evaluation of NSP system are quite complicated, memory intensive and time consuming as well. However, any technique, which computes reliability of NSP systems, can easily be applied to series/parallel systems as well. Many of the series-parallel (or parallel-series) system are represented through *Reliability Logic or Block Diagram.* However, particularly for NSP systems, simpler ways to represent the system through a graph like structure.

A network graph G= (V, E) consists of a set of vertices (or nodes) |V| or n and a set of edges (or links) |E| or e. If an edge connects two vertices *i* and *j*; *j* is said to be adjacent to *i*. The n number of nodes in the graph is assigned number 1, 2, 3...n sequentially. The e number of links of the network can be arbitrarily and sequentially assigned numbers. One of the earliest DARPA (Defence Advance Research and Project Agency, USA) communication network graph model is shown in Figure 1.1, Figure 1.2, and Figure 1.5. Here, |V| = n = 5 and |E| = e = 7 and source node 's' can be number '1' while the destination node 'f' could be represented by '5'. With this graph model, depending on the state (working or failed) of vertices (or nodes) and / or edges (or links) with specified probability, the network can be considered either working or failed with estimated probability.

On the basis of reliability, networks/systems modelled through graphs have been classified as:

- Undirected network
- Directed network
- Mixed network.

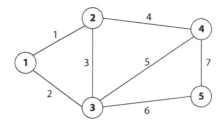

Figure 1.1 An undirected reliability graph of a network.

1.1.1 Undirected Network

It is a connected graph G for a system wherein nodes are connected by undirected edges. An undirected edge is an edge with no head or tail (no arrow shown). Undirected edges in a graph are used to indicate two-way communication links between nodes. They are represented as *unordered node pairs* (i, j) joined by the communication link or edge. An edge is said to be incident upon two nodes if the two nodes are joined by the edge.

Example 1.1: The graph in Figure 1.1 is an example of an undirected network where, node-set and edge-set are:

V = {**1, 2, 3, 4, 5**}, and
E = {(**1, 2**), (**1, 3**), (**2, 1**), (**2, 3**),(**2, 4**), (**3, 1**), (**3, 2**), (**3, 4**),
    (**3, 5**), (**4, 2**), (**4, 3**), (**4, 5**), (**5, 3**),(**5, 4**)}
    = {*1, 2, 3, 4, 5, 6, 7*}

1.1.2 Directed Network

It is another form of a system representation through connected graph G wherein each edge has an orientation. Obviously, a source node would not have any edge incidents on it whereas a destination node would not have any edge emerging out of it. Some text also refers directed edges as arcs representing a unidirectional communication links between two nodes depicting the information flow in the direction that an arc points. An arc from node *i* to node *j* is represented as an ordered pair (i, j), where *i* is called the tail and *j* is called the head of the arc. Figure 1.2 is an example of a directed network, where node-set and edge set are:

V= {**1, 2, 3, 4, 5**}, and
E = {(**1, 2**), (**1, 3**), (**2, 3**), (**2, 4**), (**3, 4**), (**3, 5**), (**4, 5**)}
    = {*1, 2, 3, 4, 5, 6, 7*}

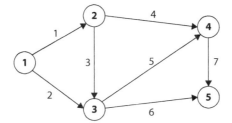

Figure 1.2 A directed reliability graph of a network.

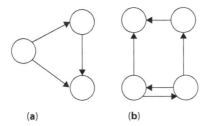

(a)   (b)

Figure 1.3 Strongly connected components.

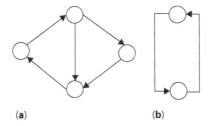

(a)   (b)

Figure 1.4 Weakly connected components.

In a directed graph, a strongly connected component is a maximal set of nodes for which there exists a directed path between every ordered pair of nodes in the component, such that the paths pass only through nodes that are also in the component. Figure 1.3 shows two examples of strongly connected components and Figure 1.4 shows two examples of components that are not strongly connected.

1.1.3   Mixed Network

A mixed network G is a graph in which some edges may be directed and some may be undirected. It is determined by the triplet (V, E, D) where V is the set of nodes, E is the set of undirected edges and D is the set of directed edges.

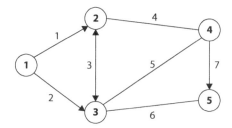

Figure 1.5 A mixed reliability graph of a network.

Table 1.1 Adjacency matrix representation of a graph.

Connection matrix Figure 1.1						Connection Matrix Figure 1.2						Connection matrix Figure 1.5					
Node	1	2	3	4	5	Node	1	2	3	4	5	Node	1	2	3	4	5
1	0	1	1	0	0	1	0	1	1	0	0	1	0	1	1	0	0
2	1	0	1	1	0	2	0	0	1	1	0	2	0	0	1	1	0
3	1	1	0	1	1	3	0	0	0	1	1	3	0	1	0	1	1
4	0	1	1	0	1	4	0	0	0	0	1	4	0	1	1	0	1
5	0	0	1	1	0	5	0	0	0	0	0	5	0	0	1	0	0

The underlying undirected graph is obtained by deleting the orientation of the arcs in D. An orientation of a mixed graph means, that we orient the undirected edges (and leave the directed ones). Figure 1.5 shows such depiction.

Summarily, each item (component/part/subdivision etc…) of a system can be represented by a two terminal graph. Then the logical interconnection of various items form a network like structure and is better known as a *probabilistic graph* of the system due to the associated probability of success/failure of its each items, and this structure can also be designated as a *system* or a *network* (Misra, 1992) .To analyse such networks is an extremely difficult, time consuming and laborious task, almost impossible to do manually. Thus, the use of computer becomes absolutely necessary for which one would need a computer-coding scheme representing the network that can easily and suitably be manipulated by the algorithms in addition to computer-programs to provide a solution to the problem.

The commonly used schemes to code these networks have been: *incidence matrix, adjacency matrix* and *adjacency list* representation. However, the most popular, simplest and easily manipulative coding scheme for a moderate size network has been the adjacency matrix or connection matrix scheme. The connection matrices for the some cases are as shown in Table 1.1.

1.2 Large versus Complex System

At this juncture, it would be worthwhile to distinguish between- what is large and complex?

1.2.1 Large System

As stated at the beginning that the word system connotes any assemblage of functional units and may be used to denote a complete installation or equipment. A system can be represented by a graph where a nodes-represents a component/unit/subsystem and a link represents their functional connectivity.

When used in relation to a system, the word *large* connotes anything, which is greater than the average size, extent, quantity, or amount in comparison to another similar thing or some reference object. Hence, it is a relative word and it is hard to specify a system's *largeness* in the absence of a reference.

Let the network shown in Figure 1.6 represents a communication network with the *transmitter*, s, sending data or information to a *receiver*, f.

These (s, f) points have been connected through a number of intermediate links and *relay-transmitters*. There may be hundreds and thousands of *relay-transmitters* connecting the *transmitter* and the *receiver* help them to communicate. This configuration could be representing a large network. Therefore, the largeness is in relation to the number of units or elements that a system consists of. A large system need not necessarily be a complex system.

1.2.2 Complex System

The word *complex* connotes a structure consisting of interconnected or interwoven parts or elements, which are difficult to analyse, understand, or handle.

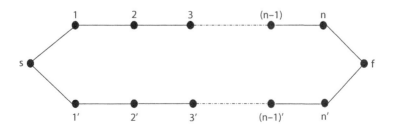

Figure 1.6 A large network.

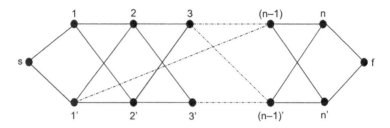

Figure 1.7 A large and complex network.

Therefore, a *complex* system is a system, which consists of interconnected or interwoven parts (components) such that it becomes difficult to analyse it in respect of its reliability or a particular problem due to the constraints imposed by the existing techniques, algorithms, software (such as programming languages, operating systems) and hardware (such as memory).

To *further* clarify the complexity of a network in a clearer and simpler way; let us consider the system given in Figure 1.7, which is obtained from Figure 1.6 by introducing some interconnecting links between the *relay-transmitters* pair.

The information now could be sent through many several alternative paths created by the addition of interconnections. On adding more interconnections, there would be an exponential rise in the number of paths to carry the information from *s* to *f*. In other words, the complexity of a network increases with the additions of new interconnecting links transforming a large network to become more and more complex.

In reliability engineering, the large network shown in Figure 1.6 is simply a series-parallel arrangement of units, which can be analysed easily with the help of well-known probability laws of intersection and union. Such types of systems can be decomposed and are reducible to a single entity.

However, the system shown in Figure 1.7 is not reducible through series and parallel models and as such is known as non-series parallel system. Such a system not only requires better approaches and methodologies but also requires a better hardware and software platform for its analysis. SP or PS networks are generally non-complex systems whereas NSP systems fall in complex system category. The complexity of the NSP systems increases with the insertion of more and more interconnecting links connecting various nodes of the system.

1.2.3 Large and Complex System

Therefore, a large and complex system is one, which has not only multitude of system elements but has several interconnecting links as well. Summarily, the whole explanation of large and complex systems could be put in the following way:

A system may be a large system but not necessary be complex if it is reducible and has necessarily a SP (or PS) structure. The reliability of such systems can be evaluated very fast and the time to obtain reliability does not vary polynomially. However, if a system has lots of interconnections and is not reducible is called as a complex system. The complexity of the system increases, time to obtain reliability varies non deterministic polynomial in time.

1.3 Network Reliability Measures: Deterministic versus Probabilistic

Diverse network reliability problems entail different performance measures for the system, which are classified based on the network models. Some networks, such as urban road networks, entail traffic characteristic like waiting time, travel time, congestion etc. Transportation networks are usually studied to determine the maximum capacity flow between (s, f) node and/or characteristic of shortest path. For some cases, transmission speed and capacity could be the performance measure of interest. One can refer to (Sheir, 1991) for an overview of the subject. However, reliability theory, in general, and in this text, in particular, studies the network based on one of the most important network reliability measure, viz., specified node-set connectivity in probabilistic sense.

(Frank & Frisch, 1970) and (Wilkov, 1972) made earlier attempts to provide various definitions of system reliability. They identified two distinct classes of reliability measures:

- Deterministic, and
- Probabilistic.

The deterministic criteria made use of discrete measures to define the reliability of a network. The assumption made when dealing with deterministic measures is that the network is subjected to a destructive force or an enemy who has complete knowledge of the topology of the network. The purpose of this intelligent enemy is to destroy or disrupt network communication. Thus the main measure of reliability is the least amount of damage the enemy must be able to inflict to render the network inoperative.

Deterministic measures thus can be viewed as simple bounds on the reliability of the network, since they are often measured as the network's worst-case vulnerability to failure. For example, in the (s, f) connectivity reliability problem, two deterministic measures of reliability are the number of edges and the number of nodes that must be destroyed or removed to disrupt the communication between the specified nodes. The minimum number of edges that must be removed in order to disconnect the nodes s and f is simply the number of edges in a minimum cardinality (s, f)-cut. The minimum number of nodes that must be removed to disconnect s and f is the (node) connectivity between the vertices s & f.

Both of these measures are computable in polynomial time. However, one of the main problems with deterministic measure is that it gives rise to some counterintuitive notions of network reliability. For example, consider the graphs shown in Figure 1.8.

According to one deterministic measure that uses (node) connectivity as a measure of the graph's reliability, the graphs of Figure 1.8(a) and (b) are equally reliable since the (s, f)-connectivity of each graph is three. However, an intuition leads one to believe that graph (a) is the more reliable of the two.

The same problem arises when the cardinality of a minimum (s, f)-cut set is used as a measure of unreliability. Consider the graphs shown in Figure 1.9. Both graphs (a) and (b) have a minimum cardinality (s, f)-cut of size one. This deterministic measure therefore implies that both are equally reliable. This is again counterintuitive, as one expects graph (a) to be the more reliable of the two. This leads to the notion that a more intuitively acceptable measure of reliability might be a *probabilistic measure*.

Therefore, for measuring the reliability of a network one can associate a statistical probability of failure/success with each of the components of the network in order to obtain a statistical measure of the overall unreliability/

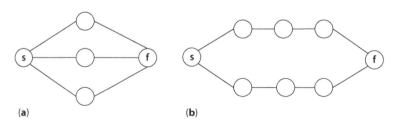

Figure 1.8 Example of deterministic reliability.

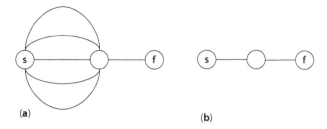

Figure 1.9 Another example of deterministic reliability.

reliability of the network. This notion supports an accepted definition of reliability as: *"the probability that a given system or device is operational".* This measure of reliability may be interpreted as a long-term average availability. That is, over a specified period of time, what is the probability that the network will remain operational? This also includes a fairly prevalent notion of reliability as the probability that a network is operational at any given moment of time. To avoid conflicts that arise with various levels of operation within a network's hierarchy, only the topology of the network is considered. This allows a network to be modelled by a graph where the nodes of the graph represent the communication centres and communication links are represented by its edges.

The probabilistic methods for determining the reliability of a network generally assume the failure of edges and/or nodes as random events. Using predetermined probabilities that the edges and/or nodes are operational; the probability that the network remains operational is often of interest. A network is considered operational, if it is connected. The probability that the network is connected is often called *probabilistic connectedness*. This *probabilistic model* is often more appropriate than the *deterministic model* since it results in a probability that the network is connected at any point in time.

Based on the probabilistic connectedness of a specified set of nodes, the following three measures are in vogue in reliability texts as reliability measures:

1.3.1   Terminal-pair Reliability Measure

For any arbitrary network, *terminal pair reliability* (TR) is the probability that a communication path exists between two specified pair of nodes, viz., source node, s, and destination or terminal node, f. Network reliability and System reliability are the other terms being used synonymously for TR in the literature (Colbourn, 1987), (Misra, 1992).

1.3.2   All-Terminal Reliability Measure

All-terminal reliability requires that every node must be able to communicate with every other node of the network. It is defined as the probability that for every pair of nodes (x, y), $\forall$ x and y $\in$ n, in the network, a path exits from node x to y. This is equivalent to stating it as the connectivity problem in graph theory. In the literature, *global reliability* and *g-reliability* are the other terms often used synonymously for *all-terminal reliability*.

The all-terminal reliability problem deals with communication among all nodes in a network. In other words, it is the probability of existence of a minimal set of edges such that all nodes of the network graph remain connected. A graph is connected if there is at least one path between every pair of nodes i.e., in this case a minimal operational sub graph is an operational spanning tree. For a spanning tree to be operational all of its edges must be operational (since it is a minimal operational sub graph), and therefore a spanning tree is in a *failed state* if any of its edges fail. A graph would have several spanning trees and the number of spanning trees grows exponentially with the graph size (Christofides, 1975), (Deo, 1979).

1.3.3   k-terminal Reliability Measure

k-terminal reliability requires that a set of *k*-specified set of nodes of the network are able to communicate with each other and it is defined as the probability that a path exists between every pair of nodes belonging to the specified set of *k* nodes of the network. In other words, *k-terminal reliability* is the probability that a specified set of k-nodes is able to communicate with each other. It is evident that both the above measures, namely, *g-reliability* and *k-terminal reliability* are the generalized form of two-terminal reliability measure.

1.4   Common Assumptions

Two major and common assumptions are made in order to make the problem of computing probabilistic connectedness more tractable.

- The first assumption is related with *statistical independence* of edge failure (or success).
  Contention: The assumption that edge failures are statistically independent implies that the probability of a link being operational is independent of the states of the other links in

the network. The assumption is that link failures are caused by random events and that all links are affected individually. However, this assumption may not be valid while modelling a real communication network, since links in one particular area may fail due to natural causes such as a major storm or an earthquake. However, this assumption is often made because information about the dependencies of link failures is extremely difficult to obtain. In fact, such dependencies may not be known. Without the assumption of statistical independence the problem becomes much more difficult to solve. As a result this assumption is often made, even when modelling networks for which it is known that link failures are not independent.

- The second assumption is that nodes are *perfectly reliable,* i.e., their probability of failure is zero or negligible.
  Contention: The assumption that nodes are perfectly reliable may, at first, seem unreasonable. However, there are reasons for adopting it. Node failures necessarily induce edge failures, and moreover introduce failures that are statistically dependent. Hence the assumption of statistical independence requires the assumption of perfectly reliable nodes.

Much of the development in the area of network reliability has been done under the assumption of perfectly reliable nodes with unreliable links. However, if it is necessary to make the assumption that nodes do fail, the methods discussed in this book could be modified appropriately in order to accommodate such assumption.

1.5 Approaches for NSP Network Reliability Evaluation

Evaluation of reliability measures has attracted a lot of attention from researchers and many approaches have been developed over the past few decades. The literature on reliability evaluation of networks, considering only connectivity as performance criterion, can broadly be classified into two paradigms, viz., (Misra, 1992), (Misra, 1993) .

- The paradigm that does not require knowledge of minimal path (or cut) sets in advance (Non Path or Cut sets based).

- The paradigm in which one of the prerequisite is- the enumeration of all possibilities through which a specified sets of nodes can communicate (or not communicate) with each other, i.e., which uses pathsets (two-terminal or spanning trees, or k-tree) or cutsets (two-terminal or global or k-cutsets) as the starting point (Minimal Path or Cut based).

Figure 1.10 shows a brief but representative categorization of existing NSP reliability evaluation approaches and Table 1.2 provides a categorised and representative bibliography (details of which can be found at the end of this book) work based on this classification. The detailed methodology of each of these methods is outside the scope of this text. However, we provide a brief description of some of them.

1.5.1   Non Path or Cut Sets Based Techniques

1.5.1.1   State Enumeration Technique

The state enumeration method is the simplest of all methods and is based on the concept of state of the system. It was once widely used until the use of graph theory and other approaches were become known for network reliability evaluation. This method evaluates network reliability from probabilities associated with success states out of the 2^n possible system states which in turn depend on the states of 'n' number of components (edges and/or nodes) in the network. These 2^n possible system states are identified for being success or failure states of the system and the reliability of the system can be evaluated as:

$$R = \sum_{i=1}^{n_1} \left(\prod_{j \in S_i} \left(p_j \right)_{operational} \prod_{k \in S_i} \left(1 - p_k \right)_{non-operational} \right) \qquad (1.1)$$

As a state of the system is governed by the state of its elements where some elements would be operational and others non-operational, thus, in the above expression, n_1 denotes the number of system success states out-of-2^n possible states; p_j and p_k are the reliabilities (success probabilities) of the element constituting i^{th} success state out-of- n_1 states. In other words, the product term constitutes the product of success and failure probabilities of the constituent elements of the network to provide the success probability of that particular success state of the system.

The final reliability expression resulting from success (or failure) states is quite unwieldy and requires a lot of time to calculate reliability value from

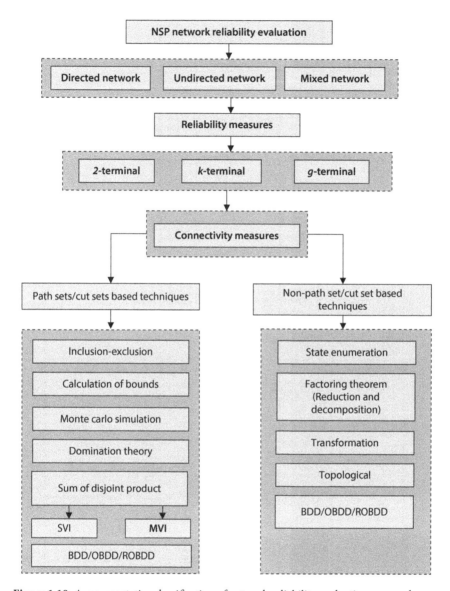

Figure 1.10 A representative classification of network reliability evaluation approaches.

the expression with associated round-off errors. This method is obviously unwieldy and unacceptably slow, as it requires an evaluation of probabilities associated with all system success states out-of-the 2^n possible system states. In other words, enumeration of all system states becomes very large and cumbersome even for small networks; this method is seldom used for reliability evaluation (Elsayed, 1996), (Misra, 1992).

Table 1.2 A categorised bibliography for NSP network reliability evaluation techniques.

Technique	Reliability		
	2-Terminal	K-Terminal	g-Terminal
Inclusion exclusion	(Kim et al., 1972), (Lin et al., 1976), (Buzacott & Chang, Dec 1984), (Locks, Dec 1985), (Buzacott, 1987)		(Buzacott & Chang, Dec 1984) (Buzacott, 1987)
Calculation of bounds	(Brecht & Colbourn, 1986), (Beichelt & Spross, 1989), (Hsieh, Sep 2003) (Sebastio et al., Nov 2014)	(Brecht & Colbourn, 1986)	(Brecht & Colbourn, 1986), (Provan, 1986)
Monte Carlo	(Easton & Wong, 1980), (Lin & Donaghev, 1993), (Sanseverino & Moreno, 2002), (Hui et al., 2003), (Cancela et al., 2010) (Zenklusen & Laumanns, 2011), (Botev et al., 2013)	(Elperin et al., 1991), (Cancela & Khadiri, 1998) (Cancela & Khadiri, 2003), (Hui et al., 2003) (Adjabi & Bouchama, 2011)	(Hui et al., 2003)
Domination theory	(Willie, 1980), (Locks, Dec 1985)		
SDP	(Abraham, 1979), (Locks, Dec 1985), (Beichelt & Spross, Apr 1987), (Locks, Oct 1987), (Heidtmann, 1989), (Veeraraghavan & Trivedi, Aug 1991), (Soh & Rai, 1991), (Rai et al., 1995), (Zhao et al., 1995) (Luo & Trivedi, 1998), (Luo & Trivedi, 1998), (Chatelet et al., 1999),	(Chaturvedi & Misra, 2002), (Mishra & Chaturvedi, 2009)	(Chaturvedi & Misra, 2002), (Mishra & Chaturvedi, 2009)

Method			
SDP	(Jane & Yuan, 2001),(Chaturvedi & Misra, 2002), (Chaturvedi & Misra, 2002) (Yeh, Feb2007), (Zuo et al., 2007), (Mishra & Chaturvedi, 2009) (Xing et al., 2012), (Yeh, 2015)	(Chaturvedi & Misra, 2002), (Mishra & Chaturvedi, 2009)	(Chaturvedi & Misra, 2002), (Mishra & Chaturvedi, 2009)
State enumeration	(Corinne & Manouvrier, 1999)		
Factoring	(Moskowitz, 1958), (Nakazawa, 1976), (Rosenthal, 1977), (Theolougou & Carlier, 1991), (Choi & Jun, 1995), (Wang & Zhang, 1997), (Rebaiaia et al., November 2009), (Rebaiaia & Daoud, 2013)	(Satyanarayana, 1982), (Wood, 1985)	(Satyanarayana & Chang, 1983), (Theolougou & Carlier, 1991), (Choi & Jun, 1995), (Wang & Zhang, 1997)
Transformation method	(Ramamoorty & Balgopal, May 1970), (Rosenthal & Frisque, 1977), (Gadani, 1981), (Gadani & Misra, 1982), (Wang & Sun, 1996)		
Topological method	(Misra & Rao, 1970), (Misra, 1970), (Satyanarayan & Prabhakar, 1978), (Aggarwal & Satyanarayan, 1984), (Resende, Dec 1988)	(Satyanarayana, 1982)	
BDD/OBDD/ROBDD	(Kuo et al., 1999), (Yeh et al., 2002), (Rauzy, 2003), (Chang et al., 2004), (Rebaiaia & Daoud, 2013)	(Yeh et al., 2002), (Rebaiaia & Daoud, 2012)	

1.5.1.2   Network Decomposition Technique

Among various techniques to evaluate network reliability, factoring theorem based approach stands out distinctly as one of the useful and popular approach. This approach was originally proposed by (Moskowitz,
1958) but was formally introduced for developing algorithms for reliability evaluation of series-parallel and non-series parallel networks
with single or two modes of failures by (Misra, 1970). The factoring
theorem states:

$$R(G) = p_e * R(G|e \text{ is functional}) +$$
$$(1-p_e) * R(G|e \text{ is not functional}) \quad\quad (1.2)$$
$$= p_e * R(G_e) + (1-p_e) * R(G-e)$$

The decomposition formula (1.2), which forms the basis for network
reduction, decomposes a large size network into smaller set of manage-
able sized networks. The main strategy applied in factoring technique is
to identify and to factor out such edges, which are bi-directional in their
orientation in a given network graph. By doing so, one decomposes a NSP
network to a series of SP/PS networks whose reliabilities can easily be computed. If a network is factored on a selected edge e, two networks graphs
G_e and $(G - e)$ would then be obtained. Depending up on the structure of
these two graphs whether SP/PS reducible or not, it would need a further
factorization on another edge (which is generally the case for large and
complex networks) in an iterative manner until all sub graphs of the network have been successfully converted to SP/PS-reducible graphs. In fact,
we need to determine reliability of 2^x-sub networks in a network consisting
of x number of bi-directional edges.

This approach has inherent limitation of its applicability to networks,
which possess even fewer bi-directional edges, as the number of sub graphs
that would be required to evaluate for their reliability would grow, exponentially, similar to the phenomenon of 'states-explosion' as the number
of elements increases observed in state enumeration technique. Further
algorithms based on this approach do not offer us a compact reliability
expression and impracticable for large systems. Even Misra Matrix method
(Misra, 1970), fastest method to date for SP-networks and would be discussed in next chapter, does not stand well with large and complex NSP
networks when combined with decomposition theorem. For instance, the
network of Figure 1.11 comprised of 21 nodes and 33 links is estimated to
require an evaluation of more than 250 thousand series-parallel networks.
Therefore, the computational time becomes enormously large even with

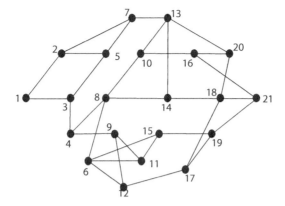

Figure 1.11 A test example (21 Nodes and 33 Links).

this type and size of systems. Hence the scope of this approach is limited to either small systems or systems with fewer bi-directional elements.

1.5.1.3   *Probability Transformation Technique*

These are basically reduction and approximate technique, but have been improved upon to provide reasonably accurate results from an engineering point of view. The procedure consists of simplifying complex and large structures by converting them into equivalent series-parallel configurations, which can be conveniently handled. The transformation techniques currently available in the literature: star-delta, delta-star, and quadrilateral star-delta or delta-star transformation techniques.

Generally, the equations for delta-star and star-delta transformations are derived by matching the probabilities of successful communication between given a set of nodes. A closed form solution is possible with delta-star; however we need a simple and rapid iterative procedure to solve three simultaneous non-linear algebraic equations in case of star-delta transformation. As a network is transformed, its complexity is reduced at each stage of simplification and finally we would be left with an equivalent edge with its reliability or unreliability equal to system reliability or unreliability.

(Rosenthal & Frisque, 1977) proposed Delta-Star transformation to 2-terminal reliability problems. (Gadani & Misra, 1981), (Gadani & Misra, 1982) and (Misra, 1992) provide various transformation techniques, viz., Delta-Star, Star-Delta, and Quadrilateral-Star, and discuss their utility to evaluate system reliability and other parameters of interest for both- maintained and non-maintained systems. But we shouldn't forget that these are all approximate yet economical methods of system reliability estimation for a large and

complex network. The numerical results of number of graph transformations, run-time, and accuracy for the approximate algorithms can be seen in
(Gadani, 1980), (Gadani & Misra, 1982), (Shooman & Kershenbaum, 1992).

Yet another method known as *topological* method, originally proposed
by (Misra & Rao, 1970) and subsequently provided in a formal and com-
puterized algorithm by (Satyanarayan & Prabhakar, 1978), cannot be used
economically for large networks as the 2-terminal reliability problem,
the simplest of the various reliability problems, is shown to be NP-hard
(Provan & Ball, 1983), (Satyanarayan & Wood, 1983), (Aggrawal & Barlow,
1984), (Aggarwal & Satyanarayan, 1984), (Proven & Ball, 1984), (Yoo &
Deo, 1988)and topological algorithms proposed to solve this problem are
usually computationally intensive. The problem remains NP-hard even
for planar networks (Vertigan, 1990) Interested readers may refer (Misra,
1992) Chapter 6 –Reliability Evaluation Techniques - for various reliability
evaluation algorithms.

1.5.1.4   *Binary Decision Diagram Based Technique*

Binary Decision Diagram (BDD) is a state-of-art of data structures to
encode and to manipulate Boolean functions. Reliability, Risk and dependability studies are heavy consumers of Boolean functions. Boolean functions are represented by a directed acyclic graph or network with restriction
on the ordering of decision variables in a graph. BDD is based on a decomposition of Boolean function called the Shannon expansion. A function 'f'
can be decomposed in terms of a variable 'x' as:

$$f = x.f_{x=1} + \bar{x}.f_{x=0}$$

A node and its descendants in BDD represent a Boolean function 'f',
where for node label 'x', one outgoing edge is directed to the sub graph
representing, $f_{x=1}$, and the other to $f_{x=0}$. The basic idea is to choose an edge
(component) and break the model down into two cases: the first assumes
the component has failed, the second assumes it has not failed. For each
case, a new reliability graph is built by taking into account the behaviour
of the chosen edges.

An ordered binary decision diagram (OBDD) is a BDD with the constraint that the variables are ordered and every source to sink path in the
OBDD visits the variables in ascending order. A reduced ordered binary
decision diagram (ROBDD) is an OBDD where each node represents a
distinct Boolean expression. But due to poor representation of engineering
failure logic, still BDD approach is in the development phase. The application of BDD in reliability evaluation is relatively new development in

the area of reliability engineering. The introduction of BDD in risk analysis, whose primary modelling tools have been FTA and ETA, has renewed their algorithm framework (Misra, 2008).

Summarily, most of the NPOC technique based algorithms tend to be less efficient and uneconomical as compared to the algorithms based on POC approach (Grnarov *et al.*, 1980). Sometimes, they offer approximate solution and are not suited for reliability evaluation of large and complex networks.

1.5.2 Minimal POC Based Techniques

A minimal path set is generally used in the sense of a minimal chain of elements of the network required to establish continuity between a specified set of terminals (nodes or vertices). However, the minimal path sets may also consist of acyclic graphs in case of flow networks (Misra & Prasad, 1982) instead of just being a simple chain structure of constituent elements. These path sets could be for 2-terminal connectivity, k-terminal connectivity or all-terminal connectivity.

The system reliability can also be computed indirectly by taking advantages of duality in graphs, i.e., a minimal path in dual graph will be the cut in original. In other words, instead of computing reliability we can compute unreliability in the sense of a minimal set of elements whose failure ensures network failure. This set we call as *minimal cut sets* of the network. These cut sets could be for the disruption of 2-terminal connectivity, k-terminal connectivity or all-terminal connectivity.

Therefore, *success of all the components* in at least one minimal path set ensures system success whereas *failure of all components* in a minimal cut set ensures system failure. A vast majority of methods to evaluate network reliability belong to POC paradigm. These techniques work in a two-step procedure, viz.,

- Enumeration of minimal path sets or cut sets of the network, and
- Combining path sets or cut sets logically using the laws of probability.

1.5.2.1 Inclusion-Exclusion Technique

This is one of the earliest techniques using the probability laws of unionization and idempotence to compute network reliability expression. Taking an example of a two-terminal reliability measures for instance, the success of all the components in at least one minimal path set ensures system success, whereas failure of all components in a minimal cut set ensures system failure. Therefore, If the set of all minimal path or cut sets between a specified pair of nodes viz., source and sink, for a network, G are known, then the terminal reliability, $R(G)$, is given by,

$$R(G) = \begin{cases} P\left(\bigcup_{i=1}^{m} X_i\right), \text{if } X_i \text{ are minimal parth sets.} \\ 1 - P\left(\bigcup_{i=1}^{n} C_i\right), \text{if } C_i \text{ are minimal cut sets.} \end{cases} \tag{1.3}$$

Where, m is the total number of path sets of network and n is the total number of cut sets of the network and $P(.)$ describes the probability function. The right hand side of expression of Eq. (1.3) can be evaluated using inclusion-exclusion principle, i.e.,

$$P\left\{\bigcup_{i=1}^{m} X_i\right\} = \begin{bmatrix} \sum_{i=1}^{m} P(X_i) - \sum_{i=1}^{m} \sum_{j=1, j\neq 1}^{m} P(X_i \cap X_j) + \cdots + \\ \left((-1)^{m-1} \sum_{i=1}^{m} \sum_{j=1, j\neq 1}^{m} \cdots \sum_{r=1, r\neq 1, j, k, \dots, (r-1)}^{m} P(X_i \cap X_j \dots \cap X_r)\right) \end{bmatrix} \tag{1.4}$$

1.5.2.2   Monte-Carlo Simulation Based Technique

Monte Carlo (MC) Simulation has been applied effectively for analysing the variety of engineering applications and reliability engineering is not an exception. In this approach, system reliability indices can be obtained as the expected value of a test function applied to a system state. This function, called *System Function* or *System Structure Function*, determines whether a specific configuration of the system based on its component's states corresponds to an operating or failed state, i.e.,

Let there be a state vector, $x = (x_1, x_2, x_3, \dots, x_n)$, where,

$$x_i = \begin{cases} 1, \text{ if component } i \text{ is functioning.} \\ 0, \text{ if component } i \text{ has failed.} \end{cases}$$

The structure function $\Phi(x)$ is defined by

$$\Phi(x) = \begin{cases} 1, \text{ if system is functioning.} \\ 0, \text{ if system has failed.} \end{cases} \tag{1.5}$$

The reliability is then defined as the probability that $\Phi(x) = 1$ (i.e., as a ratio of number for which $\Phi(x) = 1$ (success) based on the states of components to the total number of simulation runs in a number of simulation runs.

Note that the structure function can also be expressed in terms of minimal path (or cut) sets, i.e., Let X_1, X_2, ..., X_l be the complete list of all minimal path sets, and let C_1, C_2, ...,C_m be the complete list of all minimal cut sets of a *monotone* system, (Gertsbakh & Shpungin, 2009) then

$$\Phi(x) = 1 - \prod_{j=1}^{l} \left(1 - \prod_{i \varepsilon X_j} x_i \right),$$

and

$$\Phi(x) = \prod_{j=1}^{m} \left(1 - \prod_{i \varepsilon C_j} (1 - x_i) \right)$$

In short, the simulation approach is performed by following the following broad steps: determine the state of each component and, by the application of a structure function, and depending on the chosen reliability measure, assess if the system has succeeded or failed using some search algorithm such as depth-first search or so. A single simulation run generates either a system success or failure, and multiple simulation runs can be used to determine reliability estimation.

1.5.2.3   *Domination Theory Based Technique*

The approach first appeared in (Barlow, 1982), and is generally known as domination theory. The notion of dominations was discovered in the process of seeking a reduction in the complexity of the inclusion-exclusion formula for calculating the probability that all components are functioning in at least one of a given networks minimal path sets or cut sets. When applied to a reliability computation, each of the intersections appearing in the inclusion-exclusion formula represents the collection of components appearing in one or more events of the intersection in question, and each term in the expansion of $P\{\bigcup_{i=1}^{m} X_i\}$ contributes elements of the form p^k or $-p^k$ to the reliability polynomial. While the inclusion-exclusion formula provides an explicit expression for the reliability polynomial, it can entail substantial computational complexity. The generation of the (say m) minimal path (or cut) sets of a given system involves an algorithm that is exponential in m, and the number of different intersections of m sets is also exponential in m. What results is a doubly exponential algorithm for computing system reliability. From this inconvenient truth, and the need for something simpler, domination theory was born.

In domination theory first we list out all minimal path sets representing the working components of the network. The union of these components in a fixed collection of minimal path sets is called a formation. Further, i-formation is defined as a union of the components in a collection of i minimal path sets. A particular formation can also be referred as even or odd if it is the union of an even or odd number of minimal path sets respectively. Whereas, the signed domination of a given union of minimal path sets is simply the difference between the number of even and odd formations for that union. Thus the domination theory can be viewed as an accounting mechanism that helps one to keep track of the basic elements of the inclusion-exclusion calculation.

1.5.2.4   Reliability Bounds Technique

Since in a large complex and interconnected network, the number of path sets or cut sets can be exceedingly very high, say in thousands, therefore it would not be practical proposition to calculate reliability based on full expansion of the unionization of all the path sets or cut sets. Alternatively, one can work on the basis of bounds on system reliability obtained from path sets or cut sets and terminate the process of reliability computation at a stage when we find that consideration of any additional path sets or cut sets does not improve the accuracy any further.

Let X_1, X_2, ..., X_l be the complete list of all minimal path sets, and let C_1, C_2, ...,C_m be the complete list of all minimal cut sets of a *monotone* system. Denoting p_i the reliability of ith component and R(G) as the system reliability and if all system components are statistically independent, then, R(G) would be bounded by (Barlow & Proschan, 1975).

$$\prod_{i=1}^{m}\left(1-\prod_{j\in C_i}\left(1-p_j\right)\right) \le R(G) \le 1-\prod_{k=1}^{l}\left(1-\prod_{j\in X_k} p_j\right) \quad (1.6)$$

In other words, the upper bound on system reliability would be the reliability of a fictitious network made up of the parallel connections of several series subsystems consisting of each minimal path sets of the original network. Likewise, the lower bound would be the reliability of system obtained by the series connections of several parallel subsystems formed by the minimal cut sets of the original network. By doing so, there would be many components that repeat themselves in the branches of these fictitious networks formed by minimal path/cut sets. But they are treated as independent and distinct components in these systems. Therefore, this technique of reliability estimation appears to be promising and provides a practical and an economical method of assessing network reliability for small to moderate size networks.

1.5.2.5   Sum-of-disjoint Product Based Technique

The techniques based *on Sum-of-disjoint product* (SDP) have been often used effectively and efficiently in evaluation to provide a compact reliability expression. These techniques start with a Boolean polynomial formed by either success terms (e.g., path sets) or failure terms (cut sets). This class of techniques relies on Boolean algebra manipulation to convert a path/cut sets polynomial, consisting of un-complemented system variable, into a set of *exclusive and mutually disjoint* (emd) terms. The algebraic sum of these emds provides the reliability expression, i.e.,

$$R(G) = P\left\{\bigcup_{i=1}^{m} X_i\right\} = \left\{P\left\{X_1 \cup \overline{X}_1 X_2 \cup \overline{X}_1 \overline{X}_2 X_3 \cup \ldots \cup \overline{X}_1 \overline{X}_2 \overline{X}_3 \ldots \overline{X}_{m-1} X_m\right\}\right.$$
$$= \left\{\begin{array}{l} P(X_1) + P(\overline{X}_1 X_2) + P(\overline{X}_1 \overline{X}_2 X_3) + \cdots + \\ P(\overline{X}_1 \overline{X}_2 \overline{X}_3 \ldots \overline{X}_{m-1}) \end{array}\right. \tag{1.7}$$

Where, a bar over a variable in equation (1.7) denotes its complement. Note that while evaluating the product terms in equation (1.7), the laws of probability play a major role in providing a compact expression. This can be expended in a similar manner if spanning trees or *k*-trees or their dual terms are known.

Historically speaking, the foundation of a serious effort in minimizing system reliability expression using SDP approach was laid by (Aggarwal et al., 1975) (known as AMG-algorithm), mainly keeping in mind the fact, that the system reliability has to be determined repetitively during the design phase of a system and it was felt necessary to obtain the reliability expression in compact form that can be easily handled and computed fast. Another consideration that went in favour of compactness of the reliability expression was to minimize the round off errors in multiplicative computations involving un-complemented variables in reliability expression that were vogue at that time. This was the first ever attempt to obtain a compact reliability expression involving both complemented and un-complemented variables. Subsequently, four years later, (Abraham, 1979) modified AMG-algorithm to provide even lesser number of terms in the system reliability expression. Hundreds of papers have appeared in the literature thereafter, each one claiming to provide less number of terms in the network reliability expression than before for a given test problem. In fact this exercise is necessary in order to reduce computational time for TR evaluation of large and complex networks. Furthermore, network reliability evaluation is generally a routine procedure while designing networks and may have to be used repetitively many times.

The SDP based techniques can be classified into two categories, viz.,

i. Those, which use single variable inversion (SVI) and,
ii. Those, which employ multiple variable inversions (MVI).

In contrast to SVI technique, MVI technique inverts a part of the product of variables instead of a single variable at a time. This provides fewer numbers of disjoint terms, each of which covers a greater domain of Boolean structure function than is possible with single variable inversion.

The biggest advantages of the SDP techniques lie in their simplicity and independency with regard to the input they accept to generate mutually disjoint terms, which in turn have one-to-one relationship with the network reliability expression. The input to SDP approaches is a Boolean function formed by network variables (nodes and/or links) representing either *path sets, cut sets, spanning trees* or *k-trees or their duals*. Therefore, depending on the input function, the result would be in the form of *two-terminal, all-terminal* or *k-terminal* reliability polynomial. We utilize this advantage of SDP approaches for evaluating *k-terminal* reliability and *all-terminal* reliability of a network in subsequent chapters by providing a unified framework as well.

Exercises

1.1   Represent the adjacency matrix and connection matrix for the network given in Figure Ex. 1.1; also check whether it can be solved by *series-parallel* (SP) *or parallel-series* (PS) reduction technique for reliability evaluation.

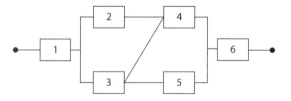

Figure Ex. 1.1 A complex network.

1.2   Enumerate the number of states of the network shown in Figure Ex. 1.1, by assuming the binary states (0-fail, 1-success) of the elements #1 to #6. Identify what are the success and failure states from such enumerations between the 'round' terminals.

1.3   Using the Decomposition method, draw the sub graphs of the RBD of the system shown in Figure Ex. 1.2 by taking element #2 as pivotal element.

Figure Ex. 1.2 A parallel network.

References

Abraham, J.A., 1979. An Improved Algorithm for Network Reliability. *IEEE Transaction on Reliability*, Vol. R-28(1), pp. 58–61.

Aggarwal, K.K., Misra, K.B. & Gupta, J.S., 1975. A fast Algorithm for Reliability Evaluation. *IEEE Transaction on Reliability*, Vol. R-24(1), pp. 83–85.

Aggarwal, A. & Satyanarayan, A., 1984. An (O/E) Time Algorithm for Computing the Reliability of a Class of Directed Networks. *Operations Research*, Vol. 32, pp. 493–517.

Aggrawal, A. & Barlow, R.E., 1984. A Survey of Network Reliability and Dominion Theory. *Operations Research*, Vol.32, pp. 478–492.

Barlow, R.E., 1982. *Set Theoretic Signed Domination for Coherent Systems*. Operation Research Centre Report No. 82-1. Berkeley: University of California.

Barlow, R. & Proschan, F., 1975. *Statistical Theory of Reliability and Life Testing: Probability Models*. Holt,Rinehart and Winston,Inc.

Christofides, N., 1975. *Graph Theory- Algorithm Approach*. New York: Academic Press, New York.

Colbourn, C.J., 1987. *The combinatorics of Network Reliability*. New York: Oxford University Press.

Deo, N., 1979. *Graph Theory with Applications to Engineering and Computer Science*. New edition ed. PHI.;

Elsayed, E.A., 1996. *Reliability Engineering*. USA: Addison Wesley Longman, Inc.

Frank, H. & Frisch, I.T., 1970. Analysis and Design of Survivable Networks. *IEEE Transactions on Communications*, Vol. COM-18, pp. 501–519.

Gadani, J.P., 1980. *On Some Aspects of Power System Reliability Analysis*. Ph.D Thesis. Indian Institute of Technology, Roorkee(India).

Gadani, J.P. & Misra, K.B., 1981. A network Reduction and Transformation Algorithm for the Assessment of System Effectiveness Indices. *IEEE Transactions on Reliability*, Vol R-30(1), pp. 48–57.

Gadani, J.P. & Misra, K.B., 1982. Quadrilateral Star Transformation: an Aid for Reliability Evaluation of Large Complex Systems. *IEEE Transaction on Reliability*, Vol. R-31(1), pp. 49–59.

Gertsbakh, I. & Shpungin, Y., 2009. *Models of network reliability. Analysis, Combinatorics and Monte Carlo*. CRC Press.

Grnarov, A.L., Klienrock, L. & Gerla, M., 1980. A New Algorithm for Symbolic Reliability in Communication Networks. In *Proc. Pacific Telecomm. Conf.*, 1980.

Misra, K.B., 1970. An Algorithm for Reliability Evaluation of Redundant Networks. *IEEE Transaction on Reliability*, Vol. R-19(4), pp. 146–151.

Misra, K.B., 1992. Reliability Analysis and Prediction: A Methodology Oriented Treatment. *Elsevier*.

Misra, K.B., ed., 1993. *New Trends in System Reliability Evaluation*. Elsevier.

Misra, K.B., 2008. *Handbook of Performability Engineering*. London: Springer Verlag,London Limited. DOI: 10.1007/978-1-84800-131-2.

Misra, K.B. & Prasad, P., 1982. Comment on Reliability Evaluation of Flow Networks. *IEEE Transaction on Reliability*, Vol. R-31(2), pp. 174–176.

Misra, K.B. & Rao, T.S.M., 1970. Reliability Analysis of Redundant Networks Using Flow Graphs. *IEEE Transaction on Reliability*, Vol. R-19(1), pp. 19–24.

Moskowitz, F., 1958. The Analysis of Redundancy Networks. *AIEE Transaction on Communications Electronics*, pp. 627–632.

Provan, J.S. & Ball, M.O., 1983. The Complexity of Counting Cuts and of Computing the Probability that a Graph is Connected. *SIAM J. of Computing*, Vol. 12, pp. 777–788.

Proven, J.S. & Ball, M., 1984. Computing Network Reliability in Time Polynomial in the Number of Cuts. *Operations Research*, Vol. 32, pp. 516–526.

Rosenthal, A. & Frisque, A.D., 1977. Transformations for Simplifying Network Reliability Calculations. *Networks*, Vol. 7, pp. 97–111.

Satyanarayan , A. & Wood, R.K., 1983. A Linear Time Algorithm for Computing k- terminal Reliability in Series- Parallel Networks. *SIAM Journal of Computing*, Vol. 14, pp. 818–832.

Satyanarayan, A. & Prabhakar, A., 1978. New Topological Formula and Rapid Algorithm for Reliability Analysis of Complex Networks. *IEEE Transaction on Reliability*, Vol. R-27(2), pp. 82–100.

Sheir, D.G., 1991. *Network Reliability and Algebraic Structure*. New York: Oxford University Press, New York.

Shooman, M.L., 1968. *Probabilistic reliability: an engineering approach*. New York: McGraw-Hill.

Shooman, M. & Kershenbaum, A., 1992. Methods for Communication-Network Reliability Analysis: Probablistic Graph Reduction. In *Proc. Annual Reliability and Maintainability Symposium.*, 1992.

Singh, B. & Proctor, C.L., 1976. Reliability Analysis of Multi-state Device Networks. *Proc. A. Reliability and Maintainability Symposium*, pp. 31–35.

Vertigan, D., 1990. *The Computational Complexity of tutte Invariants for Planar Graphs.* England: Mathematical Institute, University of Oxford.

Wilkov, R.S., 1972. Analysis and Design of Reliable Computer Networks. *IEEE Transactions on Communications*, Vol. COM-20, pp. 660–678.

Yoo, Y.B. & Deo, N., 1988. A Comparison of Algorithms for Terminal Pair Reliability. *IEEE Transaction on Reliability,* Vol. 37(2), pp. 210–215.

2

Reliability Evaluation of General SP-Networks

Reliability has become a key factor in the design and operation of modern large, complex, and expensive systems. It is no longer economically feasible to over design system facilities and to introduce excessive redundancy. Since 1950s, the mathematical theory of reliability started receiving a great deal of attention from engineers and mathematician. (Moor & Shannon, 1956), presented their first significant paper on mathematical modules of multi component system. In their paper, they examined that by proper incorporation of redundant units a network of high reliability could be constructed using relatively less reliable components. Subsequently, several papers have been published on the reliability evaluation of redundant and majority voting systems. A large number of techniques exist to improve the system reliability. Some of the important techniques have been:

- Parts improvement method,
- Effective and creative design,
- Use of overrated components,
- Structural redundancy.

The parts improvements technique involve with the improvement of reliability of at least the most critical, if not all, components. However, cost involved in the applications of new production techniques and automation required for this alternative thereof limits its use. Moreover, whatever improvement we may employ, production of a perfect part (100 % reliability) is almost impossible. Besides, this approach becomes unwieldy when one deals with large and complex systems. The effective and creative design approach needs some careful thinking on the part of design engineer to create a new or improved system with high reliability. Use of overrated component approach obviously would restrict its use due to the cost constraints and the availability of component with the requisite ratings.

However, structural redundancy provides a very effective means of improving system reliability by incorporating alternative routes at the component or subsystem levels. It not only needs comparatively less skill on the part of designer but also provides a quick solution to achieve desired level of reliability, if no constraint on space, weight, volume, cost etcetera are demanded. In a nutshell, if the state-of-art is such that either it is not possible to produce highly reliable components or the cost of producing such components is very high, we can improve the system reliability by the technique of introducing redundancies by deliberate creation of alternative parallel paths, if the design allows doing so.

Wide-ranging applications of redundancy in system design can be found in almost all types of systems, viz., interconnected power systems, protective schemes in nuclear reactors, data processing systems etcetera. The list is endless. However, when a system is formed from units connected in series, parallel and in mixed configurations of series-parallel or parallel-series, a suitable and efficient method of calculating its reliability becomes essential.

Therefore, both in system analysis and design, the following aids and tools are of great importance:

- A set of applicable mathematical models,
- Concept and procedure for estimating system reliability and comparing alternative designs, and
- Efficient computer programs to conduct an effective and efficient reliability analysis; and predict the overall reliability of such systems consisting of arbitrary or mixed redundancies viz., active, standby and/ or k-out-of-m.

There are several methods available to evaluate the overall reliability of such systems. As pointed out in *Chapter 1, Section 1.1* that any technique, which can evaluate reliability of NSP systems, can undoubtedly be applicable to SP systems, i.e., path sets or cut sets based approaches, decomposition and reduction techniques or composite methods etc. However, these methods are found to be less efficient in dealing with these types of systems.

(Misra & Rao, 1970), presented a procedure for reliability evaluation of redundant networks using flow graphs. This was the first time that the graph theory was used for reliability evaluation for systems and was considered a breakthrough in the area of reliability evaluation. In another companion paper by Misra, (Misra, 1970) a matrix method was introduced using properties of graphs. This technique computes the overall system reliability very fast and efficiently with minimum effort on the part of the user and without keeping a track of any sequence of operators. It was considered to be a major breakthrough in the reliability evaluation techniques that do not rely on path or cut sets enumeration but on the basics of series-parallel reduction rule. The approach is still considered to be one of the fastest approaches to date for evaluating reliability of SP-systems. This approach (Misra, 1970) was extended to non-series parallel configurations using factoring theorem.

Another important advantage we draw from the above algorithm is to obtain a reducible large and complex system to a non-reducible system, in the form of its connection matrix wherein non-zero elements of the matrix represent the equivalent reliabilities of the units connected between a pair of nodes. It is not without a reason as no practical system is solely a non-reducible system, as it would have different types of redundancies and parallelism at subsystems or components level, and sometimes at systems level as well. This connection matrix of the non-reducible system can be utilized to enumerate *path sets, cut sets, spanning trees* and *k-trees* for which these algorithms inherently require the connection matrix of non-reducible model, as would be described later in Chapter 3.

This chapter briefly introduces the various types of failure distributions useful in reliability analysis and management, module representation of reliability graphs, and Misra Matrix method (Misra & Rao, 1970) by suitably modifying and extending its applicability to the systems having mixed redundancies.

2.1   Notation and Assumptions

The notations useful for this chapter are:

m	= number of units in a redundant module.
E_i	= Event that units i operates successfully.

$\overline{E}_i$ = Event that units i have failed.

$p_i(t)$ = The reliability or probability of success of ith unit.

$q_i(t)$ = The unreliability or probability of failure of ith unit.

$R_{series}(t)$ = Reliability of a series module.

$R_{parallel}(t)$ = Reliability of a parallel module.

$R_{standby}(t)$ = Reliability of a standby module.

$R_{km}(t)$ = Reliability of a *k-out of-m*: G module.

While describing the methodology to evaluate SP-system reliability, we make the following assumptions:

   i.   The logical manner or configuration in which modules have been connected to form the system is known.

   ii.   The units in a module are statistically independent, i.e., the failure of one component does not affect the probability of failure of other component.

  iii.   The units in standby module are identical whereas in other redundant modules they may have similar or/and dissimilar units.

  iv.   The reliability or the hazard rate pattern of each unit in the system and the relationships among the units, in the form of a reliability graph, are known. Additionally, either the reliability or the failure rate distribution parameters of the unit is known.

   v.   Mission time is implicit in the system reliability calculation.

2.2   Unit-Reliability and Failure Models

Every system whatsoever big, can be divided into several parts and units. The failure of system as a whole or a part, all depends upon the functional interactions of system components. Besides, the behavioural characteristics exhibited by one class of components differ from those exhibited by the other class of components. Each unit of the system may contribute significantly to the over-all reliability of the system. Thus it is imperative to have a mathematical model representing the failure characteristics of units. This also helps in comparing different behavioural patterns and to draw definite and general conclusions for similar units. Here we briefly describe the four commonly employed hazard rate model used in reliability analysis and design.

2.2.1   Constant-Hazard Model

The simplest case that we consider is the constancy of failure rate with time. For an ith component with constant hazard rate, this model takes the form: $h_i(t) = \lambda_i$ Where, λ_i is a constant and is independent of time, and would have the reliability expression as:

$$p_i(t) = e^{-\lambda_i t} \qquad (2.1)$$

An example that exhibits this characteristic is electronic components and this model has been used extensively in reliability research and studies.

2.2.2   Linear-Hazard Model

The linear-hazard model is the simplest among the time-dependent model for reliability analysis and design. Unlike the constant hazard-model, which assumes that units do not deteriorate with time, this module assumes that the rate, at which the random failures of units occur, linearly increases with time. Many mechanical components that are under stresses fail due to wear-out and deterioration. The general form of this model for some unit i, is given as:

$$h_i(t) = a_i + b_i$$

and the component reliability can be written as:

$$p_i(t) = e^{-(a_i t + b_i t^2/2)} \qquad (2.2)$$

2.2.3   Weibull-Hazard Model

There are many situations in which the failure rate cannot be approximated by a straight line. In such cases, the Weibull model can be used to fit the non-linear behaviour of $h_i(t)$. This model is expressed as:

$$h_i(t) = a_i t^{b_i}$$

This gives us the reliability expression as:

$$p_i(t) = e^{-\frac{a_i t^{b_i+1}}{b_i+1}} \qquad (2.3)$$

This model has two parameters, viz., scale parameter, a, which affects the amplitude and the shape parameter b. The *characteristic life*, (at which the 63.2% failures are expected to be observed in a population or at which the failure probability is 0.632) and a commonly used term with this distribution, given in terms of its parameter is $\theta = \left(\dfrac{b+1}{a}\right)^{\frac{1}{b+1}}$ time

unit. This is the most general representation as it can generates a wide range of hazard modes for various values of parameters a and b. This model also includes the two previously discussed forms, i.e., b = 0, would produce the constant-hazard model and b =1 could represent a linearly increasing hazard model.

2.2.4   Extreme Value-Hazard Model

This model can be represented by:

$$h_i(t) = a_i e^{b_i t}$$

and the reliability expression for some component i is given by:

$$p_i\left(t\right) = e^{\frac{a_i}{b_i}\left(e^{b_i t}-1\right)} \tag{2.4}$$

2.3   Module Representation of Reliability Graphs

The section describes the most commonly used models in reliability engineering and can be termed as *basic building blocks* of a much bigger systems. A module is defined to be a unit, or simply several connected units in different configurations. A configuration permitted, as a module is limited to either of the following:

2.3.1   Single-Unit Module

A single unit module is a module, which consists of a solitary unit. The module reliability is the reliability of unit itself. The connection of this module, end to end, yields a model known as series model.

2.3.2   Multi-Unit Module

Several units connected in various configurations form this module. However, depending on the interrelationship, the units may have, this module is sub classified into following models:

Figure 2.1 Series model.

2.3.2.1   Series Model

The series model is the most commonly encountered model and is also the simplest configuration to analyse. Apart from at the working stage of a system, this model is being used to depict the system at early design stages where the details on design are gradually evolving. In this model, all units must operate successfully if the system is to function. Since, upon the failure of any one-unit, the system fails. The dependency or independency of failure would make no difference. *The reliability of this model would always be less than or equal to the least reliable unit.* The block diagram representation of the model is shown in Figure 2.1 and the reliability of this module,, is given by (2.5). Equation (2.5) is also known as the product rule in reliability engineering.

$$R_{series}(t) = \begin{cases} P\{E_1 \cap E_2 \cap E_3 \cap \ldots \cap E_m\} \\ \text{on the assumption of independent t events, this becomes} \\ P(E_1).P(E_2).P(E_3)\ldots P(E_m) \\ \displaystyle\prod_{i=1}^{m} p_i(t) \end{cases} \tag{2.5}$$

Example 2.1: A power supply contains three rectifiers in series. Each rectifier has a distribution with shape parameter b equal to 1.2 but different characteristic lives given by 12000 hours, 15000 hours and 21000 hours, respectively. Determine the design-life of the power supply for a reliability requirement of 0.90.

Solution: Since, the characteristic life, $\theta_i = \left(\dfrac{b_i+1}{a_i}\right)^{\frac{1}{b_i+1}}$, Equation (2.3) can be rewritten as:

$p_i(t) = e^{-\left(\frac{t}{\grave{e}_i}\right)^{b_i+1}}$, where $b_1 = b_2 = b_3 = 1.2$, and $\theta_1 = 12000$, $\theta_2 = 15000$, $\theta_3 = 21000$, and system reliability, $R_s(t_d) = 0.90$, $t_d = ?$

Therefore, the reliability of the series system of three Weibull units at $t = 5000$ hours is given by:

$$R_s\left(t_d\right)=e^{-\left[\left(\frac{t_d}{12000}\right)^{2.2}+\left(\frac{t_d}{15000}\right)^{2.2}+\left(\frac{t_d}{21000}\right)^{2.2}\right]}=0.90,$$

Solving for t_d yields the design-life of power supply, $t_d = 3219.737$ hours.

2.3.2.2   Parallel Model

A system with m number of units is said to be an m-unit parallel model if the successful functioning of any one of the units lead to the module success. This type of structure is also known as active redundant model. In reliability sense, such a system could be represented as shown in Figure 2.2. The reliability of this model is given by equation (2.6):

$$R_{parallel}\left(t\right)=\begin{bmatrix}P\left\{E_1\cup E_2\cup E_3\cup\ldots\cup E_m\right\}\\ 1-P\left\{\overline{E}_1\cap\overline{E}_2\cap\overline{E}_3\cap\ldots\cap\overline{E}_m\right\}\\ 1-P\left(\overline{E}_1\right).P\left(\overline{E}_2\right).P\left(\overline{E}_3\right)\ldots P\left(\overline{E}_m\right)\\ 1-\prod_{i=1}^{m}q_i\left(t\right)\\ 1-\prod_{i=1}^{m}\left(1-p_i\left(t\right)\right)\\ 1-\left(1-p\left(t\right)\right)^{m}\end{bmatrix}\qquad(2.6)$$

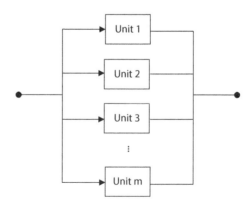

Figure 2.2 Parallel model.

However, this model would not be a true representative of many practical situations. For instance, in a communication system with three transmitters, the average message load may be such that at least two transmitters must be operational at all times to avoid message loss. Resistors and capacitors can also create design problems when they are put actively in parallel. The failure of one of two such components operating in parallel would change the circuit constants. Under such circumstances, another type of modules known as standby and k-out-of-m model are more appropriate and practical to use.

Example 2.2: A pressure gauge has been observed to Weibull failure distribution with a shape parameter of 1.1 and a characteristic life of 15000 hours. If two such gauges are used in redundant configuration, then determine the reliability of the system for 5000 hours.

Solution: The units are identical with p_1 (5000) = p_2 (5000) = 0.9052. Therefore, the reliability of pressure gauge system, R_s (5000) = p_1 (5000) + p_2 (5000) – p_1 (5000) $*$ p_2 (5000) = 0.9910.

2.3.2.3   Standby Model

Unlike the parallel model, wherein all units are operating at any given time, in this model, one or more standby units wait to take over the operation from the on-line operating unit as soon as this unit fails. The standby units replace the failed unit instantaneously on failure of operative unit in sequence, either manually or automatically such that the proper system operation continues uninterrupted. Hence the reliability of operator or sensing device and switching mechanism become critical and must be very high. A general m-unit standby model is shown in Figure 2.3.

Assuming that all units are identical, the reliability of this model is given by equation (2.7) as:

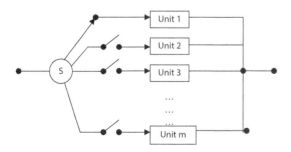

Figure 2.3 Standby model with common switching device.

$$R_{standby}(t) = p(t)\left[1 + \sum_{j=1}^{m-1} \frac{\left(\left|\ln p(t)\right|\right)^{j}}{j!}\right] \qquad (2.7)$$

Note that the above equation is valid under the assumption with perfect switch and no failure in the standby mode. Due to the fact that the standby unit becomes alive only after the failure of on-line unit, the reliability of this module would be higher than that of a module having equal number of units in parallel in active redundant mode of operation. Several recent and old texts provide on variations on such model such as (Misra, 1992), (Misra, 1993), (Elsayed, 1996), (Ebeling, 2011).

Example 2.3: A printing company has three presses with one operating and other two are in standby. Each press is identical with a failure rate of 0.02 failures per hour. The company received an order that require 75 hour of continuous time on a press. Determine the reliability of the printing support while order is being processed.

Solution: Here, total number of units in the standby configuration is m = 3. For constant failure rate, 0.2231. Using equation (2.7), the reliability of print-

ing support, $R_s(75) = 0.2231 \times \left(1 + \dfrac{\left|\ln(0.2231)\right|}{1!} + \dfrac{\left|\ln(0.2231)\right|^2}{2!}\right) = 0.8088$.

2.3.2.4 k-out-of-m Model

Another important practical model is one where to avoid failure of the system; more than one of its parallel units are required to function. If any *k* out of *m* units of the models are essential to function than such models are known as *k-out-of –m: Good* or simply *k-out-of –m: G* models as *k* units are supposed to be *Good*, out of the *m* units.

On the other hand, if *k* units out of *m*, must fail (or *Bad*) for a system to fail, the model is known as *k-out-of –m: B* model.

In general, a *k-out-of –m: G* model can also be modelled on the basis of *(m-k+1)-out-of –m: B* model. A schematic representation of *k-out-of –m: G* model is shown in Figure 2.4.

For this module, where the units are identical and statistically independent, the binomial distribution can be used to evaluate module's reliability, i.e., if *p(t)* is the success of each unit, than the probability that *k* out of *m* units would be successful is given by:

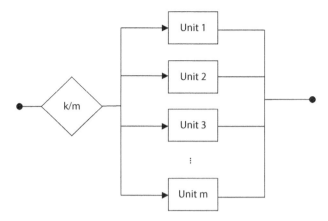

Figure 2.4 k-out-of-m model.

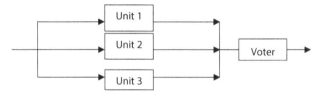

Figure 2.5 Voting system.

$$R_{k/m}(t) = \sum_{i=k}^{m} \binom{m}{i} p(t)^i * \left(1 - p(t)\right)^{m-i} \qquad (2.8)$$

In this type of module, there may be a crossover point where the single-component reliability will be greater than the *k-out-of –m* system reliability and configuration does not provide any benefit unless the component reliability is more than the crossover point reliability. If R is the single component reliability, then the cross over point can be determined by solving:

$$R(t) = \sum_{i=k}^{m} \binom{m}{i} R(t)^i * \left(1 - R(t)\right)^{m-i}$$

Example 2.4: In the design of computer systems, increased reliability can be achieved through the use of triple redundancy (consisting of three identical units with reliability of R each and a *2-out-of–3 configuration*) feeding into a common voting system with a reliability of R_v as shown in the Figure 2.5. Prove that the system reliability is given by $R^2(3–2R) \times R_v$.

Solution: As the units are identical, we can use equation (2.8) with k = 2, m = 3 and p(t) = R, i.e.,

$$R_{2/3} = \sum_{i=2}^{3} \binom{3}{i} R^i (1-R)^{3-i} = R^2 (3-2R),$$

Since, the voter is in series with the 2-out-of-3 redundant system, therefore the reliability of triple redundant system = $R^2(3-2R) \times R_v$

Example 2.5: In the above example, if R_v = 0.9, determine the crossover point reliability.

Solution: The crossover point can be found by solving $R_{2/3} = R =$ $\sum_{i=2}^{3} \binom{3}{i} R_i (1-R)^{3-i} = R^2 (3-2R)$, which gives R=0.5. It means that if the unit reliability is below 0.5, the system reliability will be worse than

0.5 where as if unit reliability is > 0.5 then the system reliability will be better than 0.5. At crossover point, the system reliability is $R^2(3-2R)R_v$ = $0.5^2(3-2 \times 0.5) \times 0.9 = 0.45$.

There are several other approaches exist to calculate the reliability of such systems. (Balaguruswami & Misra, 1976), provided an approach for evaluating the exact reliability with different unit failure probabilities and with general type of failure distributions of the constituent units. (Barlow & Heidtmann, 1984) proposed that reliability of this model could be computed exactly by expanding a generating function *g(z)* and collecting the terms corresponding the power of 'z' varying from *k* to *m*. The recursive use of probability law of union or SDP techniques can also be applied to solve *k-out-of -m* redundancy problem (Locks, 1984).

Example 2.6: Consider a 3-out-of-4 configuration with dissimilar units. Determine the reliability expression and system reliability for reliability of the units as 0.6, 0.7, 0.8, and 0.9, respectively.

Solution: If the units are labelled as 1, 2, 3, and 4 then working of the following units together will yield system success, viz., E_1 = {1, 2, 3} or E_2 = {1, 2, 4} or E_3 = {1, 3, 4} or E_4 = {2, 3, 4}. Unionizing these situations would yield, reliability of 3-out-of-4: G system with dissimilar units as,

$$R_s(t) = p_1(t)p_2(t)p_3(t) + p_1(t)p_2(t)p_4(t) + p_1(t)p_3(t)p_4(t) + p_2(t)p_3(t)p_4(t)$$
$$- 4\, p_1(t)\, p_2(t)p_3(t)p_4(t) + p_1(t)\, p_2(t)p_3(t)p_4(t)$$

$$R_s(t) = 0.6 \times 0.7 \times 0.8 + 0.6 \times 0.7 \times 0.9 + 0.6 \times 0.8 \times 0.9 \times$$
$$+ 0.7 \times 0.8 \times 0.9 - 4 \times 0.6 \times 0.7 \times 0.8 \times 0.9 \times$$
$$+ 0.6 \times 0.7 \times 0.8 \times 0.9 = 0.7428$$

For identical units with equal reliability, $p_1(t) = p_2(t) = p_3(t) = p_4(t) = p$
$R_s(t) = 4p^3 - 3p^4$

JG Algorithm for k-out-of-m System: In this text, we describe an approach by (Jain & Gopal, 1985), which would update the reliability of such model recursively as the units are added one by one to in a system configuration. The basic recursion formula of the algorithm is:

$$R_{k,k+i}(t) = R_{k,k}(t) + \sum_{j=1}^{i} R_{k+j,k+j}(t) \left[\sum_{jl=l}^{j+k-1} \prod_{l=1}^{j} \frac{q_{jl}(t)}{P_{jl}(t)} \right] \qquad (2.9)$$

Where, $R_{k,k+i}(t)$ is the reliability of a k-out-of- $(k + i)$: G system. By varying i from $i = 0$ to $i = m\text{-}k$, we can determine the reliability of *k-out-of-m* model. If the units are identical, than equation (2.9) could be simplified as:

$$R_{k,k+i} = \left[p(t) \right]^k + \sum_{j=1}^{i} \left[p(t) \right]^{k+j} \left[\binom{j+k-1}{i} \left[\frac{q(t)}{p(t)} \right]^j \right] \qquad (2.10)$$

It also offers the solution exactly in $\binom{m}{k}$ terms. For instance, using JG algorithm the following equations would evolve from the recursive use of equation (2.9) for k-out-of-4:G system for k =1, 2, 3, i.e.,

for $k = 1, 1 - \text{out} - \text{of} - 4$:G, $R_{1,4} = R_{1,1} + R_{2,2} \left[\dfrac{q_1}{P_1} \right] + R_{3,3} \left[\dfrac{q_1 q_2}{P_1 P_2} \right] + R_{4,4} \left[\dfrac{q_1 q_2 q_3}{P_1 P_2 P_3} \right]$

for $k = 2, 2 - \text{out} - \text{of} - 4$:G, $R_{2,4} = R_{2,2} + R_{3,3} \left[\dfrac{q_1}{P_1} + \dfrac{q_2}{P_2} \right] + R_{4,4} \left[\dfrac{q_1 q_2}{P_1 P_2} + \dfrac{q_1 q_3}{P_1 P_3} \dfrac{q_2 q_3}{P_2 P_3} \right]$

for $k = 3, 3 - \text{out} - \text{of} - 4$:G, $R_{3,4} = R_{3,3} + R_{4,4} \left[\dfrac{q_1}{P_1} + \dfrac{q_2}{P_2} + \dfrac{q_3}{P_3} \right]$

Where, $R_{i,i} = R_1 \times R_2 \dots R_i$

Example 2.7: Determine the reliability of a 3-out-of-4 configuration with dissimilar units using JG algorithm with the data given in earlier example.

Solution: The Reliability of 3 – out – of – 4:G,

$$R_{3,4} = R_{3,3} + R_{4,4}\left[\frac{q_1}{p_1} + \frac{q_2}{p_2} + \frac{q_3}{p_3}\right]$$

$$= 0.6 \times 0.7 \times 0.8 \times 0.6 \times 0.7 \times 0.8 \times 0.9 \times \left[\frac{0.4}{0.6} + \frac{0.3}{0.7} + \frac{0.2}{0.8}\right]$$

$$= 0.7428$$

2.4   Misra Matrix Method

This section presents a method for general but large SP system comprising various redundancies. At the basic level, where only parallel redundancies are assumed to exist in the system, the following steps are being followed (Misra, 1970), (Misra, 1992):

1. Given the reliability of each unit in the system and relationships between the units in the form of a reliability graph, the method starts with the development of a weighted connection matrix [C] *on fly* i.e., while the data about the system is being read from a file or inputted by the user into the computer, the elements of the connection matrix gets updated. The input data consists of such information about each unit on its
   - Starting node,
   - Finishing node, and
   - Reliability of the unit.
2. While reading the data of a unit, if it is found that a non-zero entry already exists for that position in the connection matrix [C] then the reliability of the new unit is combined using the union law and the entry at that position is updated. In other words, all units connected between any pair of nodes, say, i and j are being replaced by a single unit having an equivalent reliability value as determined by using equation (2.6) between this pair of nodes.
3. Finally the weighted matrix [C] obtained so would have a property that for any non-zero entry in [C] there exists one and only one link between any pair of nodes.
4. Further, to minimize the storage requirement, the column corresponding to source node in [C] matrix stores the

out-degree information of each node whereas the row corresponding to the sink node is utilized for storing the in-degree information of each node.

5. The algorithm starts with the elimination process of entries in the connection matrix [C] with a node, say, i, that has its out-degree and in-degree equal to unity. After eliminating and updating the entry in matrix [C], another node having the property of equal and unity in-out degree is looked for elimination.

6. The process continues till all such nodes will get exhausted. At this point, matrix [C] would have only one non-zero entry corresponding to the element C (source, terminal) of [C] which would be the overall reliability of the systems.

We modify input information about the system feed to the computer and the vital step 5 of the original algorithm wherein the units connected in parallel are replaced with an equivalent unit. This modification would make it more general and applicable to the existence of the type of redundancies discussed in the previous sections.

2.5   Algorithm

The steps in the extended and modified algorithm are summarized as under:

1. Read number of nodes, n and
2. Initialize weighted connection matrix $[C]_{nxn}$ with all element set to zero.
3. Read the data in the following manner for each unit in the system:
   i. Node numbers to which the unit is connected.
   ii. Read either Reliability or the type of failure distribution of unit viz., exponential, Rayleigh (Linear), Weibull or Extreme value.

If reliability of the unit is given then go to next step, Otherwise, read distribution parameters (a, b) and time, t. Calculate the reliability, $p_{xyi}(t)$, say, for a unit i connected between nodes x and y for the following hazard rate functions:

$$P_{xyi}(t) = \begin{cases} \exp\left(-a_{xyi}t\right) & \text{if the } h_i(t) = a_i, \text{for constant} \\ \exp\left(-a_{xyi}*t + b_{xyi}\,t^2/2\right), & \text{if } h_{xyi}(t) = a_{xyi} + b_{xyi}t, \text{for linear (Rayleigh)} \\ \exp\left(-\dfrac{a_{xyi}*t^{b_{xyi}+1}}{b_{xyi}+1}\right), & \text{if } h_{xyi}(t) = a_{xyi}t^{b_{xyi}}, \text{ for Weibull} \\ \exp\left(-\dfrac{a_{xyi}}{b_{xyi}}\left(e^{b_{xyi}t}-1\right)\right), & \text{if } h_{xyi}(t) = a_{xyi}e^{b_{xyi}t} \text{ for extreme value.} \end{cases} \tag{2.11}$$

Update connection matrix [C] if, element $C(x,y) = 0$, then $C(x,y) = p_{xyi}(t)$, Otherwise, update the value of $C(x,y)$ in the following manner:

$$C(x,y)_{new} = \begin{cases} \text{Active Redundancy} \\ C(x,y)_{old} + p_{xyi}(t) - C(x,y)_{old}*p_{xyi}(t) & (2.12) \\ \text{Standby Redundancy (identical units case only) } p(t) = p_{xyi}(t)\,\forall xyi \\ \left[C(x,y)_{old} = \dfrac{\left(\left|\ln p(t)\right|\right)^r}{r!} \right], \qquad \text{for } r > 1 & (2.13) \\ k - out - of - m : G \\ C(x,y)_{old}*p(t), \qquad \text{for } 2 \le i \le k & (2.14) \\ \text{and,} \\ \text{(i) for identical units:} \\ C(x,y)_{old} + \left[p(t)\right]^i \left[\binom{m}{ii-k}\left[\dfrac{q(t)}{p(t)}\right]^{ii-k}\right], \text{for } k+1 \le ii \le m-k & (2.15) \\ \text{(ii) for non-identical units:} \\ C(x,y)_{old} + \prod_{jj=1}^{i} P_{jj}(t)\left[\sum_{jl=1}^{ii-1}\prod_{ii=1}^{ii-k}\dfrac{q_{jl}}{P_{jl}}\right], \text{for } k+1 \le ii \le m-k & (2.16) \end{cases}$$

4. Define in and out degrees for each node in [C].
5. Eliminate the node z that has degrees $in_{zz} = out_z = 1$.
6. Transfer the product $C(i,z) * C(z,j)$ to location by modifying the old $C(i,j)$ entry using

$$C(i,j)_{new} = C(i,j)_{old} + C(i,z)*C(z,j) - C(i,j)_{old}*C(i,z)*C(z,j) \tag{2.17}$$

Also reset the entries $C(i,z) = C(z,j) = 0$.

7. Check whether all the intermediate nodes have been eliminated: if not, go to step 6. Otherwise print out the element $C(Source, \sin k)$ of the [C], which is the reliability of the network
8. Stop.

We illustrate the above algorithm by taking some examples.

Example 2.8: To illustrate the above algorithm, let us consider a fairly complicated reliability graph, of 8 nodes and 16 units from (Henley & Williams, 1973) with modifications, shown in Figure 2.6. The reliability of each unit is given in Table 2.1. The tags of units have been attached with an arbitrarily order to input the system data to the computer and to show the versatility of the algorithm.

Solution: It is apparent from Figure 2.6, that module consisting of units number 11, 13, 15 is a *2-out-of-3 model* whereas units number 14 and 16 constitue *a stanby module*. The development of matrix [C] as the data supplied sequentially has been shown below in a tabular form for brevity, wherein the highlighted entry show an alteration in the element's value upon addition of a new unit.

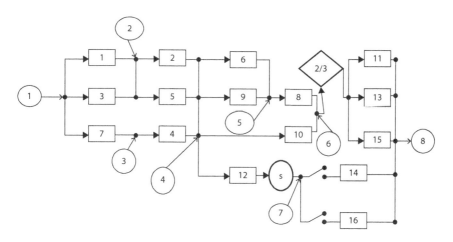

Figure 2.6 Reliability logic diagram of a 16 units systems.

Table 2.1 Reliability of units for system shown in figure 2.6.

Unit$_i$	R$_i$	Unit$_i$	R$_i$	Unit$_i$	R$_i$	Unit$_i$	R$_i$
1.	0.80	5.	0.85	9.	0.62	13.	0.85
2.	0.75	6.	0.82	10.	0.88	14.	0.90
3.	0.70	7.	0.90	11.	0.85	15.	0.85
4.	0.87	8.	0.89	12	0.75	16.	0.90

Matrix [C] initialized. 8×8

0	0	0	0	0	0	0	0
0	0	0	0	0	0	0	0
0	0	0	0	0	0	0	0
0	0	0	0	0	0	0	0
0	0	0	0	0	0	0	0
0	0	0	0	0	0	0	0
0	0	0	0	0	0	0	0
0	0	0	0	0	0	0	0

Unit no.# 1 is added between nodes 1-2.

0	0.8	0	0	0	0	0	0
0	0	0	0	0	0	0	0
0	0	0	0	0	0	0	0
0	0	0	0	0	0	0	0
0	0	0	0	0	0	0	0
0	0	0	0	0	0	0	0
0	0	0	0	0	0	0	0
0	0	0	0	0	0	0	0

Unit no. #2 added between nodes 2-4

0	0.8	0	0	0	0	0	0
0	0	0	0.75	0	0	0	0
0	0	0	0	0	0	0	0
0	0	0	0	0	0	0	0
0	0	0	0	0	0	0	0
0	0	0	0	0	0	0	0
0	0	0	0	0	0	0	0
0	0	0	0	0	0	0	0

Element C(1,2) updated on addition of Unit no. #3 using (2.12): active redundancy

0	0.94	0	0	0	0	0	0
0	0	0	0.75	0	0	0	0
0	0	0	0	0	0	0	0
0	0	0	0	0	0	0	0
0	0	0	0	0	0	0	0
0	0	0	0	0	0	0	0
0	0	0	0	0	0	0	0
0	0	0	0	0	0	0	0

Unit no. # 4 added between nodes 3-4

0	0.94	0	0	0	0	0	0
0	0	0	0.75	0	0	0	0
0	0	0	0.87	0	0	0	0
0	0	0	0	0	0	0	0
0	0	0	0	0	0	0	0
0	0	0	0	0	0	0	0
0	0	0	0	0	0	0	0
0	0	0	0	0	0	0	0

Element C(2, 4) updated on addition of Unit no. #5 using (2.12): active redundancy

0	0.94	0	0	0	0	0	0
0	0	0	0.9625	0	0	0	0
0	0	0	0.87	0	0	0	0
0	0	0	0	0	0	0	0
0	0	0	0	0	0	0	0
0	0	0	0	0	0	0	0
0	0	0	0	0	0	0	0
0	0	0	0	0	0	0	0

Unit no. #6 added between nodes 4-5.

0	0.94	0	0	0	0	0	0
0	0	0	0.9625	0	0	0	0
0	0	0	0.87	0	0	0	0
0	0	0	0	0.82	0	0	0
0	0	0	0	0	0	0	0
0	0	0	0	0	0	0	0
0	0	0	0	0	0	0	0
0	0	0	0	0	0	0	0

Unit no. #7 added between nodes 1-3.

0	0.94	0.9	0	0	0	0	0
0	0	0	0.9625	0	0	0	0
0	0	0	0.87	0	0	0	0
0	0	0	0	0.82	0	0	0
0	0	0	0	0	0	0	0
0	0	0	0	0	0	0	0
0	0	0	0	0	0	0	0
0	0	0	0	0	0	0	0

Unit no. #8 added between nodes 5-6.								Element C(4, 5) updated on addition of Unit no. #9 using (2.12): active redundancy							
0	0.94	0.9	0	0	0	0	0	0	0.94	0.9	0	0	0	0	0
0	0	0	0.9625	0	0	0	0	0	0	0	0.9625	0	0	0	0
0	0	0	0.87	0	0	0	0	0	0	0	0.87	0	0	0	0
0	0	0	0	0.82	0	0	0	0	0	0	0	0.9316	0	0	0
0	0	0	0	0	0.89	0	0	0	0	0	0	0	0.89	0	0
0	0	0	0	0	0	0	0	0	0	0	0	0	0	0	0
0	0	0	0	0	0	0	0	0	0	0	0	0	0	0	0
0	0	0	0	0	0	0	0	0	0	0	0	0	0	0	0

Unit no. # 10 added between nodes 4-6.								Unit no. #11 added between nodes 6-8.							
0	0.94	0.9	0	0	0	0	0	0	0.94	0.9	0	0	0	0	0
0	0	0	0.9625	0	0	0	0	0	0	0	0.9625	0	0	0	0
0	0	0	0.87	0	0	0	0	0	0	0	0.87	0	0	0	0
0	0	0	0	0.9316	0.88	0	0	0	0	0	0	0.9316	0.88	0	0
0	0	0	0	0	0.89	0	0	0	0	0	0	0	0.89	0	0
0	0	0	0	0	0	0	0	0	0	0	0	0	0	0	0.85
0	0	0	0	0	0	0	0	0	0	0	0	0	0	0	0
0	0	0	0	0	0	0	0	0	0	0	0	0	0	0	0

Unit no. #12 added between nodes 4-7.								Element C(6, 8) updated on addition of Unit no. #13 using (2.14-2.16): 2-out-of-3							
0	0.94	0.9	0	0	0	0	0	0	0.94	0.9	0	0	0	0	0
0	0	0	0.9625	0	0	0	0	0	0	0	0.9625	0	0	0	0
0	0	0	0.87	0	0	0	0	0	0	0	0.87	0	0	0	0
0	0	0	0	0.9316	0.88	0.75	0	0	0	0	0	0.9316	0.88	0.75	0
0	0	0	0	0	0.89	0	0	0	0	0	0	0	0.89	0	0
0	0	0	0	0	0	0	0.85	0	0	0	0	0	0	0	0.7225
0	0	0	0	0	0	0	0	0	0	0	0	0	0	0	0
0	0	0	0	0	0	0	0	0	0	0	0	0	0	0	0

Unit no. # 14 added between nodes 7-8 using (2.8).								Element C(6, 8) updated on addition of Unit no. #15 using (2.10)							
0	0.94	0.9	0	0	0	0	0	0	0.94	0.9	0	0	0	0	0
0	0	0	0.9625	0	0	0	0	0	0	0	0.9625	0	0	0	0
0	0	0	0.87	0	0	0	0	0	0	0	0.87	0	0	0	0
0	0	0	0	0.9316	0.88	0.75	0	0	0	0	0	0.9316	0.88	0.75	0
0	0	0	0	0	0.89	0	0	0	0	0	0	0	0.89	0	0
0	0	0	0	0	0	0	0.7225	0	0	0	0	0	0	0	0.93925
0	0	0	0	0	0	0	0.9	0	0	0	0	0	0	0	0.9
0	0	0	0	0	0	0	0	0	0	0	0	0	0	0	0

Element C(7, 8) updated on addition of Unit no. #16							
0	0.94	0.9	0	0	0	0	0
0	0	0	0.9625	0	0	0	0
0	0	0	0.87	0	0	0	0
0	0	0	0	0.9316	0.88	0.75	0
0	0	0	0	0	0.89	0	0
0	0	0	0	0	0	0	0.93925
0	0	0	0	0	0	0	0.994824
0	0	0	0	0	0	0	0

Matrix [C] at the end of data read operation

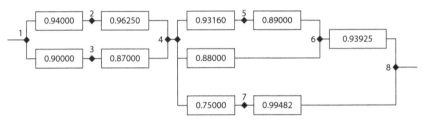

Figure 2.7 Reduced system at the end of data-read.

A reduced system can easily be constructed from matrix [C] as shown in Figure 2.7

Now the reliabilty evaluation process starts from step#5 onwards. The tabular from shows these steps with respective Figures of reduced system side by side after sequential elimination of nodes. It is worthwhile to note that at each step the size of [C] reduced by one.

Matrix [C] with in/out degrees of each node and elimination of node 2 begins.							
2	0.94	0.9	0	0	0	0	0
1	0	0	0.9625	0	0	0	0
1	0	0	0.87	0	0	0	0
3	0	0	0	0.9316	0.88	0.75	0
1	0	0	0	0	0.89	0	0
1	0	0	0	0	0	0	0.93925
1	0	0	0	0	0	0	0.994824
0	1	1	2	1	2	1	2

Node 2 gets eliminated and respective element's value also gets updated.						
2	0.9	0.90475	0	0	0	0
1	0	0.87	0	0	0	0
3	0	0	0.9316	0.88	0.75	0
1	0	0	0	0.89	0	0
1	0	0	0	0	0	0.93925
1	0	0	0	0	0	0.994824
0	1	2	1	2	1	2

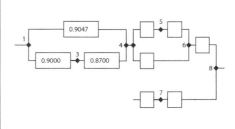

Node 3 gets eliminated and equivalent transmittance between node 1 & 4 gets computed					
1	0.979331	0	0	0	0
3	0	0.9316	0.88	0.75	0
1	0	0	0.89	0	0
1	0	0	0	0	0.93925
1	0	0	0	0	0.994824
0	1	1	2	1	2

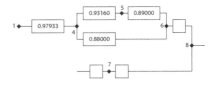

Node 5 gets eliminated and equivalent transmittance between node 4 & 6 gets computed.				
1	0.979331	0	0	0
2	0	0.979495	0.75	0
1	0	0	0	0.93925
1	0	0	0	0.994824
0	1	1	1	2

Node 6 gets eliminated.			
1	0.979331	0	0
2	0	0.75	0.919991
1	0	0	0.994824
0	1	1	2

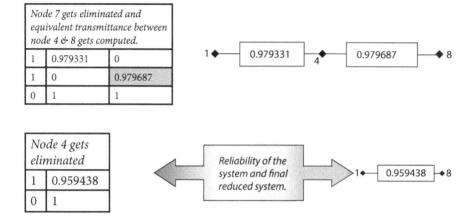

Node 7 gets eliminated and equivalent transmittance between node 4 & 8 gets computed.		
1	0.979331	0
1	0	0.979687
0	1	1

Node 4 gets eliminated	
1	0.959438
0	1

As a second example, we consider a more realistic system- a Fire Detector System.

Example 2.9: Reliability logic diagram of a pneumatic system (Chaudhari *et al.*, 2001) shown in Figure 2.8.

It consists of 3 parts: heat detection, smoke detection, and a manually-operated alarm button. In the heat-detection section, there is a circuit with 4 s-identical fuse plugs, FP_1, FP_2, FP_3, FP_4, which are used to force the air out of the circuit, if the temperature experienced exceeds 72°C. The circuit is connected to pressure switch, PS. The PS begins functioning when at least 1 of the plugs operate, and transmits a signal to the start relay, SR, to produce alarm and thereby causing a system shut down. The smoke-detector, SD, has three units (SD_1, SD_2, SD_3) which are connected to a voting unit (VU) through a logical 2-out-of-3 system. Thus, at least 2 smoke detector must give a fire signal before the fire alarm is activated. For the successful transmission of an electrical signal from heat detection and/or smoke detector, the DC source must be working. In the manual activation section, there is an operator OP, who should always be prsent. If the operator observes a fire, then the operator turns-on the manual-switch, MS, to relieve pressure in the circuit of the heat-detection section. This activates the PS, which in turn gives an electrical signal to SR. We solve this example by actually executing the program (can be downloaded from www.scrivenerpublishing.com) for the data file as shown in the box. The program needs the following information.

The first line of the data file shows the total number of nodes in the system, which is 8 in this case. The next line onwards, we give node numbers

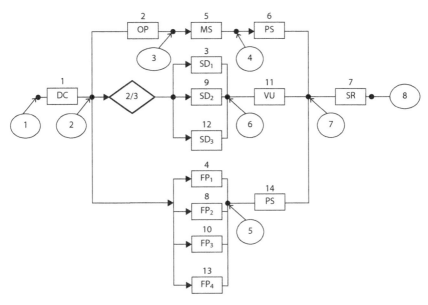

Figure 2.8 Reliability block diagram of fire detector system.

to which a unit is connected; specify that the unit follows a certain failure distribution (d) i.e., w for the Weibull; the Weibull parameters a, and b; time; and the type of module. For k-out-of-m module one more parameter is specified, i.e., the value of k. Note at line number 4, 10 and 13 of data file where the parameter k is 2.

```
Example 2.9: Data-Input File: illustration 2.m
8
1 2 d w 1.5 0.5 0.2 0
2 3 d w 1.5 0.5 0.2 0
2 6 d w 1.8 0.8 0.2 2 2
2 5 d w 2.3 1.3 0.2 1
3 4 d w 1.6 0.6 0.2 0
4 7 d w 1.6 0.6 0.2 0
7 8 d w 1.7 0.7 0.2 0
2 5 d w 2.2 1.2 0.2 1
2 6 d w 1.7 0.7 0.2 2 2
2 5 d w 2.1 1.1 0.2 1
6 7 d w 1.9 0.9 0.2 0
2 6 d w 1.8 0.8 0.2 2 2
2 5 d w 2.0 1.0 0.2 1
5 7 d w 1.6 0.6 0.2 0
```

We run the program at the *Matlab®*. prompt by writing:

> *>> misMatMethod*
> ---
> *if you get this error:...*
> *Error in ==> C:...\formCMat.m*
> *On line 27 ==> cij (unit(i-1).node(1),unit(i-1).node(2))= ...*
> *CHECK:The data file must be terminated where the data ends.*
> *In other words the total line in the file must be equal to the num-*
> *ber of units in the system*
> *Check the blinking cursor at the end of data file.*
> *For this, use PgDn key on the keyboard.*
> ---
> *Checked. So proceed...?: 1 (Yes)/0:1*
> *The data input file: illustration2.m*
> *The Result file : illustration2Res.m*
> *The CMAT file after data of each unit read*
> *(LEAVE BLANK FOR NOT NEEDED)):*
> *The CMAT file thereafter each node elimination*
> *(LEAVE BLANK FOR NOT NEEDED)):*
> *The System Reliability is: 0.856303.*
> *The computation time is = 0.651000 seconds.*
> ---

The output file, illustration2Res.m, contains the following information of the system:

************ THE SYSTEM DETAIL ******************

MODULE NO.#: 1, which is consisted of 1 units connected in series, in between nodes [1 and 2], respectively.
 The reliabilities of units of this module are: [0.914441], respectively.

MODULE NO.#: 2, which is consisted of 1 units connected in series, in between nodes [2 and 3], respectively.
The reliabilities of units of this module are: [0.914441], respectively.

MODULE NO.#: 3, which is consisted of 3 units connected in 2 out -of- 3 configuration, in between nodes [2 and 6], respectively.
The reliabilities of units of this module are: [0.946306 0.937230 0.946306], respectively.

MODULE NO.#: 4, which is consisted of 4 units connected in parallel, in between nodes [2 and 5], respectively.

The reliabilities of units of this module are: [0.975621 0.971425 0.966520 0.960789], respectively.

MODULE NO.#: 5, which is consisted of 1 units connected in series, in between nodes [3 and 4], respectively.
The reliabilities of units of this module are: [0.926681], respectively.

MODULE NO.#: 6, which is consisted of 1 units connected in series, in between nodes [4 and 7], respectively.
The reliabilities of units of this module are: [0.926681], respectively.

MODULE NO.#: 7, which is consisted of 1 units connected in series, in between nodes [7 and 8], respectively.
The reliabilities of units of this module are: [0.937230], respectively.

MODULE NO.#: 8, which is consisted of 1 units connected in series, in between nodes [6 and 7], respectively.
The reliabilities of units of this module are: [0.954102], respectively.

MODULE NO.#: 9, which is consisted of 1 units connected in series, in between nodes [5 and 7], respectively.
The reliabilities of units of this module are: [0.926681], respectively.
The C matrix of the above system is:

0.000000 0.914441 0.000000 0.000000 0.000000 0.000000 0.000000 0.000000
0.000000 0.000000 0.914441 0.000000 0.999999 0.990738 0.000000 0.000000
0.000000 0.000000 0.000000 0.926681 0.000000 0.000000 0.000000 0.000000
0.000000 0.000000 0.000000 0.000000 0.000000 0.000000 0.926681 0.000000
0.000000 0.000000 0.000000 0.000000 0.000000 0.000000 0.926681 0.000000
0.000000 0.000000 0.000000 0.000000 0.000000 0.000000 0.954102 0.000000
0.000000 0.000000 0.000000 0.000000 0.000000 0.000000 0.000000 0.937230
0.000000 0.000000 0.000000 0.000000 0.000000 0.000000 0.000000 0.000000

The System Reliability is = 0.856303

2.6   Implementation and Documentation

The modified and general algorithm presented in this chapter has been programmed in *Matlab*®. The program has the following modules:

2.6.1   Main Module

This module requires at least two files that shall have the information of the system for which the reliability evaluation to be performed. The first file will have the input data for the system while the second file is kept reserved for output. The other two files are optional and are meant to keep a track of iterations made in [C] throughout the input operation and post-processing of [C] during the node elimination process.

For reading inputs, forming [C] during every unit-data read and processing the [C] thereafter, it calls several other supporting routines for viz.,

    i. for inputting system information and building matric [C]-> *formCMat*
    ii. for post-processing [C], it calls -> *processCmat*
    iii. for outputting the System's detail-> *systemDetail*

Before the program begins to process [C], it validates the inputs. On finding any discrepancy in the input data, it prompts a user with warning messages for the following inconsistencies in the data exist:

    i. A unit connected between a node-pair is specified to belong to a parallel or a standby module; and no other unit has been specified thereafter in the data input between this node-pair. As per the definitions of parallel and standby module, the program expects at least two units in these configurations.
    ii. A unit connected between a node-pair is specified to belong to a k-out-of-m module; and the data supplied for the units connected between this node pair is $\leq k$ or $> m$.

2.6.2   Function formCmat

The calling format of this routine is:

function [cMAT,nNodes, module,error1] =
formCMat(dataFin,[cMatfout])

It accepts one input argument viz., the system data input file name. The other argument for outputting [C] at each data read is optional.

It provides four output arguments viz., the [C] at the end of data read operation, number of nodes in the system, modules in the systems and an error flag which turns-on on finding the inconsistency in the input data. Variable *module* is an array of structures, which contains the following information:

- Number of units in a module,
- Node-pair numbers to which a module is connected,

- Type of configuration of modules, viz., series (0), parallel (1), k-out-of-m (2) or standby (3) where the number inside thr round brackets are the configuration-type identifiers,
- Minimum number of units needed for a module success. It is initialized with unity except for the type-2 configuration, k-out-of-m, for which value of k is to be supplied in the input file (*See* illustration 2.2).
- Total number of units in a module, and
- Reliabilities of each unit in a module.

As pointed out earlier that [C] builds up takes place *on fly*, the data read operation is done by this routine. The input would contain the information of the system and each unit. At system level, the number of nodes in the system has to be known whereas at unit level, the following information would be required in sequence:

- Node-pair to which a unit is connected.
- Whether reliability of the unit or the distribution that the unit follows is known? The program differentiates it by sensing the next data input. A character p signifies that probability of success of this unit is known whereas a character d implies that the unit follows a distribution pattern.
- Once the input is read as p, the next data would be the value of reliability of the unit otherwise program seeks for the type of distribution and distribution parameters for the type of distribution specified.

The program capable of distinguishing four types of failure distributions described in Section 2.2. However, the flexibility inherent in modular programming makes it a trivial issue as the list can always be appended with new types of distributions.

The following letters are used to identify hazard rate distribution types in data input:

c   Constant
r   Rayleigh (Linear)
w   Weibull
e   Extreme value

Based on the character specified, the reliability equations (2.11) are used to calculate the reliability of the unit.

Further, if between any pair of nodes, if the unit(s) has already been added than depending upon the module type, it uses the appropriate equation from (2.12), (2.13), (2.14) and (2.16) to calculate the module reliability. This value of reliability for each module appears in [C] at the end of data-read.

2.6.3 Function processCmat

The calling sequence of this routine is:

function rel = processCmat(cmat, nNodes,[cmatFile]).

The function accepts in two parameters, the matrix [C] and number of nodes in the system. The third parameter is an optional parameter and is used to store intermediate value of matrix [C], wherein besides there is a change in the value of elements of [C], the size of [C] also reduces by 1 at the end of each, iteration.

When [C] would have a single element, the value contained would be the reliability of the system. This value is outputted by this function.

2.6.4 Function systDetail

Once the system reliability has been computed, this function helps in producing the output of the type shown for the illustration 2.2. The declaration of this routine is as under:

function systDetail(fn,cmat,module,sysRel)

2.7 Remarks

The versatility and applicability of Misra Matrix has been demonstrated by extending it for more general SP-networks, where a unit or module can follow any type of failure patterns. The following facts indicate the supremacy of this method over the other approaches:

1. If we intend to apply path sets based approach on illustration 2.1 then the original graph of the system of 16 units shown in Figure 2.6 would have a total of 55 path sets. The number of path sets and path sets unions required for computing the system reliability, therefore, would be $2^{55}-1$, which is far in excess of 10^{16}.

2. However, the reduced graph of the same system shown in Figure 2.7 would have only six minimal path sets. Similarly,

the reduced graph of example 2.2, which could be drawn easily by using [C], would have a total of eight minimal path sets.

Hence, one could have a second thought to apply the path sets based technique, viz., sum of disjoint product based approach discussed in later chapters. But it is worth to mention that not only it might demand a further reduction procedure but would also require a SDP based approach to find disjoint terms. Therefore, the application of path sets enumeration method to the original or reduced graph for SP- systems is very time consuming, if not difficult. The Misra Matrix Method (Misra, 1970), (Misra, 1992) does both the tasks in one go. Hence, there are no exaggerations in saying that the method is much and more superior to the entire family of the methods available till date to evaluate the system reliability of SP- networks.

A sample input-output of the program to compute system reliability for example 2.2 has been shown. The modifications incorporated in the original algorithm (Misra, 1992) have made the algorithm more versatile and would be useful in system analysis and design.

However, the approach described in this chapter is applicable only for SP-networks. In case of NSP-networks, our strategy for system reliability evaluation would be through path and cut sets enumeration and the process of computing SDP terms, which has one to one relationship with reliability expression.

Exercises

2.1   Reduce the SP-network shown in Figure Ex. 2.1 and obtain the reliability expression for a series-parallel system. What will be the reliability of this system assuming that the reliability of each element is 0.95.

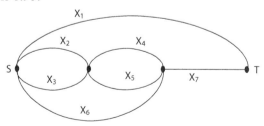

Figure Ex. 2.1 A series-parallel system.

2.2   Evaluate the reliability of the network shown in Figure Ex. 2.2. The reliability of each element is shown inside the parenthesis.

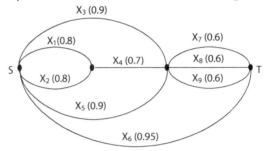

Figure Ex. 2.2 A series-parallel system.

2.3   Evaluate reliability of the network shown in Figure Ex. 2.3. The reliability of each element is shown above the boxes.

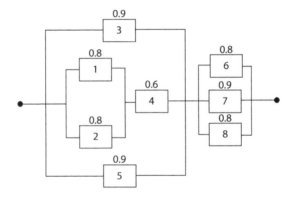

Figure Ex. 2.3 A series-parallel network.

2.4   If 2/3-redundant block and standby block is replaced with active parallel redundant blocks with equal number of units as in original in Figure 2.6, then determine the reliability of the system?

References

Balaguruswami, E. & Misra, K.B., 1976. Reliability Calculations of Redundant Systems with Non-identical Units. *Microelectronics and Reliability*, Vol. 15, pp. 135–138.

Barlow, E.R. & Heidtmann, K.D., 1984. Computing k-out-of-n system Reliability. *IEEE Transaction on Reliability*, Vol. R-30(4), pp. 322–323.

Chaudhari, G., Kuolung, H. & Nadar, A., 2001. A New Approach to System Reliability. *IEEE Transaction on Reliabilty,* Vol. 50(1).

Ebeling, C.E., 2011. *An Introduction to Reliability and Maintainability Engineering.* New York: Tata McGraw-Hill.

Elsayed, E.A., 1996. *Reliability Engineering.* USA: Addison Wesley Longman, Inc.

Henley, E.J. & Williams, R.A., 1973. *Chapter 12: Process Reliability Analysis by Flow Graph Methods in Graph theory in Modern Engineering.* NY: Acad. Press.

Jain, S.P. & Gopal, K., 1985. Recursive Algorithm for Reliability Evaluation of k-out-of-n: G System. *IEEE Transaction on Reliability,* Vol. R-34(2), pp. 144–146.

Locks, M.O., 1984. Comments on: Improved Method of Inclusion Exclusion Applied to k-out-of-n System. *IEEE Transaction on Reliability,* Vol. R-33(4), pp. 321–322.

Misra, K.B., 1970. An Algorithm for Reliability Evaluation of Redundant Networks. *IEEE Transaction on Reliability,* Vol. R-19(4), pp. 146–151.

Misra, K.B., 1992. Reliability Analysis and Prediction: A Methodology Oriented Treatment. *Elsevier.*

Misra, K.B., ed., 1993. *New Trends in System Reliability Evaluation,* Elsevier.

Misra, K.B. & Rao, T.S.M., 1970. Reliability Analysis of Redundant Networks Using Flow Graphs. *IEEE Transaction on Reliability,* Vol. R-19(1), pp. 19–24.

Moor, E.F. & Shannon, C.E., 1956. Reliable Circuits Using Less Reliable Relays. *Journal of the Franklin Institute,* (9), pp. 191–208.

3

Path Sets Enumeration

The network reliability is usually concerned with the task of evaluating the *terminal reliability* or the probability of establishing communication between a set of specified nodes, which is often carried out using either path sets or cut sets of a probabilistic graph.

Although there is plethora of methods that exist to evaluate reliability measures, the most widely used technique in vogue still remains through *path sets* or *cut sets* and therefore enumeration of path sets (or spanning trees, or k-trees, let us call as path sets or success terms, in general) or its dual cut sets are the most fundamental step in evaluating the reliability measures of a network. Therefore, to make network reliability computation using path or cut sets competitively attractive, we must have an efficient method for enumerating path or cut sets as these path sets or cut sets are used to obtain system reliability expression in a compact form by employing SDP techniques.

The methods for enumerating path sets can broadly be divided into two categories:

    a. By utilizing and exploitation of the information contained in the matrix representation of a network graph, and

b. Graph Traversal or Exhaustive Search Technique by using a suitable data structure containing the information of the network graph.

Generally, the methods based on first category do not require the knowledge advanced mathematics or graph theory.

Although there are several data structures available for a network graph representation, in this text, we represent a network graph through the connection /adjacency/incidence matrix whose size is dictated by the number of nodes and/or links in a network. This actually results in storing a single matrix of (n × n) or (n × l) size and avoids using other complex form of representations of a network such as link-list or tree and their manipulations thereof for path sets generation.

In order to distinguish links from the nodes in all the test problems, we have shown nodes by bold numbers and links by the numbers in normal print.

3.1   Enumeration of (s, f) Connected Path Sets

For small size networks, one can easily enumerate the path or cut simply by visual inspection. However, increase in the network size and complexities necessitate in applying some logics, mathematics and graph theoretic. In many networks, one is usually interested to compute reliability between a specified pair of nodes, and all other remaining nodes.

Any network graph, directed or undirected, can be represented by its connection or adjacency or incidence matrix. The connection matrix contains a total of 2*l number of non-zero elements, if the graph is undirected or (l + number of bi-directional elements) otherwise. Non-zero elements in each row are the nodes, which are adjacent to the node addressed by that row index. On the other hand, the incidence is node by link matrix whose size is dictated by the number of nodes and links in the network graph. The elements of this matrix can be either 0/1 or -1/1. Reading the matrix row-wise (remember the 'a' row represents a particular node of the network graph), and encountering a 0 or -1 in any column implies that the particular link does not join this node whereas a 1 implies it does.

Before we delve into the methods of enumerations of (s, f) terminal pair paths, there are certain useful properties of the network graph utilized for such enumerations such as:

i. The degree of a node is the number of branches incident on it. For directed network graph, there will an in-degree and an out-degree for each node.

ii. The paths for any terminal pair of the network graph are combinations of branches of different order. The cardinality (number of elements) of such path sets ranges from 1 to (n-1) and cut set ranges from 1 to (L+1) where L = (l-n+1), the number of basic loops in the graph.

iii. A subnet graph corresponding to a combination is said to be a path if
- It touches both the terminal nodes, i.e., both the terminal nodes must be of degree one.
- It does not contain any loop, and
- It represents a connected graph.

iv. For a subnet graph representing a path, the intermediate nodes in the subnet graph should be of degree two only.

v. If a subnet graph which has any intermediate node of degree other than 2 or 0 represents either a disconnected graph or a non-minimal path.

These simple observations have favoured researchers to devise methods to look for all path sets between any specified pair of nodes of a given network viz., in general source and sink. Here, we will describe some simple to computer-requiring methods for network graph to fulfil these objectives.

3.1.1   Method 1: Using Powers of Connection matrix

The method starts with the connection matrix representation of the network graph. This matrix is algebraically (remember, not numerically) multiplied iteratively by itself. The maximum cardinality path, i.e., (n-1), possible in the network dictates the number of times this multiplication to continue. Besides, at each multiplication, one must apply the laws of Boolean algebra such as commutative, absorption, identity, and idempotent. In a multiplication, if number of elements turns out to be lesser than the order of the forming matrix, those elements are discarded. The elements corresponding to the specified node pair(s) in the matrix of each order would represent the path sets of different order from one node to another. Collecting these terms with the removal of redundant terms would be number of minimal path sets enumerated by this approach. Note that, this matrix can also provide the path sets of different order for every pair of nodes by extracting the elements of specified node pair(s) in each order of the matrix.

Let us illustrate this method through an example.

Example 3.1: Consider the ARPA network shown in Figure 3.1 below. Enumerate the path sets of the network using the powers of its connection matrix

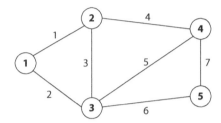

Figure 3.1 Example ARPA network.

Solution: The connection matrix of the network is, (Note that the elements are branch numbers labels).

$$CM = \begin{bmatrix} 0 & 1 & 2 & 0 & 0 \\ 1 & 0 & 3 & 4 & 0 \\ 2 & 3 & 0 & 5 & 6 \\ 0 & 4 & 5 & 0 & 7 \\ 0 & 0 & 6 & 7 & 0 \end{bmatrix}$$

Due to symmetry of the matrix, only lower diagonal terms of the resultant matrix are shown.

$$CM^2 = \begin{bmatrix} 0 & 23 & 13 & 14+25 & 26 \\ - & 0 & 12+45 & 35 & 36+47 \\ - & - & 0 & 34+67 & 57 \\ - & - & - & 0 & 56 \\ - & - & - & - & 0 \end{bmatrix}$$

$$CM^3 = \begin{bmatrix} 123 & 254 & 145 & 324+135+267 & 136+147+257 \\ - & 123+345 & 467 & 125+367 & 126+456+357 \\ - & - & 123+345+567 & 124 & 347 \\ - & - & - & 345+567 & 346 \\ - & - & - & - & 567 \end{bmatrix}$$

$$CM^4 = \begin{bmatrix} 1245 & 1345+2467 & 2345+2567+1467 & 1367 & 1456+2347+1357 \\ - & 1245+3467 & 3567 & 1234+4567+1267 & 1257 \\ - & - & 1245+3467 & 1235 & 1236+3456+1247 \\ - & - & - & 1245+3467 & 1246+3457 \\ - & - & - & - & 3467 \end{bmatrix}$$

Therefore, path sets between node pair (**1, 5**) are

{2, 6} from element CM(1, 5) in CM^2

{1, 3, 6}, {1, 4, 7}, {2, 5, 7} from element CM(1, 5) in CM^3

{1, 4, 5, 6}, {2, 3, 4, 7}, {1, 3, 5, 7} from element CM(1, 5) in CM^4

Example 3.2: Enumerate the path sets from node **1** to other nodes from the powers of matrix.

Solution: By extracting the element (1, i) for i = 2, 3, 4, 5 from the different powers of connection matrix from CM to CM^4, we obtain,

Between (**1, 2**) = {1}, {2, 3}, {2, 5, 4}, {1, 3, 4, 5}, {2, 4, 6, 7}. Discarded path is a non-minimal redundant path.

Between (**1, 3**) = {2}, {1, 3}, {1, 4, 5}, {2, 3, 4, 5}, {2, 5, 6, 7}, {1, 4, 6, 7}. Discarded paths are non-minimal redundant path.

Between (**1, 4**) = {1, 4}, {2, 5}, {2, 3, 4}, {{1, 3, 5}, {2, 6, 7}, {1, 3, 6, 7}.

Between (**1, 5**) = {2, 6}, {1, 3, 6}, {1, 4, 7}, {2, 5, 7}, {1, 3, 5, 7}, {1, 4, 5, 6}, {2, 3, 4, 7}.

3.1.2   Method 2: Traversing Through Connection Matrix

Taking the connection matrix as the starting point, the method begins with scanning the first row corresponding to source node and collects the non-zeros entries in its all columns, signifying source node's connectivity with other nodes, to form 'incomplete paths' by appending each adjacent node as a separate paths. Now, for each 'incomplete path', its last element is checked for – whether it is terminal node? If so, then a path is found else every columns corresponding to the row of last element (recently appended node in the list) in the 'incomplete path' are checked for adjacent nodes. Each non-zeros entry is appended in the 'incomplete path', if not already exiting' to provide several other paths. If no non-zero entry is found corresponding to the last entry in an 'incomplete path' or a repeat of an element occurs, then that path is discarded whereas if the last entry is corresponding to the terminal node, it constitutes a path' and is stored. This process is applied to all 'incomplete paths' till there is no incomplete path remained (Ahmad, 1989). The node-wise path obtained so can easily be converted to the link-wise path thereafter.

Example 3.3: Apply the traversing through connection matrix method to the example 3.1.

Solution: The connection matrix for the network graph is:

$$CM = \begin{bmatrix} 0 & 1 & 2 & 0 & 0 \\ 1 & 0 & 3 & 4 & 0 \\ 2 & 3 & 0 & 5 & 6 \\ 0 & 4 & 5 & 0 & 7 \\ 0 & 0 & 6 & 7 & 0 \end{bmatrix}$$

By using the bold numbers for node-labels, the steps followed are:

1. From the first row, we get the following 'incomplete paths': {1, 2}, {1, 3}, i.e., the source node '1' is connected with node {2} and {3}, respectively. It has no direct connection to terminal node '5', entry being 0 (No first order path).

2. Taking Incomplete path {1, 2} and now, scanning row 2, we get two incomplete paths:
{1, 2, 1} (Discarded as node 1 repeats), {1, 2, 3} and {1, 2, 4}. (No path has its last node entry '5'-the terminal node). Similarly for {1, 3}, we get: {1, 3, 1}, {1, 3, 2} {1, 3, 4} and {1, 3, 5}.

3. Checking these 'five incomplete paths' obtained so, we found that path #1 = {1, 3, 5} has its last entry '5'. So it is path from node **1** to **5**. The remaining four incomplete paths are: {1, 2, 3}, {1, 2, 4}, {1, 3, 2}, and {1, 3, 4}.

4. Proceeding as in step 2 above and appending these incomplete paths one by one, we get:
{1, 2, 3} → {1, 2, 3, 1}, {1, 2, 3, 2}, {1, 2, 3, 4} (Incomplete path) and {1, 2, 3, 5} (Path # 2)
{1, 2, 4} → {1, 2, 4, 2}, {1, 2, 4, 3}, (Incomplete path) and {1, 2, 4, 5} (Path #3)
{1, 3, 2} → {1, 3, 2, 1}, {1, 3, 2, 3}, {1, 3, 2, 4} (Incomplete path)
{1, 3, 4} → {1, 3, 4, 2}, {1, 3, 4, 3}, {1, 3, 4, 5} (Path#4)

5. Again proceeding as in step 2 for the Incomplete paths {1, 2, 3, 4}, {1, 2, 4, 3}, {1, 3, 2, 4}, {1, 3, 4, 2}
{1, 2, 3, 4} → {1, 2, 3, 4, 2}, {1, 2, 3, 4, 3}, {1, 2, 3, 4, 5} (Path # 5),

{1, 2, 4, 3} → {1, 2, 4, 3, 1}, {1, 2, 4, 3, 2}, {1, 2, 4, 3, 4},
{1, 2, 4, 3, 5} (Path # 6),
{1, 3, 2, 4} → {1, 3, 2, 4, 2}, {1, 3, 2, 4, 3}, {1, 3, 2, 4, 5} (Path #7)
{1, 3, 4, 2} → {1, 3, 4, 2, 1}, {1, 3, 4, 2, 3}.

Now, the procedure terminates as there is no incomplete path left. Therefore, the procedure generates the following seven (1, 5) node wise and link wise path sets between (s, t) pair (1, 5) as:

{1, 3, 5}→ {2, 6}, {1, 2, 3, 5}→ {1, 3, 6}, {1, 2, 4, 5}→ {1, 4, 7}, {1, 3, 4, 5}→ {2, 5, 7}, {1, 2, 3, 4, 5}→{{1, 3, 5, 7}, {1, 2, 4, 3, 5} → {1, 4, 5, 6}, {1, 3, 2, 4, 5} → {2, 3, 4, 7}.

3.1.3 Method 3: Using Incidence Matrix

The method is based on the property (iii) stated in Section 3.1 (Mishra & Misra, 1980). The path sets for any terminal pair of the network graph are combinations of the links of different order. Path of cardinality one exists, if there is a direct link between a specified source-terminal pair of nodes and can easily be found from the incidence matrix (by scanning it column-wise for a pair of specified nodes), which is an (n × l) order 'nodes versus links' matrix representing a network graph. The paths of cardinality two or more can be obtained by generating combinations of number of links from 2 to (n–1), i.e., $C_i^l \, \forall i = 2, 3(n-1)$. Further, a column vector denoting D_i, as the degree of node i in the subnet graph, corresponding to a links-combination can be generated from the incidence matrix by adding algebraically the columns of incidence matrix corresponding to the links present in the combination.

Conditions in property (iii) provided in Section 3.1 of a network graph can be satisfied if

a. The degree of node corresponding to terminal pair of nodes in D_i must be equal to 1, i.e., a necessary and sufficient condition. This condition is exploited to reduce the labour of forming number of combinations and exhaustive search, and

b. The degree of nodes other than terminal nodes should either be equal to '0' or '2'. This is a necessary condition but not sufficient one, i.e., a combination of links satisfying this condition might render either a disconnected graph or path consists of loop or a non-minimal path. *This insufficiency imposes to check the connectivity of graph represented by a combination or the path so formed must be compared with all the previously enumerated paths that no subset of the combination under consideration is a path.*

Example 3.4: Consider the network of example 3.1 once again. Check the combination of links {1, 5, 6, 7} for the conditions a and b above.

Solution: The incidence matrix of the network graph of example 3.1 is:

$$
IM = \begin{bmatrix}
1 & 1 & 0 & 0 & 0 & 0 & 0 \\
1 & 0 & 1 & 1 & 0 & 0 & 0 \\
0 & 1 & 1 & 0 & 1 & 1 & 0 \\
0 & 0 & 0 & 1 & 1 & 0 & 1 \\
0 & 0 & 0 & 0 & 0 & 1 & 1
\end{bmatrix}
$$

The vector for this combination can be obtained by algebraically adding the columns corresponding to links present in this combination, $D = [1, 1, 2, 2, 2]$. As per conditions (a) and (b) above, it should be a path between terminal nodes, {1, 2}. But it is a non-minimal path being a superset of path {1} that joins nodes {1, 2}.

Also note that a combination i for which the degree of nodes, other than terminal nodes, in D_i is not equal to '0' or '2' can also represent either a disconnected graph or non-minimal path. But they are discarded without any checks.

Example 3.5: Enumerate the path sets from node {1} to all other nodes of the network graph given in example 3.1 using the incidence matrix of the network graph.

Solution: The first order path from node **1** to other nodes can be found from the incidence matrix by looking through all columns corresponding to node **1**. Link {1} connects node **2** and link {2} connects node **3** while other nodes are not directly connected with node **1** necessitating the generations of combinations as provided in Table 3.1

The path sets methods described above generate path sets either in random order or at most increasing order of cardinality. Apart from enumeration, the ordering of path/cut sets also plays an important role in reducing the number of disjoint terms generated to obtain a compact TR expression. An experiment described in (Soh & Rai, 1993) considers the several ordering schemes, viz.,

Table 3.1 Path Sets Enumeration using Incidence Matrix.

S. no.	Link-combinations	Column vector, D_i	Contributed path between terminal nodes	Remark
1.	13	(12100)	(1,3)	Using the incidence matrix, the Links combinations of order 2, 3, 4 are formed. Note that combination '12' is not used as it violates condition i) giving a degree of source node 1 equal to 2. Each combination is to be checked using some suitable technique for connectivity and minimality. ×'s shows the violations and hence that combination is discarded.
2.	14	(12010)	(1,4)	
3.	15	(11110)	×	
4.	16	(11101)	×	
5.	17	(11011)	×	
6.	23	(11200)	(1,2)	
7.	24	(11110)	×	
8.	25	(10210)	(1,4)	
9.	26	(10201)	(1,5)	
10.	27	(11011)	×	
11.	134	(12110)	×	Path sets are by collecting the combinations satisfying the properties, conditions and checks as mentioned in section 3.1 are:
12.	135	(12210)	(1,4)	**Between terminal nodes {1,2}**
13.	136	(12201)	(1,5)	{1], {23}. {245}, {2467}
14.	137	(12111)	×	**Between terminal nodes {1,3}**
15.	145	(12120)	(1,3)	{2}, {13}, {145}, {1467}
16.	146	(12111)	×	**Between terminal nodes {1,4}**
17.	147	(12021)	(1,5)	{13}, {25}, {135}, {234), {267}, (1367)
18.	156	(11211)	×	**Between terminal nodes {1,5}**
19.	157	(11121)	×	{26}, {136}, {147}, {257}, {1357}, {1456}, {2347}
20.	167	(11112)	×	

(Continued)

Table 3.1 Cont.

S. no.	Link-combinations	Column vector, D_i	Contributed path between terminal nodes	Remark
21.	234	(12210)	(1,4)	
22.	235	(11310)	×	
23.	236	(11301)	×	
24.	237	(11211)	×	
25.	245	(11220)	(1,2)	
26.	246	(11211)	×	
27.	247	(11121)	×	
28.	256	(10311)	×	
29.	257	(10221)	(1,5)	
30.	267	(10212)	(1,4)	
31.	1345	(13220)	×	
32.	1346	(13211)	×	
33.	1347	(13121)	×	
34.	1356	(12311)	×	
35.	1357	(12221)	(1,5)	
36.	1367	(12212)	(1,4)	
37.	1456	(12221)	(1,5)	
38.	1457	(12131)	×	
39.	1467	(12122)	(1,3)	
40.	1567	(11222)	×	Satisfies conditions but not a minimal path
41.	2345	(12320)	×	
42.	2346	(12311)	×	
43.	2347	(12221)	(1,5)	
44.	2356	(11420)	×	
45.	2357	(11321)	×	
46.	2367	(11312)	×	
47.	2456	(11311)	×	
48.	2457	(11231)	×	
49.	2467	(11222)	(1,2)	
50.	2567	(10322)	×	

   i. Decreasing Hamming distance where distance is equal to the number of variables in a term common with the reference term and reference term is the first term lexicographically in the minimal set with smaller number of variables.
   ii. Lexicographical that follows the order of alphabets used to represent path/cut sets
   iii. Increasing order of cardinality
   iv. Cardinality + Lexicographic
   v. Cardinality + Hamming distance

The outcome of the experiment was that either (Cardinality + Lexicographic) or (Cardinality + Hamming distance) gives lesser number of disjoint terms as compared to the order if a single ordering scheme is being used.

A computer program based on the path sets enumeration method, similar to the Method #2, devoid of use of any complex data structure or mathematical operations yet generates minimal path sets in increasing order of cardinality in lexicographic order between any specified pair of nodes of a network is described in Appendix 3A.1 and a *Matlab®* code which can be downloaded at www.scrivenerpublishing.com.

3.2   Enumeration of All-node Connected Path Sets: Spanning Tree

In case we want all the users to remain connected together, the global reliability quantifies the grade of service. The path sets required for global reliability evaluation are different from those required for the 2-terminal reliability evaluation. The basic difference is that for global reliability a path set must contain all the nodes of network graph, which are spanning trees of the graph. Spanning tree enumeration in a network graph is an important issue and task in many problems encountered in computer network and circuit analysis. A spanning tree of a network graph is a minimal network, which connects all nodes but without a loop. Also,

- An edge contained in certain spanning tree is called branch of that tree while an edge of the graph G not contained in that particular spanning tree is called a chord.
- For a connected graph of n nodes and l edges, spanning tree has (n-1) branches and (l-n+1) chords.
- No more than (l-n+1) chords of a spanning tree can be replaced to get another spanning tree.

- The distance between two spanning trees T_i and T_j of a graph is the number of edges of G present in one tree but not in the other.
- The maximum distance between two spanning trees of a graph is, $d_m \leq \min\{n-1, l-n+1\}$.

The simple approach to enumerate all spanning is the application of elementary tree transformation based on addition of a chord and deletion of an appropriate branch from one spanning tree of the graph through these successive exchanges (Deo, 1979) (Piekarski, 1965). Other well-known search methods such as Kruskal's and Prim's algorithms available in several elementary texts can also be used. However, we describe here some methods developed and/or employed by reliability fraternity.

3.2.1 Method 1: Using the Cartesian Product of the Node Cut Sets

This method is proposed in (Aggarwal & Rai, 1981) and uses the Cartesian product of (n-1) vertex cut sets whose elements are the links connected any of the (n-1) nodes of the given graph, i.e.,

$$C = \times_{i=1}^{n-1} C_i \,,$$

Where C_i is a vertex cut set of the graph and C is a set of sub graph of G with (n-1) links. It should be noted that any circuit of G with (n-1) branches will have an even number of identical appearances in C and will have to be removed from the C.

Example 3.6: Enumerate the all spanning trees of the network graph shown in Example 3.1.

Solution: Let us select nodes **1, 2, 4,** and **5.** The vertex cut sets in terms of links of these nodes are, {1, 2}, {1, 3, 4}, {4, 5, 7} and {6, 7}.

Now, we obtain the Cartesian product of vertex cut sets one-by-one in an iterative manner and discarding the entries with repeated element, i.e, link.

$C = \{1, 2\} \times \{1, 3, 4\} = \{\{1, 3\}, \{1, 4\}, \{1, 2\}, \{2, 3\}, \{2, 4\}\}$

$C = C \times \{4, 5, 7\} = \{\{1, 3\}, \{1, 4\}, \{1, 2\}, \{2, 3\}, \{2, 4\}\} \times \{4, 5, 7\}$

$= \{\{1, 3, 4\}, \{1, 3, 5\}, \{1, 3, 7\}, \{1, 4, 5\}, \{\{1, 4, 7\}, \{1, 2, 4\}, \{1, 2, 5\}, \{1, 2, 7\}, \{2, 3, 4\}, \{2, 3, 5\}, \{2, 3, 7\}, \{2, 4, 5\}, \{2, 4, 7\}\}$

C = C × {6, 7} = {{1, 3, 4}, {1, 3, 5}, {1, 3, 7}, {1, 4, 5}, {{1, 4, 7}, {1, 2, 4}, {1, 2, 5}, {1, 2, 7}, {2, 3, 4}, {2, 3, 5}, {2, 3, 7}, {2, 4, 5}, {2, 4, 7}}× {6, 7}, finally

C = {{1, 3, 4, 6}, {1, 3, 6, 7}, {1, 3, 5, 6}, { 1, 3, 5, 7}, {1, 3, 6, 7}, {1, 4, 5, 6}, {1, 4, 5, 7}, {1, 4, 6, 7}, {{1, 2, 4, 6}, {1, 2, 4, 7}, {1, 2, 5, 6}, {1, 2, 5, 7}, {1, 2, 6, 7}, {2, 3, 4, 6}, {2, 3, 4, 7}, {2, 3, 5, 6}, {2, 3, 5, 7}, {2, 3, 6, 7}, {2, 4, 5, 6}, (2, 4, 5, 7}, {2, 4, 6, 7}}

Therefore, the method correctly generates 21 spanning trees of the network graph.

3.2.2   Method 2: Using the Incidence Matrix

This is an extension of the method described in Section 3.1.3 for enumerating all the (s, f) path sets (Samad, 1987) with observing and noting some properties of a network graph with respect to a spanning tree:

i.   The order of a sub graph touching all the nodes of a graph would be (n-1), i.e., it will have (n-1) links. Thus, combinations $_{n-1}^{m}C$ (where m is the number of links in the network) will contain all the trees of the graph with each combination belong to either of the following:
   • A spanning tree
   • A sub graph with loops,
   • A disconnected sub graph.
ii.   A tree cannot have any branch with both end-vertices of degree one.
iii.   Further, a branch having one vertex of degree one is removed from the tree then the sub graph left will always be connected. In other words, the sequential removal of branch at every stage removes only one node from the sub graph.
iv.   A connected graph with (n-1) branches may have loop if the number of vertices is equal to or less than (n-1).
v.   In a disconnected graph, there is at least one branch removal of which will cause the removal of two nodes of the network. This implies that a graph is disconnected then a sequential branch removal process will cause removal of two nodes for some particular branch of the network graph.

Therefore, to generate spanning trees of a network graph, the following steps are followed:

1. Column vectors for combinations $\,_{n-1}^{m}C$ are generated from the incidence matrix by adding algebraically (n–1) columns of the incidence matrix of the network graph.
2. Each column vectors generated so are tested for whether it represents a (i) sub graph with loop(s) (ii) a disconnected sub graph, otherwise it is a spanning tree.
3. A zero entry in a particular column vector would represent a sub graph with loop(s) signifying to drop this combination.
4. If an entry in a particular column vector is greater than or equal to 1, then it may either be a disconnected graph or a spanning tree. One can use a sequential removal of branch from this combination to test for a disconnected sub graph. The sequential branch removal is done till only two branches are left and at each removal the column vector has to be updated. If a sequential branch removal causes to remove two nodes signifying an isolated branch (disconnected graph), then this combination is dropped. Also, if a branch removal does not remove a node implying the combination forms a circuit in the graph.

The method is explained with the following example.

Example 3.7: Apply the incidence matrix approach to enumerate spanning trees of the network graph given in example 3.1.

Solution: Starting with the incidence matrix of the network graph, the various valid/invalid combinations formed with their respective sub graphs are shown in the following Table 3.2. Here m=7, n=5. The enumerated valid combinations providing spanning trees are 21 as shown in Table 3.2

$$IM = \begin{bmatrix} 1 & 1 & 0 & 0 & 0 & 0 & 0 \\ 1 & 0 & 1 & 1 & 0 & 0 & 0 \\ 0 & 1 & 1 & 0 & 1 & 1 & 0 \\ 0 & 0 & 0 & 1 & 1 & 0 & 1 \\ 0 & 0 & 0 & 0 & 0 & 1 & 1 \end{bmatrix}$$

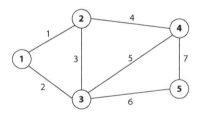

3.3   Number of Spanning Trees

In this section, we describe some methods to have a count on the number of spanning trees a network graph would have if one is interested to know

Table 3.2 Spanning trees enumeration using incidence matrix.

Branch combinations	Network sub graph	Algebraic sum column vector
1 2 3 4		2 3 2 1 0
1 2 3 5		2 2 3 1 0
1 2 3 6		2 2 3 0 1
1 2 3 7		2 2 2 1 1
1 2 4 5		2 2 2 2 0

(Continued)

Table 3.2 Cont.

Branch combinations	Network sub graph	Algebraic sum column vector
1 2 4 6		2 2 2 1 1
1 2 4 7		2 2 1 2 1
1 2 5 6		2 1 3 1 1
1 2 5 7		2 1 2 2 1
1 2 6 7		2 1 2 1 2

(*Continued*)

Table 3.2 Cont.

Branch combinations	Network sub graph	Algebraic sum column vector
1 3 4 5		1 3 2 2 0
1 3 4 6		1 3 2 1 1
1 3 4 7		1 3 1 2 1
1 3 5 6		1 2 3 1 1
1 3 5 7		1 2 2 2 1

(Continued)

Table 3.2 Cont.

Branch combinations	Network sub graph	Algebraic sum column vector
1 3 6 7		1 2 2 1 2
1 4 5 6		1 2 2 2 1
1 4 5 7		1 2 1 3 1
1 4 6 7		1 2 1 2 2
~~1 5 6 7~~		1 1 2 2 2

(Continued)

Table 3.2 Cont.

Branch combinations	Network sub graph	Algebraic sum column vector
~~2 3 4 5~~		1 2 3 2 0
2 3 4 6		1 2 3 1 1
2 3 4 7		1 2 2 2 1
2 3 5 6		1 1 4 1 1
2 3 5 7		1 1 3 2 1

(*Continued*)

Table 3.2 Cont.

Branch combinations	Network sub graph	Algebraic sum column vector
2 3 6 7		1 1 3 1 2
2 4 5 6		1 1 3 2 1
2 4 5 7		1 1 2 3 1
2 4 6 7		1 1 2 2 2
2̶ 5̶ 6̶ 7̶		1 0 3 2 2

(*Continued*)

Table 3.2 Cont.

Branch combinations	Network sub graph	Algebraic sum column vector
3 4 5 6		0 2 3 2 1
3 4 5 7		0 2 2 3 1
3 4 6 7		0 2 2 2 2
3 5 6 7		0 1 3 2 2
4 5 6 7		0 1 2 3 2

before deciding to enumerate them for certain application, e.g., design of electrical circuits, reliability analysis, graph with a maximum number of spanning trees etc.

The well-known *Cayley's Theorem* in graph theory provides the number of labelled spanning trees in a complete graph as n^{n-2}, where a labeled tree is a tree with its vertices are assigned unique numbers from 1 to n. Cayley's theorem provides a way to count the spanning trees in a complete labeled graph, whereas the *Matrix Tree Theorem* applies to labelled graphs in general and is a generalization of Cayley's formula.

3.3.1 Matrix Tree Theorem

If G is a connected labelled graph with adjacency matrix A and degree matrix D, then the number of unique spanning trees of G is equal to the value of any cofactor of the matrix $H = [D - A]$. Matrix H is also referred as *Laplacian, Lucacian* or *Kirchoff* matrix.

The degree matrix $D = (d_{ij})$ is defined as

$$d_{ij} = \begin{cases} \text{degree}(v_i) \text{if } i = j \\ 0 \text{ elsewhere} \end{cases}$$

The (i, j) cofactor of an nxn matrix M is defined to be $(-1)^{i+j} \det(M(i\,|\,j))$, where $M(i\,|\,j)$ is the (n–1) × (n–1) matrix formed by deleting row *i* and column *j* of matrix M.

Example 3.8: Use the Matrix theorem to count the number of spanning trees in the network graph of example 3.1, reproduced below:

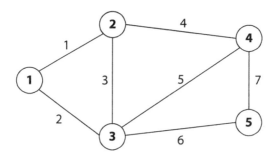

Solution: The adjacency matrix of the network graph is:

$$A = \begin{bmatrix} 0 & 1 & 1 & 0 & 0 \\ 1 & 0 & 1 & 1 & 0 \\ 1 & 1 & 0 & 1 & 1 \\ 0 & 1 & 1 & 0 & 1 \\ 0 & 0 & 1 & 1 & 0 \end{bmatrix}, D = \begin{bmatrix} 2 & 0 & 0 & 0 & 0 \\ 0 & 3 & 0 & 0 & 0 \\ 0 & 0 & 4 & 0 & 0 \\ 0 & 0 & 0 & 3 & 0 \\ 0 & 0 & 0 & 0 & 2 \end{bmatrix}$$

$$H = D - A = \begin{bmatrix} 2 & -1 & -1 & 0 & 0 \\ -1 & 3 & -1 & -1 & 0 \\ -1 & -1 & 4 & -1 & -1 \\ 0 & -1 & -1 & 3 & -1 \\ 0 & 0 & -1 & -1 & 2 \end{bmatrix},$$

and (1,1) cofactor of H is $\det \begin{bmatrix} 3 & -1 & -1 & 0 \\ -1 & 4 & -1 & -1 \\ -1 & -1 & 3 & -1 \\ 0 & -1 & -1 & 2 \end{bmatrix} = 21$ provides the

number of spanning trees of the network graph.

Another method to find the number of spanning tree is provided by (Kelmans & Chelnokov, 1974). If $\mu_1 \geq \mu_2 \geq \mu_3 \geq \ldots \geq \mu_n (= 0)$ be the eigenvalues of H, then number of spanning trees would be equal to:

$$\text{number of spanning trees} = \frac{1}{n} \prod_{i=1}^{n-1} \mu_i.$$

Example 3.9 and Solution: Considering the above example again, the eigenvalues of $eigen(H) = [-0.0000 \quad 1.5858 \quad 3.0000 \quad 4.4142 \quad 5.0000]$, and product of its eigenvalues (except zero) comes out to be 105. Therefore the number of spanning trees would be, $\frac{105}{5} = 21$.

Generally, the methods described here may not be feasible for enumeration or counting the number of spanning trees, especially for large and special graphs found in various applications for which one would resort to some other computationally efficient methods other than those described in this text. Besides, for comparing the numbers of spanning trees in different classes of graphs, exact formula are needed. Even though there are several other known methods for counting the number of spanning trees, further research is still on, and interested readers may research on this subject from the literature.

3.4   Enumeration of k-node Connected Path Sets: k-Trees

A k-tree can be defined as a tree that covers all the k-specified set of vertices of a network graph G. A k-tree might be a spanning tree and vice-a-versa. The vertices such that the deletion of these does not disturb the k-connectedness of these k-specified nodes can be referred as redundant nodes. The number of such redundant vertices may or may not be equal to n−|k|. The method to enumerate k-trees described here needs the spanning trees of the given network graph and follows the following steps (Rath & Soman, 1993) :

1. Enumerate all the spanning trees of the network graph.
2. Specify k-set of vertices and identify the vertices (redundant vertices) not contained in the specified k-set.
3. For each redundant vertex, form a set of link(s) incident on it.
4. Compare each spanning tree elements with each set of link(s) in a sequential manner. If the number of common element is one, delete it from that particular spanning tree. If the difference of elements at any juncture is more than one, then keep the spanning tree as it is.
5. Take the recurring instances of a term once and non-recurring instances as it is. The terms after this process represent all k-trees for a specified node-set.

Example 3.10: Enumerate k-trees for the specified node set {**1, 3, 4**} for the network graph of example 3.7.

Solution: The redundant node-set for the network graph is {**2, 5**}. The link-set connected to node {**2**} is {1, 3, 4} and with {**5**}, it is {6, 7}. These link sets are compared with 21 spanning trees of the network graph enumerated earlier to produce nine k-trees for the specified node-set {**1, 3, 4**} as presented in Table 3.3.

Table 3.3 Generating k-Trees.

| Spanning trees | Comparing with | | k-trees for node connectivity {1, 3, 4} |
	{1, 3, 4} with column #1	{6, 7} with column #2	
1 2 4 6	1 2 4 6	1 2 4	1 2 4
1 2 4 7	1 2 4 7	~~1 2 4~~	
1 2 5 6	2 5 6	2 5	2 5
1 2 5 7	2 5 7	~~2 5~~	
1 2 6 7	2 6 7	2 6 7	2 6 7
1 3 4 6	1 3 4 6	1 3 4	1 3 4
1 3 4 7	1 3 4 7	~~1 3 4~~	
1 3 5 6	1 3 5 6	1 3 5	1 3 5
1 3 5 7	1 3 5 7	~~1 3 5~~	
1 3 6 7	1 3 6 7	1 3 6 7	1 3 6 7
1 4 5 6	1 4 5 6	1 4 5	1 4 5
1 4 5 7	1 4 5 7	~~1 4 5~~	
1 4 6 7	1 4 6 7	1 4 6 7	1 4 6 7
2 3 4 6	2 3 4 6	2 3 4	2 3 4
2 3 4 7	2 3 4 7	~~1 3 4~~	
2 3 5 6	2 5 6	~~2 5~~	
2 3 5 7	2 5 7	~~2 5~~	
2 3 6 7	2 6 7	~~2 6 7~~	
2 4 5 6	2 5 6	~~2 5~~	
2 4 5 7	2 5 7	~~2 5~~	
2 4 6 7	2 6 7	~~2 6 7~~	

Appendix 3A.1: Enumeration of Path Sets Algorithm, Illustration and *Matlab*® Code Notation

In this description, the following notations are being used:

f: Destination or sink node
l: Number of links
n: Number of nodes
s: Source node
V: Set of vertices or nodes
L: Set of edges or links
(.) Set of elements.
{.} A set

[A]: 2- dimensional 0/1 element dynamic array whose first dimension grows with each iterations of the algorithm whereas the second is fixed and equal to the number of nodes in the network.

[P]: 2- dimensional dynamic array. During the iterative process, its rows grow depending on the number of nonzero element found in the current iteration. The second dimension expands by one in each iterative step.

[AA], [PP]: Temporary storage for A and P, respectively.
X_i: ith row of [X]
$X_{i,j}$: Element in ith row and jth column of [X]
Y^r: Value of element at rth position in vector Y
[ ]: A null matrix or a vector with no elements.

Let us take a simple example ARPA network to illustrate the concept for the development of *Matlab*® code:

Illustration 3A.1: The ARPA network has been shown in Figure 3A.1 (a), (b) for undirected and directed cases respectively. The source has been assigned the number 1 while the destination is given the number 5. Connection matrix for Figure 3A. 1 (a) and (b) would be as shown in Table 3A. 1.

Let us consider Figure 3A. 1 (a) to enumerate path sets. The steps to follow are shown in a tabular form in Table 3A. 2 for the sake of brevity. We start with source node, 1, and store it in a matrix [P]. Matrix [A] is the row of connection matrix corresponding to the source node. [PP] contains [P] with each entry of [P] appended by the non-zeros locations of [A].

As A has non-zeros at locations 2 and 3, we append [P] with these values and stored it in [PP]. We take out rows of connection matrix corresponding

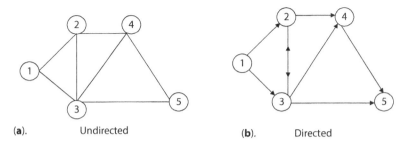

Figure 3A 1: ARPA network (Undirected, Directed).

Table 3A.1 Adjacency matrix.

Connection Matrix Figure 3A.1(a)						Connection Matrix Figure 3A.1(b)				
Node	1	2	3	4	5	Node	1	2	3	4	5
1	0	1	1	0	0	1	0	1	1	0	0
2	1	0	1	1	0	2	0	0	1	1	0
3	1	1	0	1	1	3	0	1	0	1	1
4	0	1	1	0	1	4	0	0	0	0	1
5	0	0	1	1	0	5	0	0	0	0	0

to the last element in each row of [PP] i.e., 2nd and 3rd rows by setting elements (1 & 2) of 2nd row and elements (1 & 3) of 3rd row to zero (marked with star). We store these modifications in rows in matrix [AA]. It completes one cycle of the search.

As a next step, we update [P] by [PP] and [A] by [AA]. At this point, we perform two checks viz.,

i.   Whether the last element in any row(s) of [PP] contains sink node and,

ii. Whether all entries in that row(s) of [AA] are zero.

Depending on the observations, we draw the following conclusions:

•   If last value in some row(s) of [PP] is the sink node number, then path set(s) has been found and we remove this row(s) from [PP] and [AA] before updating them into [P] and [A]. In this case, row(s) of [AA] might or might not have all values zero e.g., it could be seen in iteration number two for

Table 3A.2 Steps to enumerate path sets for the network of Figure 3A.1(a).

Iteration No.	[P]	[A]	[PP]	[AA]
1.	1	0 1 1 0 0	1 2 1 3	0* 0 1 1 0 0* 1 0 1 1
2.	1 2 1 3	0 0 1 1 0 0 1 0 1 1	1 2 3 1 2 4 1 3 2 1 3 4 *135*	0* 0* 0 1 1 0 0* 1 0 1 0* 0 0*1 0 0 1 0* 0 1 *01010*
3.	1 2 3 1 2 4 1 3 2 1 3 4	0 0 0 1 1 0 0 1 0 1 0 0 0 1 0 0 1 0 0 1	1 2 3 4 *1 2 3 5* 1 2 4 3 *1 2 4 5* 1 3 2 4 <u>*1 3 4 2*</u> *1 3 4 5*	0 0* 0* 0 1 *0 0 0*1 0* 0* 0* 0 0* 1 *0 0 1 0*0* 0 0* 0* 0 1 0* 0 0* 0* 0 *0 0 0*0*0*
4.	1 2 3 4 0 0 0 0 1 1 2 4 3 0 0 0 0 1 1 3 2 4 0 0 0 0 1		*1 2 3 4 5* *1 2 4 3 5* *1 3 2 4 5*	

*Replacement of Element with Zero.

path set {1, 3, 5}, and in iteration number three for path set {1, 3, 4, 5} and are shown in bold and italic.

- However, if some row(s) of [AA] has all zeros but [PP] does not have last element as sink node number, this implies formation of loop(s). This can be seen for the set {1, 3, 4, 2} in iteration number three, which is shown in bold and underlined. Hence, we discard this set(s) also and proceed further with the remaining entries in [PP] and [AA]. We stop the procedure when the iterative count becomes one less than the number of nodes in the network. Thus, the minimal path sets of the above example would be:

{1, 3, 5}, {1,2, 3, 5}, {1,2, 4, 5}, {1, 3, 4, 5}, {1, 2, 3, 4, 5}, {1, 2, 4, 3, 5} and {1,3,2,4,5} respectively.

Similar steps could be followed for directed case as well and the method would give six minimal path sets with the omission of path set {1, 2, 4, 3, 5}.

The following points may be noted for the illustration outlined above:

i. Size of [AA] is fixed and equal to the nodes in the graph.
ii. Maximum size of [PP] = total non-zeroes entries in [A] * Iteration number (i.e., cardinality of the path)
iii. At any point of time, the length of P would be equal to the (iteration count +1).
iv. If at any point, if a particular row of [PP] contains sink node number implying a valid path set.
v. In [AA] if all elements in a row are zero and last node in PP is not sink implying Invalid path set. Otherwise a valid path set.

For assigning branch number, we replace the upper diagonal elements of connection matrix by 1, 2, 3…l sequentially, as shown in Table 3A. 3. In other words, the non-zero elements in adjacent matrix are the link-number assigned to them. However, we have to consider whole adjacent matrix if the links are possessing directions too.

Table 3A.3 Assignment of branch number (undirected).

Connection matrix Figure 3A.1(a)					
Node	1	2	3	4	5
1	0	1	2	0	0
2	-	0	3	4	0
3	-	-	0	5	6
4	0	-	-	0	7
5	0	0	-	-	0

The conversion to get link-wise path sets is straightforward. The path sets for undirected case then turn out to be:

{2, 6}, {1, 3, 6}, {1, 4, 7}, {2, 5, 7}, {1, 3, 5, 7}, {1, 4, 5, 6}, and {2, 3, 4, 7}

The procedure to enumerate path sets, described generates path sets in increasing order of their cardinality and in lexicographic order- a condition, which is helpful in achieving a compact network reliability expression in form of sum of disjoint products (*sdp*). The ordering of path sets for the illustration, as claimed, could easily be checked. Albeit the method uses connection matrix but it does not require performing any complicated matrix operations. The other feature of the algorithm is that it automatically assigns branch numbers to the network branches, if the path sets are desired in terms of branch number, therefore, providing less burden on the user end. The highlights of the method presented above may be summarized as follows:

- It can find path sets for a specified pair of nodes.
- The iterative count also depicts the cardinality of a path set, if found. Thus, setting the iterative count $\leq (n - 1)$ can generate path sets of desired order of cardinality.
- Path sets are obtained in increasing order of their cardinality and Lexicographic order.
- It can also convert path set in terms of network nodes to network links.

We write each step of the idea outlined above in a systematic and algorithmic manner.

Algorithm: Various steps involved in the algorithm are as follows:

1. Generate adjacency matrix [ADJMAT] from the network data.
2. Set kk = 1, where kk is the cardinality of the path set, initialize array P with source node, A= row of [ADJMAT] corresponding to the source node.
3. Set i =1, j = 1, IlengthPrv = 0 (Number of elements in I on previous iteration), initialize PP = [ ] and AA= [ ] empty vector.
4. I = Find all nodes that are adjacent to the last node number in P_i by finding the

   index of non-zero elements in A_i. Ilength = number of elements in I, r =1 (for indexing elements in I).
5. PP_j = [P_i I^r], augment P_i with I^r, the rth value contained in I.

   AA_j = I^r row of [ADJMAT] with all elements, corresponding to the entries in PP_j, are set to zero.

   if I^r == Sink Node, path = PP_j and if conversion to branch wise needed, call functions for (i) assigning branch number and (ii) converting path set branch wise.

   elseif all values in AA_j==0 and I^r ≠ Sink Node → an invalid path set.
6. Repeat from step 5 for next j and r, *until j ≠ Ilength + IlengthPrv*
7. Repeat from step 4 *until next i≠ number of rows in P*, *IlengthPrv = IlengthPrv + Ilength*.

8. Release memory that correspond to valid path sets and/or invalid path sets in PP, and AA; replace P=PP, A=AA;
9. Repeat from step 3 for next kk *until kk < total nodes* in the network else Stop.

In order to implement the algorithm, it is necessary to code the network which includes assigning number to the branches.

Assigning Numbers to Branches

The diagonal entries in matrix [ADJMAT] are all zeros and number of non-zeros elements in upper-diagonal is equal to the number of branches present in the undirected graph. Thus, only upper or lower diagonal entries may be utilized for assigning number to the branches in the network. The steps involved are as follow:

1. If UNDIRECTED, extract and store the upper diagonal values of [ADJMAT] in B, else set B= [ADJMAT]
2. Assign decimal number sequentially starting from 1 onwards by tracing each non-zero value column-wise in B.

Path Sets in Terms of Network Links

The conversion of node-wise path sets to the branch-wise path sets is done as follows:

(*PTH: path set nodewise, PTHBR: path set branchwise*) ,Initialize to [ ] at the beginning.

1. Set i=1, lenPth = length (cardinality) of Path set
2. TMP=[PTH^i PTH $^{(i+1)}$], initialize X with ith and (i+1)th value of PTH
3. If UNDIRECTED, Sort TMP in increasing order of values.
4. Augment PTHBR = [PTHBR B$_{TMP^1, TMP^2}$]
5. Repeat step 2, *until next i ^{1} lenPth-1 else STOP*

In order to demonstrate the algorithmic steps in details, once again we revert to the ARPA network shown in Figure 3A. 1.

Illustration 3A.2: Let us begin with *Figure 3A. 1.* (a). The steps are as follows:

Undirected

The algorithm starts with building the adjacency matrix as shown in Table 3A. 4. The iterations start from step 2 onwards.

Table 3A.4 Adjacency matrix (Undirected).

Nodes ⇒ ⇓	1 •	2 •	3 •	4 •	5 •
1 •	0	1	1	0	0
2 •	1	0	1	1	0
3 •	1	1	0	1	1
4 •	0	1	1	0	1
5 •	0	0	1	1	0

1. **Iteration, kk = 1**

   P = 1(sourceNode), sinkNode =5, A = 0 1 1 0 0

   3. i = 1 , j = 1, IlengthPrv = 0, P_1 = 1, A_1 = 0 0 1 1 0, AA=PP= [ ],
   4. I= 2 3, Ilength = 2, r=1
   5. I^1=1, PP_1=1 2, AA_1 = 0 0 1 1 0
   6. j=2, r=2
      5. I^2 = 3, PP_2= 1 3, AA_2 = 0 1 0 1 1
      6. j = 3, r = 3, j>2, true
   7. i=2 > 1 row in P, true
   8. P =[1 2; 1 3] ; A =[0 0 1 1 0; 0 1 0 1 1], AA=[ ], PP=[ ].

2. **Iteration, kk = 2**

   3. i = 1, j =1, IlengthPrv = 0, P_1 = 1 2, AA_1 = 0 0 1 1 0
   4. I = 3 4, Ilength = 2, r = 1
   5. I^1 = 3, PP_1 = 1 2 3, AA_1 = 0 0 0 1 1
   6. j = 2, r = 2
      5. I^2 = 4, PP_2 = 1 2 4, AA_2 = 0 0 1 0 1
      6. j = 3, r = 3, j > 2 true
   7. IlelngthPrv = 2, i = 2
      4. I = 2 4 5, Ilength = 3, r = 1
      5. I^2 = 2, PP_3 = 1 3 2, AA_3 = 0 0 0 1 0
      6. j = 4, r =2
         5. I^2 = 4, PP_4 = 1 3 4, AA_4 = 0 1 0 0 1
         6. j = 5, r =3
         5. I^3 = 5, PP_5 = 1 3 5, AA_5 = 0 0 0 1 0, **Path Set Found.**
         6. j = 6, r = 4, j > 5 true

7. IlengthPrv = 5, i= 3 > rows in P, true

8. P = [1 2 3; 1 2 4; 1 3 2; 1 3 4], A = [0 0 0 1 1; 0 0 1 0 1; 0 0 0 1 0; 0 1 0 0 1], AA= [ ], PP = [ ].

3. **Iteration, kk = 3**

3. i = 1, j =1, IlengthPrv = 0, P_1 = 1 2 3, AA_1 = 0 0 0 1 1

4. I = 4 5, Ilength = 2, r = 1

5. I^1 = 4, PP_1 = 1 2 3 4, AA_1 = 0 0 0 0 1

6. j = 2, r =2

    5. I^2 = 5, PP_2 = 1 2 3 5, AA_2 = 0 0 0 1 0, **Path Set Found.**

    6. j = 3, r = 3, j > 2 true

7. IlengthPrv = 2, i =2

    4. I = 3 5, Ilength = 2, r = 1

    5. I^1 = 3, PP_3 = 1 2 4 3 , AA_3 = 0 0 0 0 1

    6. j = 4, r = 2

    5. I^2 = 5, PP_4 = 1 2 4 5 , AA_4 = 0 0 1 0 0, **Path Set Found.**

    6. j = 5, r =3, j > 4 true

    7. IlengthPrv = 4, i = 3

    4. I = 4, Ilength = 1, r = 1

    5. I^1 = 4, PP_5 = 1 3 2 4 , AA_5 = 0 0 0 0 1

    6. j = 6, r =2, j > 5 true

    7. IlengthPrv = 5, i = 4

    4. I = 2 5, Ilength = 2, r = 1

    5. I^1= 2, PP_6 = 1 3 4 2 , AA_6 = 0 0 0 0 0, I^1 = 5 **Invalid Path Set.**

    6. j = 7, r = 2

    5. I^2= 5, PP_7 = 1 3 4 5 , AA_7 = 0 0 0 0 0, **Path Set Found.**

    6. j = 8, r = 3, j > 7 true

    7. IlengthPrv = 7, i = 5 > rows in P true

8. P = [1 2 3 4; 1 2 4 3; 1 3 2 4], A=[0 0 0 0 1; 0 0 0 0 1 ;0 0 0 0 1], AA = [ ], PP = [ ]

4. **Iteration, kk=4**

3. i = 1, j = 1, IlengthPrv = 0, P_1 = 1 2 3 4, AA_1 = 0 0 0 01

4. I = 5, Ilength = 1, r = 1

5. I^1= 5, PP_1 = 1 2 3 4 5 , AA_1 = 0 0 0 0 0, **Path Set Found**

    6. $j = 2, r = 2, j > 1$ true

    7. IlengthPrv = 1, i = 2

        4. I = 5, Ilength = 1, r = 1

        5. $I^2 = 5$, PP$_2$ = 1 2 4 3 5, AA$_2$ = 0 0 0 0 0, **Path Set Found.**

        6. $j = 3, r = 2, j > 2$ true

        7. IlengthPrv = 2, i = 3

        4. I = 5, Ilength = 1, r = 1

        5. $I^3 = 5$, PP$_3$ = 1 3 2 4 5, AA$_3$ = 0 0 0 0 0, **Path Set Found.**

        6. J = 4, r = 2, j > 3 true

        7. Ilength = 3, i = 4 > rows in P true

    8. P = [ ], A = [ ], PP= [ ], AA = [ ]

    9. kk = 5 (= = total number of nodes) **Stop.**

Hence the algorithm finds a total of seven path sets viz. *{1 3 5}, {1 2 3 5}, {1 2 4 5}, {1 3 4 5}, {1 2 3 4 5}, {1 2 4 3 5} and {1 3 2 4 5}*, respectively.

Directed

Similar steps are being followed for the directed case, too i.e., we start with the adjacency matrix of the directed graph as shown in Table 3A. 5.

Table 3A.5 Adjacency matrix (Directed)

Nodes ⇒ ⇓		1 •	2 •	3 •	4 •	5 •
1	•	0	1	1	0	0
2	•	0	0	1	1	0
3	•	0	1	0	1	1
4	•	0	0	0	0	1
5	•	0	0	0	0	0

Due to the only one bi-directional link between nodes 2–3, the total path sets found by algorithm are six, i.e., one at iteration number, kk = 2, two at kk = 3, and three at kk = 4. The path sets are {1 3 5}, {1 2 3 5}, {1 2 4 5}, {1 3 4 5}, {1 2 3 4 5}, and {1 3 2 4 5}, respectively.

The sample input/output (I/O) of the program for this example can be seen in the Appendix 3A.2: , that includes the following cases for path sets viz., (i) undirected and branch-wise (ii) undirected and node-wise and, (iii) output of directed and branch-wise.

Appendix 3A.2: Sample program I/O for Figure 3A.1

Data File Input: Each row of the data shows that connection with other nodes. For example, row#1 of the input says that node #1 is connected with node #2 and #3, respectively. The data is written in a file named 'exDat.m', where .m is the file extension of a Matlab file. The program is run by writing '*pathsEnum*' on the *Matlab®* command prompt.

Undirected	*OR*	*Directed*
2 3		2 3
1 3 4		3 4
1 2 4 5		2 4 5
2 3 5		5
3 4		end
end		

- **Undirected and Branchwise**

  » *pathsEnum*
  adjMatdataFile(withpath)?:d:\skcmatlab\pSet\exDat.m
  SourceNode No.?:1
  TerminalNode No.?:5
  TotalNodes?:5
  Directed/undirected: 1/0? 0
  Please specify path sets to be enumerated BranchWise or NodeWise(1 or 0):1
  TotalBranch :?:7
  FOR OUTPUT
  Please enter Output file with full path:exRes.m
  t = 0.0600
  Total path sets found= 7

  Generated output file
  2 6
  1 3 6
  1 4 7
  2 5 7

```
    1 3 5 7
    1 4 5 6
    2 3 4 7
    end
```

Total path sets found = 7

Time: 0.06000000000

Branch areNumbered as:

Node#	Node#	BrNo.#
1	2	1
1	3	2
2	3	3
2	4	4
3	4	5
3	5	6
4	5	7

- ***Undirected and Nodewise***

» pathsEnum

adjMatdataFile(withpath)?:d:\skcmatlab\pSet\exDat.m

Source Node No.?:1

Terminal Node No. ?:5

Total Nodes?:5

Directed/undirected: 1/0? 0

Please specify path sets to be enumerated BranchWise or NodeWise(1 or 0):0

FOR OUTPUT

Please enter Output file with full path: d:\skcmatlab \pSet\ exResN.m

t = 0

Total path sets found= 7

Generated output file

```
    1 3 5
    1 2 3 5
    1 2 4 5
```

```
1 3 4 5
1 2 3 4 5
1 2 4 3 5
1 3 2 4 5
end
```

Total path sets found= 7
Time: 0.00000000000
For directed case, number of bidirectional links is also entered as input if path sets to be enumerated are branch-wise.

- ***Output of Directed and Branchwise***

>> pathsEnum
adjMatdataFile(withpath)?:exDat.m
SourceNode No.?:1
TerminalNode No. ?:5
TotalNodes?:5
Directed/undirected :1/0? 1
Please specify paths to be enumerated
BranchWise or NodeWise(1 or 0):1
TotalBranch :?:7
Number of bidirectional links:? 1
FOR OUTPUT
Please enter Output file with full path:exRes.m
t = 0.0152
Total Paths found= 6

```
3 7
1 4 7
1 5 8
3 6 8
1 4 6 8
3 2 5 8
end
```

Total path sets found = 6
Time: 0.11000000000

Branch are Numbered as:

Node#	Node#	Br.No.#
1	2	1
3	2	2
1	3	3
2	3	4
2	4	5
3	4	6
3	5	7
4	5	8

Exercises

3.1   Consider the communication network shown in Figure Ex. 3.1. Construct its incidence matrix. Obtain the vector D for the combination of links {1, 2, 3, 9, 12} and apply the properties as outlined in method#3 to make your comments.

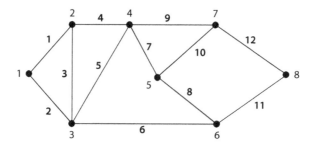

Figure Ex. 3.1 Communication network Graph.

3.2   Enumerate by visual inspection, the minimal paths for the networks shown in Figure Ex. 3.2.

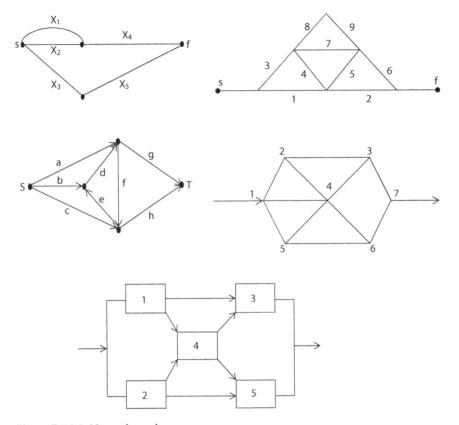

Figure Ex. 3.2 Network graphs.

3.3 Use the incidence matrix approach to enumerate path and spanning trees of the networks of above network graphs.

3.4 For the network shown in Figure Ex. 3.2, enumerate all path sets between node 2 and all other nodes using the powers of connection matrix.

3.5 Enumerate the k-trees for the node set {1, 4, 5} for the network shown in example 3.7.

References

Aggarwal, K.K. & Rai, S., 1981. Reliability Evaluation in Computer Communication Networks. *IEEE Transaction on Reliability*, Vol. R-30(1).

Ahmad, S.H., 1989. Simple enumeration of minimal tiesets of undirected graph. *Microelectronics Reliability*, Vol. 29(4), pp. 509–510.

Deo, N., 1979. *Graph Theory with Applications to Engineering and Computer Science*. New edition ed. PHI.

Kelmans, A.K. & Chelnokov, V.M., 1974. A certain polynomial of a graph and graphs with an extremal number of trees. *J. Comb Theory*, Ser. B 16, pp. 197–214.

Mishra, R.B. & Misra, K.B., 1980. Enumeration of all simple paths in a communication network. *Microelectronics and Reliability*, Vol. 20, pp. 419–426.

Piekarski, M., 1965. Listing all possible trees of a linear Graph. *IEEE Transaction on Circuit Theory*, Vol CT-12, pp. 124–125.

Rath, D. & Soman, K.P., 1993. A simple Method for Generating k - Trees of a Network. *Microelectronics and Reliability*, Vol 33(9), pp. 1241–1244.

Samad, M.A., 1987. Methods for Global reliability Evaluation of any Large Complex System. *Reliability Engineering*, Vol. 18, pp. 47–55.

Soh, S. & Rai, S., 1993. Experimental Results on Preprocessing of Path/Cut Terms in Sum of Disjoint Products Techniques. *IEEE Transaction on Reliability*, 42(1), pp. 24–33.

4

Cut Sets Enumeration

A cut set is a set of links (branches), which literally cuts the success path by severing all the possible lines of communication between the transmitting and receiving terminals. A minimal cut set of a network graph G is a set of links, whose removal or non-functioning ensures the network disconnectivity for a specified set of nodes provide removal of no proper subset of these links disconnects G. The number of path sets or cut sets in any general network depends to a large extent on the topology of the network and it would be advantageous to work with path sets or cut sets, whichever has its number less. In most of the practical systems, particularly in highly redundant and well-connected networks, the number of cut sets is usually much less than the number of path sets and it may be advantageous to work with cut sets rather than path sets in such cases.

An advance estimate of the number of path sets or cut sets helps determine the approach that one may use eventually to evaluate reliability of a given network graph. One such estimate was provided by (Aggarwal, Chopra, & Wajwa, 1982), which suggests that relatively for a network of n nodes and l links, the number of cut sets *between any pair of nodes* would be of the order of 2^{n-2}, whereas the number of path sets is of the order of 2^{l-n+2}. Note that the estimation for other types of minimal cuts (global or k-minimal) is not known. Besides, if average degree of nodes in a given network graph is more than 4, then l>2n, thereby $2^{l-n+2} > 2^{n-2}$. It means that such networks generally have a large number of path sets than the number of cut sets. Also where element reliabilities are high, cut sets based reliability evaluation provides more accurate results. Therefore, depending upon the situation, one can use either path sets or cut sets for computing a reliability measure.

The path sets enumeration technique described in Chapter 3 are equally-well applicable to enumerate cut sets as well if one can develop a *dual* of the network graph under consideration (Samad, 1987), (Shen, 1995). However, not always being possible to construct a dual graph even for a small size network is the reason for its inapplicability and unpopularity among the engineers and researchers.

The techniques of cut sets enumeration can be broadly divided into (i) Direct methods that utilize the structure of the network graph and its representation through a suitable data structure and manipulation thereafter (ii) Path sets based techniques with the use of Boolean/ set theoretic laws and concepts. These cut sets enumeration methods suffer the disadvantage of knowing of minimal path sets in advance, in order to determine cut sets. Therefore, these methods are generally not efficient. This chapter presents some methods to enumerate 2-terminal, global and k-cut set of a given network graph.

4.1   (s, f) Cut Sets Enumeration

4.1.1   Method 1: Using Connection Matrix

This algorithm to enumerate minimal cut sets is described in (Ahmad, 1990), and is an extension of the method proposed by the same author for acyclic directed graph (Ahmad, 1988). The method follows the following steps:

1. Construct the connection matrix of the network graph wherein the elements of the matrix represent the link label connecting the nodes. If the graph is reducible, reduce it with the corresponding changes in the elements in this matrix.
2. Collect all the labels appearing in the first row- a source minimal cut, and in the last column-a destination minimal cut.

3. Form a set 'S' of all columns combinations of order 1 to (n-3), n≥4 (n<4 provides the trivial cases) with columns 2 to (n-1). Delete a combination by observing:
   a. If the combination consists of only those column having zeros in the first row,
   b. If the combination consists of those rows having *non-zero* entries in the last column.
   The above rules help not only to reduce the number of combinations to be handled to generate minimal cut sets but also remove the combinations that eventually generate non-minimal cut sets. On the reduced combinations set,
4. Take one combination; collect all the links-labels appearing in the row(s) corresponding to row#1 + this combination without considering columns represented by this combination. This combination will provide another cut set.
5. Repeat step #4 for all remaining combinations.

Let us take an example to illustrate the above algorithm.

Example 4.1: Apply the above algorithm on the ARPA network graph shown in Figure 4.1.

Solution: The network graph and its connection matrix are reproduced for the sake of brevity as below:

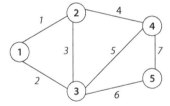

$$CM = \begin{bmatrix} 0 & 1 & 2 & 0 & 0 \\ 1 & 0 & 3 & 4 & 0 \\ 2 & 3 & 0 & 5 & 6 \\ 0 & 4 & 5 & 0 & 7 \\ 0 & 0 & 6 & 7 & 0 \end{bmatrix}$$

Figure 4.1 ARPA network.

Steps:

1. From the CM above, collecting terms from first row, {1, 2}, and last column, {6, 7}, produce two minimal cut sets.
2. Here, n = 5, Order of combinations to be formed = (5–3), i.e., 1 to 2 from the columns # 2 to # 4 of CM, i.e., all the combination of set {2, 3, 4} up to 2nd order.

   S = {{2},{3},{4},{2,3},{2,4},{3,4}}, Further;

Only combination {4} has zero entry in the first row, therefore, discarded.

Row (combination) {3,4} has non-zero entry in their last column; therefore, discard this combination and its supersets appearing in S. This gives the updated set, S ={{2},{3},{2,3},{2,4}}

3. For combination, {2} , we consider elements in rows 1 & 2 except elements that appears in column2 1 & 2, i.e., the link labels in rows, {1,2} except in columns {1, 2} are = {2, 3, 4}, Similarly, for combination {3}, we consider {1, 3} and the cut set is = {1, 3, 5, 6}

   For combination, {2, 3}, we consider {1, 2, 3} and the cut set is = {4, 5, 6}

   For combination, {2, 4}, we have {1, 2, 4} and the cut set is = {2, 3, 5, 7}. Therefore, there are six minimal cut sets produced by the algorithm: {1, 2},{6, 7}, {2, 3, 4}, {1, 3, 5, 6}, {4, 5, 6}, and {2, 3, 5, 7}.

4.1.2   Method 2: Using Minimal Path Sets

There are several methods appeared in the literature for enumeration the (s, f) minimal cutsets necessitating the knowledge of path sets a priori. We would provide the notion only for some of these methods as they are computationally cumbersome.

4.1.2.1   Using Set-theoretic Product of Path Sets

This iterative method proposed by (Schabe, 1995) is based on set-theoretic considerations and is an improvement over the method proposed by (Elias, Mokhles, & Ibrahim, 1993) who have also provided a review on the subject. In order to speed-up computation, it suggests the ordering of path according to their size (number of elements constituting a path, i.e., cardinality) starting with the path of smallest cardinality and paths of equal cardinality are ordered lexicographically. It employs the following two notions:

a. A subsystem having a single path, (e.g., series subsystem), $P_1 = \{e_1, e_2, e_3, ...e_k\}$ has $k = card(P_1)$, cutsets.

b. If a subsystem characterized by a cutset $\{C_1, C_2, C, ... C_k\}$ (not minimal) is connected in parallel with a certain path $P_{k+1} = \left\{e_{i_1}, e_{i_2}, e_{i_3}, ...e_{i_m}\right\}$, then the cutset of new system would be the cross product of sets, i.e

It takes the following broad steps:

1. If an element $e_j \in P_i \forall i = 1,2,3...P$ pathsets, then e_j is a minimal cut of cardinality one. Store it in, say, ξ and remove it from all pathsets.

2. Remove redundant and/or repetitive terms (pathsets) from the set obtained in step 1.

3. Select a path sets, obtain the set theoretic cross-product, $\xi = \{C_1, C_2, C_3, ...C_k\} \otimes \{e_{i_1}, e_{i_2}, e_{i_3}, ...e_{i_m}\}$. Minimizing it by removing the redundant and/or repetitive terms. The remaining terms are added to the cutsets list.

4. The process is continued till we obtain the cross-product with the last path set in the list.

Example 4.2: Let us consider the seven (s, f) path sets of a network graph of Figure 4.1 enumerated in Chapter 3: {2, 6}, {1, 3, 6}, {1, 4, 7}, {2, 5, 7}, {1, 3, 5, 7}, {1, 4, 5, 6}, {2, 3, 4, 7}, ordered in cardinality + lexicographically. It is evident from the minimal pat list that there is no cut of cardinality 1 (step 1). The cross-product of first two path sets gives:

$$\xi = \{2,6\} \otimes \{1,3,6\} = \{\{1,2\},\{2,3\},\{2,6\},\{1,6\},\{3,6\},\{6\}\}$$

On removing redundant terms, {1, 6}, {2, 6} and {3, 6}, the reduced set is $\xi = \{\{1,2\}, \{2,3\}, \{6\}\}$, which is used to update ξ by taking its cross-product with the next path set, i.e.,

$$\xi = \{1,4,7\} \otimes \{\{1,2\},\{2,3\},\{6\}\}$$

$$= \{\{1,2\},\{1,2,3\},\{1,6\},\{1,2,4\},\{2,3,4\},\{4,6\},\{1,2,7\},\{2,3,7\},\{6,7\}\}$$

$$\xi = \{\{1,2\},\{1,6\},\{2,3,4\},\{4,6\},\{2,3,7\},\{6,7\}\}$$

Finally, it produces six minimal cutsets as,

$$\xi = \{2,3,4,7\} \otimes \{\{1,2\},\{1,5,6\},\{2,3,4\},\{2,3,7\},\{4,5,6\},\{6,7\}\}$$

$$= \{\{1,2\},\{2,3,4\},\{2,3,5,7\}, \{1,3,5,6\},\{4,5,6\},\{6,7\}\}.$$

4.1.2.2 *Using Path Sets Matrix*

It utilizes a path matrix of order number of paths × links of the network graph whose elements are either 1 or 0 depending on the presence/absence of a link (represented by the column of path matrix) in that particular path (represented by the row of path matrix). Obviously, a column containing all ones signify the presence of a minimal cut of orders one. This column can be removed from the matrix from further considerations.

Now a test is conducted by combining (Boolean O Ring) the columns of order two at a time, checking whether any combination of such order gives a column containing all ones? If so then that combination would constitute a cut and is stored if it is found to be minimal by comparing it with the previously stored minimal cutsets. The process is repeated for next order combinations to the highest combination possible.

The 7×7 order (7 path and 7 elements) order path matrix for the network graph of example 4.1 is:

$$
\begin{bmatrix}
0 & 1 & 0 & 0 & 0 & 1 & 0 \\
1 & 0 & 1 & 0 & 0 & 1 & 0 \\
1 & 0 & 0 & 1 & 0 & 0 & 1 \\
0 & 1 & 0 & 0 & 1 & 0 & 1 \\
1 & 0 & 1 & 0 & 1 & 0 & 1 \\
1 & 0 & 0 & 1 & 1 & 1 & 0 \\
0 & 1 & 1 & 1 & 0 & 0 & 1
\end{bmatrix}
$$

One has to form the combinations of order $C_2^7, C_3^7, C_4^7, C_5^7, C_6^7,$ and C_7^7 and each combination would have to be tested for constituting a cut (by observing if a column contains all ones) and then for its minimality through the comparison with already enumerated minimal cuts. For instance, if we combine column 1 and 2, we get all ones in the first column. It means combination of links {1, 2} constitutes a cut. However, column 1 and 3 do not provide all ones after combination, hence cannot form a cut of order two.

4.1.2.3   Using Path Sets Inversion

This method was introduced by Locks (Locks, 1978) wherein the inversion is accomplished by a recursive method of combining a two-step application of De' Morgan's theorem with a subsequent minimization. For a system having 'P' minimal paths, the recursion has P stages-one for each path. At any i^{th} stage, i<=P, the minimalized inverse of first (i-1) paths is logically multiplied by the inverse of ith minimal path to form the inverse of first i number of minimal path and the process continues until i equals P. Summarily, it inverts each minimal paths, takes the Boolean product of the paths one-by-one and applies the Boolean minimization of each stage of the product cycle.

Example 4.3: Let us apply the method to network graph of example 4.1 having the seven minimal path sets as:

P= {{2, 6}, {1, 3, 6}, {1, 4, 7}, {2, 5, 7}, {1, 3, 5, 7}, {1, 4, 5, 6}, {2, 3, 4, 7}}. For first path, the inversion would be

$2,6 = \bar{2} + \bar{6}$, using De' Morgan's theorem where bar over the link's number denotes a failed link. Similarly, for second path, $1,3,6 = 1 + 3 + 6$.

The Boolean multiplication of $MC = \left(\bar{2}+\bar{6}\right) \times \left(\bar{1}+\bar{3}+\bar{6}\right) = \overline{12} + \overline{23} + \overline{26}$ $+ \overline{16} + \overline{36} + \bar{6} = \overline{12} + \overline{23} + \bar{6}$.

Now, the result obtained above as MC is again to get an updated MC through Boolean multiplication with the next inverted path. This process of Boolean multiplication continues until the last path in inverted form gets multiplied with the MC updated in the previous step. The final Boolean product, MC, would represent the minimal cutset of the network graph and is obtained in the final step by multiplying the inverted form of last path {2,3,4,7} as:

$$MC = \left(\bar{2}+\bar{3}+\bar{4}+\bar{7}\right) \times \left(\overline{12}+\overline{156}+\overline{234}+\overline{2357}+\overline{456}+\overline{67}\right)$$

$$= \overline{12}+\overline{1256}+\overline{234}+\overline{2357}+\overline{2456}+\overline{267}+\overline{123}+\overline{1356}$$
$$+\overline{234}+\overline{2357}+\overline{3456}+\overline{367}+\overline{124}+\overline{1456}+\overline{234}+\overline{2345}$$
$$+\overline{456}+\overline{467}+\overline{127}+\overline{1567}+\overline{2347}+\overline{2357}+\overline{4567}+\overline{67}$$

After performing the minimization by cancelling the duplicate and redundant terms, we get the following six terms in the MC,

$$MC = \overline{12}+\overline{234}+\overline{23}+\overline{1356}+\overline{456}+\overline{67}$$

This can easily be verified as the minimal cutset of the network graph.

4.2   Global Cut Sets Enumeration

There is not much text/literature available on enumeration of global cutsets. Here, we present a simple but powerful *g*-minimal cutsets enumeration approach which can handle undirected networks without any redundant overheads (Mishra & Chaturvedi, Global Reliability Evaluation using *g*-Minimal Cutsets, 2009). The major advantages of the algorithm are

a. It uses previous node-sets to generate next order node-sets to avoid exhaustive generation of node sets.
b. It only uses network connectivity criterion using a part of the adjacency matrix to verify that a node-sets will indeed generate a g-minimal cutset and,
c. It yields non-redundant g-minimal cutsets, thus alleviating from redundancy removal overheads.

The approach combines set theory and an iterative process to yield high efficiency. The iterative process uses the connectivity information of the network combined with previously gathered information to generate new subsets logically. The following background is needed before we present the details on algorithm.

4.2.1   Testing Connectivity of a Specified Node Set

The very question that needs an answer very frequently in this algorithms is: Is graph (s,f) connected? Is a specified set of nodes connected? Breadth First Search or Depth First Search methods ae some of the well-known methods to answer such questions. However, given the adjacency matrix of a graph, it is also possible to determine whether a graph is connected by trying various permutations of rows and the corresponding coloumns of adjacency matrix. This however is an inefficient method due to n! number of permutations. One can also use the following therorem and corollary from graph theory (Deo, 1979) :

Theorem: Let A be adjacency matrix of a simple graph G. Then ij^{th} entry in A^r is the number of different edge sequences of r edges between vertices v_i and v_j.

Corollary: If A is adjacency matrix of a graph G with n vertices, and $B = A + A^2 + A^3 \ldots + A^{n-1}$ (in the ring of integers), then G is disconnected if there exists at least one entry in B that is zero.

However, this is again an inefficient method and involves a large number of matrix multiplications. Therefore, the method utilizes the following technique that can be easily determined from adjacency matrix.

4.2.1.1   Node Fusion Technique

Method of adjacent node fusion is used to check the connectivity of a particular node sequence or combination set by taking out rows and columns corresponding to this set of nodes from the adjacency matrix of the network. Let these extracted rows and columns form a matrix [B]. Now, i^{th} and j^{th} rows of this matrix are merged, if node, i, is adjacent to node, j. We do this merging by applying the Boolean *OR* operation to i^{th} and j^{th} rows. Similar operation we apply to i^{th} and j^{th} columns. Then j^{th} row and column are deleted. We repeat this process till the exhaustion of all adjacent nodes.

The basic idea in this method is the fusion (merger) of vertices adjacent to a selected vertex in a recursive manner. The process ends when no more vertices are available to fuse further indicating that all connected component of the graph has been fused to a single vertex. In the adjacency matrix, the fusion of jth vertex to the ith vertex is accomplished by logical OR-ing operation, *i.e.*, by logically adding the jth row to the ith row as well as the jth column to ith column. Then the jth row and column are discarded from the matrix or care has been taken that they should not be considered in fusion process. The upper bound on the execution time is proportional to *n(n-1)*.

A simple example illustrates the method as follows.

Example 4.4: Let us illustrate it by taking an arbitrary network graph examples for connected and not connected case of specified node sets by taking out the rows and columns corresponding to the node set, say {1 2 3 4} and {1 2 5 7}, respectively. The steps are shown below in Table 4.1.

Table 4.1 Illustrating Node-Fusion technique.

Test set	Extracted rows and columns to form matrix [B]	Step 1	Step 2	Step 3
{1 2 3 4} (Connected)	0 1 1 0 / 0 0 1 1 / 0 0 0 1 / 0 0 0 0	Node 2 is adjacent and fused and row and column 2 deleted. 1 1 1 / 0 0 1 / 0 0 0	Repeat Step 1 1 1 / 0 0	Repeat Step 1 1
{1 2 5 7} (Not Connected)	0 1 0 0 / 0 0 0 0 / 0 0 1 1 / 0 0 0 0	Node 1 & 2 fused 1 0 0 / 0 1 1 / 0 0 0	No further fusion possible.	

The program listing of the connectivity testing using node fusion can be seen in Appendix 4A.1

4.2.2   Generation of Node Set Combination from its Lower Order Node-Sets

Let there be a graph of n-nodes and (**1, 5, 7**) be a node-set of order three. To generate all the fourth order. The highest node number in this set is node#7. By incrementing it by one till 'n' and appending it with the set (**1, 5, 7**) would provide the fourth-order sets. For instance, the fourth order node sets yielded by {**1, 5, 7**} would be: {**1, 5, 7, 8**}, {**1, 5, 7, 9**}, {**1, 5, 7, 10**}… {**1, 5, 7, n**}.

Note that in this process one need not to generate all possible node-combinations as many of the node-sets are going to be discarded using a validity check criteria and only a node-set(s) which satisfies the criteria are being used to generate next higher order sets. In other words, this process greatly reduces the number of node-sets combinations need to be generated to form minimal cutsets. The next section presents the validity check criteria.

The *Matlab*® program on generation of node set combination from its lower order node sets can be seen in Appendix 4A.1

4.2.3   Checking Validity of a Node Set

The approach is simple and takes the advantages of information that can easily be extracted from the adjacency matrix representation of a network graph. In fact, any node set of a particular order would have the following three properties, *viz.*,

  a. Eligible for both a valid node cutset formation and for generation of next order node cutset or
  b. It would be only suitable for generating next higher order node cutset or
  c. It would not be at all useful and hence, should be discarded for further consideration.

To check whether a first order node-set is useful to form a minimal cutsets and also be useful for generating higher order node-sets, we look for the graph connectivity after removing the row and column corresponding to the selected first order node set. If this criterion is satisfied, then this node would form a g-minimal cutset as well as will be used to form second order node-sets generation. Clearly, out of n nodes, few nodes may not be satisfying this criterion, thus reducing the number of generations in next stage.

However, for higher node-sets combinations, if any node-set is not connected themselves then it is discarded for further use. Otherwise, this set is further checked for its connectivity with any other node (not in the set) of the network. If not found, then this set is again discarded for further use. Otherwise, it is checked for the last condition, *i.e.*, removing sub-graph corresponding to this set whether remaining nodes are connected? These validity check criteria have proven to provide only those node-sets, which will form g-minimal cutsets. Note that all these criteria can easily be checked by the node-fusion technique described in *Section 4.2.1*. The example provided later further explains these criteria and technique.

The *Matlab*® program on validity checking of a node set can be seen in Appendix 4A.2

4.2.4   Formation of Cutset

Up to this point, we have worked on the sets of network nodes of different orders only. However, to form link cutsets, we can follow the steps given as under:

1. Take a valid node-set and collect all the branches that are connected with each node of this set.
2. Compose a single set using set-theoretic XOR-operation to form a link cutset of the network.

This procedure is repeated for each valid node set of a particular order.

The program for formation of cutset by converting node set into link cutset can be seen in Appendix 4A.2.

4.2.5   General Algorithm to Enumerate Minimal Cutsets for a Reliability Measure

The steps of the algorithm for a given network graph are (Mishra & Chaturvedi, 2009).

1. If source and terminal nodes are known than assign highest node number # N to the source node and #1 to the sink node. Otherwise, assign node number sequentially and assume highest node number #N is source node with node #1 as sink node.

2. Form adjacency matrix representation of the network. This matrix is being used to test connectivity criterion of a specified node set.

3. Check, whether after removing i^{th} node from the network $\forall$ $i = 1$ to N-1, rest of the nodes remains connected with source node? If yes, then i^{th} node forms a *g-minimal* cutset and will also be used to form next higher order node set. Store these *m*- numbers (out of N) nodes of first order node sets.

4. Generate next higher order node-sets combinations for each jth qualified node-set, $j = 1, 2...m$ obtained in previous step in the following manner:

   Define and Determine, *nHigh* = highest node number in the set, *nMax* = maximum node number connected to this node set.

   If *nHigh* $\neq$ N-1, append node set with element *nHigh*+1 to *nMax*, sequentially to form node sets. Repeat this step for all j to obtain higher order combinations for each qualified node set. Let the total number of these node sets be l.

5. Validate these l-node sets for forming *g*- minimal cutsets by testing these two conditions:

   a. Check whether p^{th} node-set, $\forall$ $p = 1, 2...l$, is connected themselves in the network? If No, repeat for next node-set. If yes, then check that each element of this node set is also connected with at least one other node of the network. If No, repeat for next node set. If yes, then

   b. Check whether removing this p^{th} node set from the network, whether the remaining nodes of the network remain connected from the source.

   If both the above conditions are satisfied then the node set is a valid node set. Store all these node-sets and repeat steps from step #4 till $(N$-1)th order node set.

6. If *2*-terminal (or *k*-terminal) node sets are required then specify *2*- (or *k*-) nodes of the network else go to step #8.

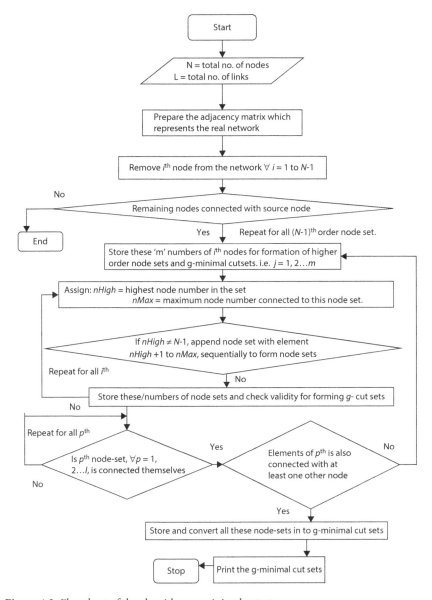

Figure 4.2 Flowchart of the algorithm: g-minimal cutsets.

7. Keep those node sets only in which at least one node of specified source-terminal nodes (or k-nodes) appears and discard all other node sets.

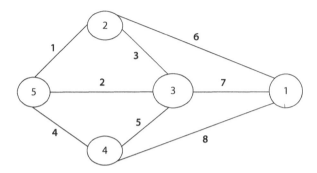

Figure 4.3 Network reliability graph of an ARPA communication network.

8. Convert all node-sets to link cutsets by using set-theoretic XOR-operation on links connected to each element of a node set.

Step #8 provides all minimal cutsets for a selected reliability measure.

The flow chart of *g*-minimal cutsets enumeration procedure is provided (Mishra, 2009).

The above steps of the algorithm have been implemented in *Matlab*. The main and associated programs for enumeration of g-minimal cutset can be downloaded from www.scrivenerpublishing.com/Chaturvedi_Network_Reliability_2016_Matlab_Programs.rar. The next section, by taking an example, describes the algorithmic steps of the method.

Example 4.5: Figure 4.3 shows an ARPA communication network of 4 sink nodes, viz., 1-4 and 5 as a source node, the undirected branches and nodes are identified with numeric characters only. Here bold numbers show the link number and node numbers are shown inside circle with normal fonts.

Solution: The steps of the method to obtain the global minimal cutsets of the given network are as follows:

Step#1: The adjacency matrix A of the reliability graph of Figure 4.3 is given below.

$$A = \begin{bmatrix} 0 & 1 & 1 & 1 & 0 \\ 1 & 0 & 1 & 0 & 1 \\ 1 & 1 & 0 & 1 & 1 \\ 1 & 0 & 1 & 0 & 1 \\ 0 & 1 & 1 & 1 & 0 \end{bmatrix}$$

Step#2: First order node set are, = [{1}, {2}, {3}, {4}]. Removing node# 1, the rest of the nodes remains connected with node #5 using the node-fusion technique. This is true for node #2, #3 and #4 as well. Therefore, the valid first order node sets are {1}, {2}, {3}, and {4}, respectively. Here, $l = 4$.

Step# 3: To generate next order node sets, nHigh and nMax with the above first order node-sets are:

Node-Set	{1}	{2}	{3}	{4}
nHigh (nMax)	1(4)	2(3)	3(4)	4(4)

Therefore, the following five, second order node sets are generated, i.e., here, $l = 5$ and thus the second order node-sets are: [{1, 2}, {1, 3}, {1, 4}, {2, 3}, {3, 4}].

Step #4: Node-fusion technique results provide that all these second order node sets, {1, 2}, {1, 3}, {1, 4}, {2, 3}, {3, 4}, are connected with themselves (can also be seen in the network). This testing can simply be done by taking the rows and columns corresponding to each node-set in sequence.

{1, 2}→ connected with other nodes {3, 4}, and removing node #1 and #2, rest of the nodes remain connected with source node #5 implying that it is a valid node sets. Similarly, {1, 3}, {1, 4}, {2, 3} and {3, 4} are also valid node sets.

Taking second-order node sets to generate third-order sets as:

Node-Set	{1, 2}	{1, 3}	{1, 4}	{2, 3}	{3, 4}
nHigh (nMax)	2(4)	3(4)	4(4)	3(4)	4(4)

and repeating *Step # 4* generates four node sets of 3rd order: {1, 2, 3}, {1, 2, 4}, {1, 3, 4}, {2, 3, 4}, respectively. However, the valid node sets satisfying the two verifying conditions are {1, 2, 3}, {1, 2, 4} and {1, 3, 4} respectively. Lastly, it generates a valid node set {1, 2, 3, 4}.

The total number of node sets generated by the algorithm is 13, i.e., [{1}, {2}, {3}, {4}, {1, 2}, {1, 3}, {1, 4}, {2, 3}, {3, 4}, {1, 2, 3}, {1, 2, 4}, {1, 3, 4}, {1, 2, 3, 4}].

Step # 5: The conversion of these node sets to link cutsets is obtained by employing the set theoretic *XOR*-operation on the links associated with each element of a node set. For instance, consider a node set {1, 2, 4}. The links connected to node {1} are {6, 7, 8}, to {2} are {1, 3, 6} and to {4} are {4, 5, 8}, respectively. Set theoretic XOR-operation provides the set {1, 3, 4, 5, 7}, which is a *g*-minimal cut set.

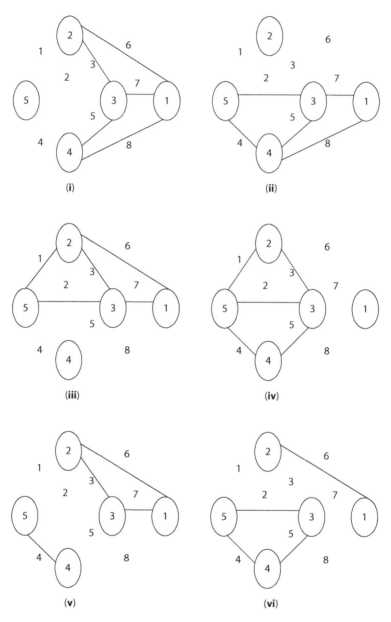

Figure 4.4 Sub-graphs of Figure 4.3 after Removal of Respective Link Cutsets.(*Continued*)

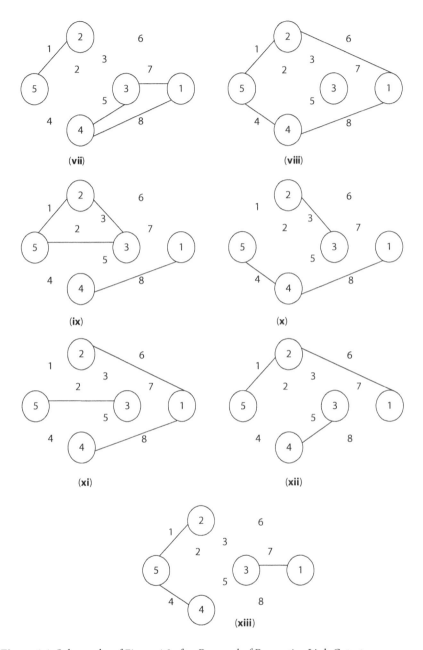

Figure 4.4 Sub-graphs of Figure 4.3 after Removal of Respective Link Cutsets.

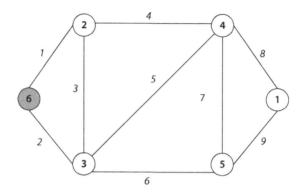

Figure 4.5 An undirected network (6 Nodes and 9 Links).

Each node set produces a unique cutset and thus 13 g-minimal cutsets are:
[{1 2 4}, {1 3 6}, {4 5 8}, {6 7 8}, {1 2 5 8}, {1 3 7 8}, {2 3 4 6}, {2 3 5 7}, {4 5 6 7}, {1 2 5 6 7}, {1 3 4 5 7}, {2 3 4 7 8}, {2 3 5 6 8}].

The resultant sub graphs after removing branches contained in g-minimal cutsets of Figure 4.3 have been shown in Figure 4.4 (i-xiii) for visualisation of resulting networks. A program sample I/O for enumeration of g-minimal cutset and evaluation of g-terminal reliability for network graph shown in Figure 4.3 can be seen in Appendix 4A.3. and Appendix 4A.4 , respectively. The details of the algorithms and their Matlab programmes are discussed in Chapter 5.

Example 4.6: Let us consider another example to enumerate minimal cutsets for other reliability measures as well for the network graph shown in Figure 4.5.

Solution: Step#1 and 2: The adjacency matrix A of the reliability network of the Figure 4.5.

Note that we have numbered 6 to source and 1 to terminal node.

Step#3: First order node set = [{1}, {2}, {3}, {4}, {5}]. Removing node #1, the rest of the nodes remains connected with node #6. This is true for node #2, #3, #4 and #5 as well. Therefore, the valid first order node sets are {1}, {2}, {3}, {4}, and {5}, respectively.

Step# 4: To generate next order node sets, *nHigh* and *nMax* are:

Node-Set	{1}	{2}	{3}	{4}	{5}
nHigh (nMax)	1(5)	2(4)	3(5)	4(5)	5(5)

Therefore, the following nine, second order, node sets are generated, *i.e.*, $l = 9$: [{1, 2}, {1, 3}, {1, 4}, {1, 5},{2, 3},{2, 4},{3, 4},{3, 5}, {4, 5}].

Step #5: {1, 2}, {1, 3} Not connected with themselves, whereas {1, 4}, {1, 5}, {2, 3}, {2, 4}, {3, 4}, {3, 5}, {4, 5} are connected with themselves (can be seen in the network of Figure 4.5). This testing can simply be done by taking the rows and columns corresponding to a node set. **{1, 4}** connected with other nodes {2, 3, 5}, and removing node #1and #4, rest of the nodes remain connected with source node #6 implying that it is a **valid** node sets. Similarly, **{1, 5}**, **{2, 4}**, and **{3, 5}** are also **valid** node sets. However, node set {2, 3} connected with other nodes {4, 5, 6} but violates condition (ii) as the remaining nodes get disconnected from the source. Similarly, {3, 4} connected with other nodes {1, 2, 5} but violates condition (ii) and {4, 5} connected with other nodes {1, 2, 3} but violates condition (ii).

Therefore, the valid second order node sets are **{1, 4}**, **{1, 5}**, **{2, 4}**, and **{3, 5}**, respectively. Taking second-order node sets and repeating **Step # 4,**

Node-Set	{1, 2}	{1, 3}	{1, 4}	{1, 5}	{2, 3}	{2, 4}	{3, 4}	(3, 5)	{4, 5}
nHigh (nMax)	2(5)	3(5)	4(5)	5(5)	3(5)	4(5)	4(5)	5(5)	5(5)

The following 10 node sets of 3rd order are generated: [{1, 2, 3}, {1, 2, 4}, {1, 2, 5}, {1, 3, 4}, {1, 3, 5}, {1, 4, 5}, {2, 3, 4},{2, 3, 5}, {2, 4, 5}, {3, 4, 5}. However, the valid node sets satisfying the two conditions are only **{1, 2, 4}**, **{1, 3, 5}** and **{1, 4, 5}**, respectively.

The steps are followed in the similar manner and generate five node sets of fourth order, *i.e.*, {1, 2, 3, 4}, {1, 2, 3, 5}, {1, 2, 4, 5}, {1, 3, 4, 5} and {2, 3, 4, 5}, respectively, giving **{1, 2, 4, 5}** and **{1, 3, 4, 5}** as valid node sets. Lastly, it generates a valid node set **{1,2,3, 4, 5}**.

Therefore using this algorithm, 15 valid node sets, i.e., [**{1}**, **{2}**, **{3}**, **{4}**, **{5}**, **{1, 4}**,**{1, 5}**, **{2, 4}**, **{3, 5}**,**{1, 2, 4}**, **{1, 3, 5}**, **{1, 4, 5}**, **{1, 2, 4, 5}**, **{1, 3, 4, 5}**, **{1, 2, 3, 4, 5}**] are been generated.

For g-terminal node sets:
Step # 8: The conversion of these node sets to link cutsets is obtained by employing the set theoretic XOR-operation on the links associated with each element of a node set. For instance, consider a node set {1, 2, 4}. The links connected to node {1} are {8, 9}, to {2} are {1, 3, 4} and to {4} are {4, 5, 7, 8}, respectively. Set theoretic XOR-operation provides the set {1, 3, 5, 7, 9}, which is a g-minimal cut set.

Each node set produces a unique cutset and thus 15 g-minimal cutsets are:

[[*1 2*}, {*8 9*}, {*1 3 4*}, {*2 3 4*}, {*4 5 6*}, {*6 7 8*}, {*6 7 9*}, {*1 3 5 6*}, {*2 3 5 6*}, {*4 5 7 8*}, {*4 5 7 9*}, {*1 3 5 7 8*}, {*1 3 5 7 9*}, {*2 3 5 7 8*}, {*2 3 5 7 9*}]. Note that the links here are labelled with italics numbers.

For 2-terminal node sets:
Specify the source node. Let it be node#1. Recall that node #6 is already assigned as source node. Discarding those node sets in which either terminal node#1 do not appear: [{1}, {1, 4}, {1, 5}, {1, 2, 4}, {1, 3, 5}, {1, 4, 5}, {1, 2, 4, 5}, {1, 3, 4, 5}, {1, 2, 3, 4, 5}]. Thus there are nine 2-terminal node sets. Following step 8 of the algorithm, the 2-terminal nine minimal cutsets are:

[[*1 2*}, {*8 9*}, {*2 3 4*}, {*4 5 6*}, {*6 7 8*}, {*1 3 5 6*}, {*4 5 7 9*}, {*1 3 5 7 9*}, {*2 3 5 7 8*}].

For k-terminal node sets:
Similar selection process of node sets is applied in case of *k*-minimal sets formation. Let us take nodes # {2, 4, 5, 6} as *k*-nodes. Discard those node sets in which any element of the *k*-nodes does not appear. then the 13 node sets are: [{2}, {4}, {5}, {1, 4}, {1, 5}, {2, 4}, {3, 5},{1, 2, 4}, {1, 3, 5}, {1, 4, 5}, {1, 2, 4, 5}, {1, 3, 4, 5}, {1, 2, 3, 4, 5}]. Note that node #**6** will appear implicitly in selecting a *k*-node set, i.e., the node sets will be same even we take nodes {2, 4, 5} as *k*-nodes. Following step 8 of the algorithm, the 13 *k*-terminal minimal cutsets are:

[[*1 2*}, {*1 3 4*}, {*2 3 4*}, {*4 5 6*}, {*6 7 8*}, {*6 7 9*}, {*1 3 5 6*}, {*4 5 7 8*}, {*4 5 7 9*}, {*1 3 5 7 8*}, {*1 3 5 7 9*}, {*2 3 5 7 8*}, {*2 3 5 7 9*}].

Appendix 4A.1: Node Fusion Technique and Generation of Node Set Combination

Node fusion technique	Generation of node set combination from its lower order node-sets
| ```
function true= isConnected(a)
true =0;tru1=1;
for i=1:size(a,1)
I=find(a(i,:)~=0);
if ~isempty(I)
a(i,I)=1;
a(I,i)=1;
end
end
while tru1
I=find(a(1,2:size(a,2))==1)+1;
if ~isempty(I)
for i=1:size(I,2)
a(1,:)=a(1,:)|a(I(i),:);
a(:,1)=a(:,1)|a(:,I(i));
end
a(I,:)=[];
a(:,I)=[];
if a==1
true=1;
return
end
else
return
end
end
``` | ```
function [SSN, SSN]=genSSN(prevSSN,maxNumNodes,nNode)
%prevSSN->previous order valid SSN
SSN = [];
nSSN =0;%Number of SSN
N2 = max(prevSSN,[],2);%or the last column of prevSSN.
N4 = max(maxNumNodes(prevSSN),[],2);
r=length(N2);% or [r,c]=size(prevSSN);
for i = 1:r
if N2(i)~=nNode %Then form SSN
if N4(i)>N2(i)
addNodes = (N2(i)+1):N4(i);
for j = 1:length(addNodes)
tmp = [prevSSN(i,:) addNodes(j)];
SSN = [SSN;tmp];
nSSN = nSSN+1;
end
end
end
end
return
``` |

Appendix 4A.2: Code for Checking Validity of a Node Set and Converting Node-Sets into Link Cutsets

Checking validity of a node set	Converting node-sets into link cutsets
| ```
function yes = validateSSN(ssn)
global adjMat snkNode
%Checks two Conditions for a valid SSN
[r,c] = size(ssn);
%Condition A (True for all degree-1 SSN so condition is checked only
for
%SSN of degree>1
if c>1
adjTmp = adjMat(ssn,ssn);
yesA2=0;
yesA1 = isConnected(adjTmp);%Is the nodes in SSN themselves
connected?
if yesA1 %check that each node in ssn is connected to at least one
other node.
[x,y] = find(adjMat(ssn,:)==1);%x contains the index of node in
ssn, y contains the node(s) connected with ssn(x(i))
for i = 1:length(ssn)
xi = find(x(i)==x);
nc = y(xi);%Nodes connected to xi th node in ssn
otherNode = setdiff(nc,ssn);
if ~isempty(otherNode)
yesA2 = 1;
break
end
``` | ```
function [validCut, nValidCuts]=branchCut(validSSN,branchToNode)
lenValidSSN = length(validSSN);
validCut = [];
nValidCuts=0;
if ~isempty(lenValidSSN)
for i = 1:lenValidSSN
[r,c] = size(validSSN{i});%r=Number of valid SSN of order 'c'
if c == 1 %Only single node SSN
for j = 1:r
valCut = branchToNode{validSSN{i}(j)};
lenCut = length(valCut);
lenValidCut = length(validCut);
if lenCut>lenValidCut
validCut{lenCut}=[];
end
validCut{lenCut} = [validCut{lenCut};valCut];
nValidCuts = nValidCuts+1;
end
else
%for more than two node SSN
for j = 1: r
valCut = branchToNode{validSSN{i}(j,1)};
for k = 2:c
valCut = setxor(valCut,branchToNode{validSSN{i}(j,k)});
``` |

```
      end
    end
    yesA = yesA1 & yesA2;
  else
    yesA = 1;
  end
  %Condition B
  if length(ssn)~=snkNode
    adjTmp = adjMat;
    adjTmp(ssn,:)=[];
    adjTmp(:,ssn)=[];
    yesB=isConnected(adjTmp);%Connected with Source?
  else
    yesB = 1;
  end
  yes = yesA & yesB;
return

      end
      lenCut = length(valCut);
      lenValidCut = length(validCut);
      if lenCut>lenValidCut
        validCut{lenCut}=[];
      end
      validCut{lenCut} = [validCut{lenCut};valCut];
      nValidCuts = nValidCuts+1;
    end
    end
  end
end
lenValidCut = length(validCut);
for i = 1:lenValidCut
  if ~isempty(validCut{i})
    validCut{i} = sort(validCut{i},2);
    validCut{i} = sortrows(validCut{i});
  end
end
```

Appendix 4A.3: Sample Program I/O for Network Graph of Figure 4.3

Each row corresponds to the number assigned to the nodes of the network. *Format:* Node Connected To Nodes Connecting Link Number Assigned In the Network i.e., first line below signifies that the source node (highest node number 5) is connected with nodes number 2, 3 and 4 with the connecting links are 6, 7 and 8 respectively. Writing 'end' terminates the data in the data input file.

Input Data File:
2 3 4 6 7 8
1 3 5 6 3 1
1 2 4 5 7 3 5 2
1 3 5 8 5 4
end

Sample Run on Matlab Prompt

>> genCutset

adjMatdataFile(withpath)?:fig4.3Dat.m

SourceNode No.? (Assign Highest Number):5

TotalBranch :?:8

FOR OUTPUT

Please enter Output file with full path:fig4.3ResGTerminal.m

TerminalNode No. ?:1

Output Data file
1 2 4
6 7 8
1 2 5 8
1 3 7 8
2 3 4 6
4 5 6 7
1 3 4 5 7
2 3 5 6 8
end
Total number of cuts = 8

>> genCutset

adjMatdataFile(withpath)?:fig4.3Dat.m

SourceNode No.? (Assign Highest Number):5

TotalBranch :?:8

FOR OUTPUT

Please enter Output file with full path:fig4.3ResGTerminal.m

Evaluating Cuts for g-Terminal Reliability

Output Data file
1 2 4
1 3 6
4 5 8
6 7 8
1 2 5 8
1 3 7 8
2 3 4 6
2 3 5 7
4 5 6 7
1 2 5 6 7
1 3 4 5 7
2 3 4 7 8
2 3 5 6 8
end
Total number of cuts = 13

Appendix 4A.4: g-Terminal Reliability Evaluation Program Sample I/O for Example of Figure 4.3

Input Data File: fig4.3ResGTerminal.m
1 2 4
1 3 6
4 5 8
6 7 8
1 2 5 8
1 3 7 8
2 3 4 6
2 3 5 7
4 5 6 7
1 2 5 6 7
1 3 4 5 7
2 3 4 7 8
2 3 5 6 8
end

Sample Matlab Prompt
>>carelKdhTst3
PleaseenterpathSet(BranchWise)filewithfulldirpath:fig4.3ResGTerminal.m
Branches in the Net:?8
Nodes in the Net:?5
Reliability of single branch:?0.9

Results Provided by the Program (Output of g-reliability Expression for the Figure 4.3 for Method HM-1 of (Chaturvedi & Misra, 2002).

```
***************DisjointSet**********SDPREL***********CUMSUMREL***
   0   0  -1   0  -1  -1  -1  -1    0.00100000000
For Cut No#= 2.
-----------------
   0   1   0   1  -1   0  -1  -1    0.00099000000     0.00199000000
For Path No#= 3.
-----------------
   1  -1  -1   0   0  -1  -1   0    0.00090000000     0.00289000000
   0   1   2   0   0   2  -1   0    0.00008910000     0.00297910000
For Cut No#= 4.
-----------------
   1  -1  -1   3   3   0   0   0    0.00089100000     0.00387010000
   0  -1   2   1  -1   0   0   0    0.00008100000     0.00395110000
   0   1   2   0   3   0   0   0    0.00000729000     0.00395839000
For Cut No#= 5.
-----------------
   0   0  -1   3   0   2  -1   0    0.00008100000     0.00403939000
   0   0   2   3   0   0   4   0    0.00000729000     0.00404668000
For Cut No#= 6.
-----------------
   0   5   0   1   5   4   0   0    0.00008019000     0.00412687000
   0   1   0   0   3   4   0   0    0.00000729000     0.00413416000
For Cut No#= 7.
-----------------
   2   0   0   0  -1   0  -1   3    0.00008100000     0.00421516000
   2   0   0   0   3   0   4   0    0.00000729000     0.00422245000
For Cut No#= 8.
-----------------
   1   0   0   7   0   7   0   3    0.00008019000     0.00430264000
   1   0   0   3   0   4   0   0    0.00000729000     0.00430993000
   0   0   0   1   0   2   0   6    0.00000729000     0.00431722000
For Cut No#= 9.
-----------------
   1   8   8   0   0   0   0   4    0.00008019000     0.00439741000
   0   1   2   0   0   0   0   4    0.00000729000     0.00440470000
For Cut No#= 10.
-----------------
   0   0   8   9   0   0   0   5    0.00000729000     0.00441199000
For Cut No#= 11.
-----------------
   0   8   0   0   0   9   0   6    0.00000729000     0.00441928000
```

For Cut No#= 12.
----
  6   0   0   0   8   7   0   0   0.00000729000   0.00442657000

For Cut No#= 13.
----
  5   0   0   7   0   0   8   0   0.00000729000   0.00443386000

Output Data file
SystemUnrel = 0.00443386000
SystemReliability = 0.99556614000

total disjoint cuts= 22

Exercises

4.1   Enumerate by visual inspection, the minimal cuts for the networks shown in Figure Ex. 4.1. Verify them by using Method 1.

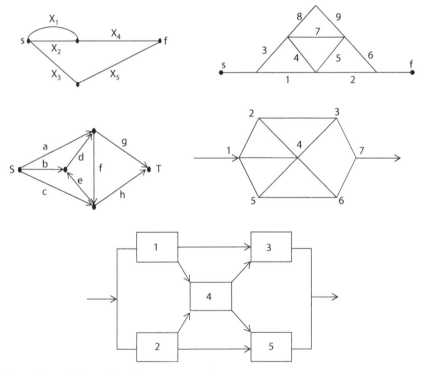

Figure Ex. 4.1 Network graphs.

4.2   Apply the approaches described in Method 2 to obtain minimal cut sets of above network graphs.

4.3   Apply the global cut sets enumeration procedure to obtain the global cut sets of the above network graphs.

References

Aggarwal, K. K., Chopra, Y. C., & Wajwa, J. S. (1982). Modification of Cut sets for Reliability Evaluation of Communication Systems. *Microelectronics and Reliability, Vol. 22*(3), 337–340.

Ahmad, S. H. (1988). Simple Enumeration of Minimal Cutsets of Acyclic Directed Graph. *IEEE Transaction on Reliability, ,R-37*, 484–487.

Ahmad, S. H. (1990). Enumeration of Minimal Cutsets of an Undirected Graph. *Microelectronics Reliability, Vol.30*(1), 23–26.

Chaturvedi, S. K., & Misra, K. B. (2002). A Hybrid Method to Evaluate Reliability of Complex Networks. *International Journal of Quality and Reliability Management, Vol. 19*(8/9), 1098–1112.

Deo, N. (1979). *Graph Theory with Applications to Engineering and Computer Science* (New edition ed.). PHI.

Elias, S. S., Mokhles, N., & Ibrahim, S. A. (1993). A New Technique in Cutset Evaluation. *Microelectronics and Reliability, Vol. 33*, 1351–1355.

Locks, M. O. (1978). Inverting and Minimalizing Path Sets and Cut Sets. *IEEE Transaction on Reliability, Vol. R-27*(2), 107–109.

Mishra, R. (2009). *Minimal Cutset based Evaluation of Reliability Measures*. Ph.D. Thesis, IIT Kharagpur (WB), India.

Mishra, R., & Chaturvedi, S. K. (2009). A Cutsets based Unified Framework to Evaluate Network Reliability Measures. *IEEE Transaction on Reliability, Vol. 56*(4), 658–666.

Mishra, R., & Chaturvedi, S. K. (2009, April). Global Reliability Evaluation using g-Minimal Cutsets. *International Journal of Performability Engineering, Vol. 5*(3), 251–258.

Samad, M. A. (1987). An Efficient Algorithm for Simultaneously Deducing Minimal Paths as well as Cuts of a Communication Network. *Microelectronics Reliability, Vol. 27*(3), 437–441.

Schabe, H. (1995). An Improved Algorithm for Cutset Evaluation from paths. *Microelectronics Reliability, Vol. 35*(5), 783–787.

Shen, Y. (1995). A New Simple Algorithm for Enumerating all mimimal Paths and Cuts of a Graph. *Microelectronics Reliability, Vol. 35*(6), 973–976.

5

Reliability Evaluation using MVI Techniques

Generally, for large and complex systems, reliability evaluation is quite a cumbersome and time-consuming process due to the large number of terms in the resulting reliability expression. Thereafter, the process of assessing numerical value from the obtained expression makes evaluation of accurate value of system reliability a difficult task due to the build-up of round-off error. However, the methods based on *sum of disjoint product* (SDP) technique have been used to tackle reliability evaluation problems more efficiently and effectively to produce a compact reliability expression. It should further be noted that this disjoint form of expression has a one-to-one mapping with the probability (reliability) expression as well (Aggarwal et al., 1975a), (Aggarwal et al., 1975b). In fact, with the advent of multiple inversions techniques, a new impetus has been given to the techniques of network reliability evaluation using path/cut sets of the network to produce a minimized form of expression. More compact the reliability expression is, more it would help tackle larger and larger system by reducing computational burden, storage requirement and the round off errors.

In this chapter, MVI based approaches KDH88 (Heidtmann, 1989) and CAREL (Soh & Rai, 1991) are presented. Other two approaches (HM–1 and HM–2) (Chaturvedi & MIsra, 2002) to evaluate reliability of large and complex systems by integrating the best features of several efficient techniques are also described. These approaches have resulted in an extensive reduction in the number of mutually disjoint terms and thus have provided a minimized and compact network reliability expression. Besides, they have not only saved CPU time appreciably but have also shown their viability to run a large problem even on a low-end PC. To demonstrate the advantage of handling such large and complex networks on relatively small computers, one can refer a comparison of approaches with earlier techniques by solving several problems of varied complexities on a low-end PC (Chaturvedi & MIsra, 2002).

5.1   Notation and Assumptions

The following notations are used in this chapter:

i	index variable; i =1, 2, 3, 4,…
E_i	Success event of ith element.
T_i	success of ith path set
m	Total number of path sets
U, V, W	A set of Boolean variables, e.g., $U = \{u_1, u_2, u_3...\}$
$R(G)$	System Reliability
$Q(G)$	System Unreliability

Besides the usual notation, the following acronyms have been used in this chapter:

$CAREL$	MVI algorithm by (Soh & Rai, 1991)
DG	Dependent Group
IG	Independent Group
$KDH88$	MVI algorithm by (Heidtmann, 1989)
$GKG–VT$	MVI algorithm by (Veeraraghavan & Trivedi, Aug 1991)
MVI	Multiple Variable Inversion
$PROB$	MVI algorithm by (Grnarov et al., 1979).
SVI	Single Variable Inversion
MCC	Minimal Conditional Cube
emd	Exclusive and Mutually Disjoint Terms

The following assumptions are implicit in this chapter:

1. Each element or a branch is in either of the two states, i.e., good or failed with known probability.
2. Nodes are perfectly reliable.
3. The path/cut sets (minimal path, spanning trees, k-trees, minimal cut sets, global cut sets, k-minimal cut sets) are known a priori.

5.2   Preliminaries

Consider a graph G (n, l) representing a network. The model is free from self-loops and directed cycles. The system can be represented by a probabilistic graph. The model may have several simple path sets between specified sets of nodes of interest. An edge or link is said to be operational or available if communication is possible via this link. If the two nodes joined by a link are unable to communicate through the link, it is said to be in a failed state. The probability that edge i is operational is denoted p_i. The probability that edge i is failed is $q_i = 1 - p_i$.

An operational sub graph is a sub graph in which sufficient edges are operational that permits the sites in question to communicate. In the two-terminal case a minimal operational sub graph is an operational (s, f)-path. A path is operational if all edges along the path are operational. Therefore, a path is in a failed state if any of the edges along it have failed. If the nodes s and f are disconnected, the graph or network is in a failed state.

5.2.1   Definitions

Some important definitions pertinent to this chapter are as follows:

Variable: A variable that can assume a Boolean value either 0 or 1, e.g., the links of networks.

Cube: It is the manner by which Boolean product of variables in a system are being represented.

Uniproduct/Minproduct: It is the product of complemented or un-complemented variables.

Subproduct/Minterm: It is the product of all variables, complemented or un-complemented form that appears exactly once.

Mixproduct: It is the product of all variables with at least one complemented (un-complemented) variable.

Dependent Group: It is a set of terms consisting of variables in which at least one variable would be contained in more one term.

Independent Group: It is a set of variables, which would have no variable common among them.

Disjoint Terms: A set of the variable(s) that appears complemented in one term and un-complemented in other term.

Both the SVI and MVI techniques accept a Boolean function of network variables (nodes and/or links) representing minimal path sets or cut sets to compute reliability measures. However, in contrast to SVI approach wherein variables are inverted sequentially one at a time, in MVI approach a group of the variables are inverted at once. In SVI, the minimization of the expression has been achieved through the ordering of path or cut sets so far. In MVI, not only the ordering of path or cut sets but the simultaneous inversions of a group of variables result into a more compact expression as compared to the expression that would be rendered by a SVI technique. In other words, the MVI techniques have a built-in feature of rendering a minimized reliability expression.

In Table 5.1, we provide some useful and pertinent Boolean lemmas, which are intrinsically used by all the MVI techniques to obtain a compact and disjoint form of Boolean/reliability expression. Let U, V, and W be three events belonging to some arbitrary event space S. Also *a* bar over an event signifies its complement of that event.

Example 5.1: Consider a MVI term $\overline{u_1 u_2 u_3 u_4}$, following the rules provided in Table 5.1, expand it to get its SVI expression.

Table 5.1 Boolean Lemmas.

S. No	Lemma	Explanation
1.	$\overline{U}V.U \equiv \varphi$	
2.	$\overline{UV}$	$\overline{UV} = \overline{U} + U.\overline{V}$
3.	$\overline{UV}.\overline{U} \equiv \overline{U}$	$(\overline{U} + U\overline{V})\,\overline{U} = \overline{U}$
4.	$\overline{UV}.U \equiv U\overline{V}$	$(\overline{U} + U.\overline{V})\,U = U.\overline{V}$
5.	$\overline{UV}.\overline{UW} = \overline{U} + U.\overline{V}.\overline{W}$	$(\overline{U} + U.\overline{V})(\overline{U} + U.\overline{W}) = \overline{U} + \overline{U}.U.\overline{W} + U.\overline{V}.\overline{U}.$ $+ U.\overline{V}.\overline{W}$
6.	$UV + UW =$ $U.(\overline{U} + (V + W))$	$U.\overline{U} + U.(V + W) = U.(\overline{U} + (V + W))$

Solution:

$$\overline{u_1 u_2 u_3 u_4} = \overline{u_1} + u_1 \overline{u_2 u_3 u_4}$$

$$= \overline{u_1} + u_1.\overline{(u_2 + u_2 u_3 u_4}$$

$$= \overline{u_1} + u_1.\overline{u_2} + \overline{u_1 u_2 u_3 u_4})$$

$$= \overline{u_1} + u_1.\overline{u_2} + u_1 u_2 \overline{(u_3 + u_3 \cdot \overline{u_4})}$$

$$= \overline{u_1} + u_1.\overline{u_2} + u_1 u_2 \overline{u_3} + u_1 u_2 u_3 \cdot \overline{u_4})$$

5.3   MVI Methods

This section presents some methods in obtaining the reliability expression for a specified reliability measure of a given network graph.

5.3.1   Method 1: KDH88

KDH88 (Heidtmann, 1989) is an MVI extension of SVI algorithm proposed by (Abraham, 1979). Using the minimal path sets, it recursively generates the disjoint terms for each path set. The recursive build-up of the terms is achieved with an inner loop within the outer loop. In the inner loop, part of the products are inverted at once instead of sequential inversion of single variable (SVI approach), thus covering a greater domain of the Boolean structure function to generate fewer terms. Each outer recursion is followed by a sequence of inner loop for each min path sets resulting in a modification of or no modification of one or more terms. Recursion of outer loop provides a portion of reliability expression contributed by a single min path sets at that instant of outer recursion. The pseudo code of the above approach would appear as:

1. *For* all Ti, i = 2, 3… m
    For all Tj, j = 1, 2… (i-1)
        If disjoint
            Continue;
        Else
            Obtain the disjoint terms and apply the disjoint process recursively for next j with each term produced in this step.
        End
        End
    End

2.   Compute reliability

Let us illustrate the above procedure by taking the sample network graphs shown in Figure 5.1 (a) (5 nodes, 8 links) and (b) (6 nodes, 9links), respectively to determine the expression for 2- terminal reliability.

Example 5.2: The enumeration methods described in Chapter 3 and Chapter 4 enumerate 9 path sets and 8 cut sets for the network of Figure 5.1(a) as follows:

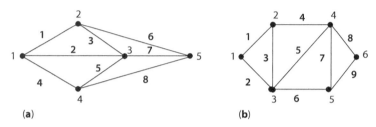

(a)   (b)

Figure 5.1 Example networks for reliability evaluation.

Path sets: {(**1**,**6**), (**2**, **7**), (**4**, **8**), (**1**, **3**, **7**), (**2**, **3**, **6**), (**2**, **5**, **8**), (**4**, **5**, **7**), (**1**, **3**, **5**, **8**), (**4**, **5**, **3**, **6**)}.

Cut sets: {(**1**, **2**, **4**), (**6**, **7**, **8**), (**1**, **2**, **5**, **8**), (**1**, **3**, **7**, **8**), (**2**, **3**, **4**, **6**), (**4**, **5**, **6**, **7**), (**1**, **3**, **4**, **5**, **7**), (**2**, **3**, **5**, **6**, **8**)}. Apply the KDH88 disjointing procedure on 7th minimal path.

Solution: Path set number seven i.e., {**4**, **5**, **7**} is to be made disjoint with all its predecessors. KDH88 would abide by the following steps by checking and making the resulting terms disjoint with previous path sets successively:

(Dropping the (,) *coma* to separate variables (here link numbers) for convenience) and utilizing the Boolean lemmas provided in Table 5.1,

i. $\overline{16} \times 457,$
(No variables are common between them).

ii. $\overline{16} \times \overline{27} \times 457 = \overline{16} \times \overline{2} \times 4\underline{57}$
(By using Boolean identity $xy.\overline{yz} = \overline{xyz}$).

iii. $\overline{16} \times \overline{2} \times \overline{48} \times 457 = \overline{16} \times \overline{2} \times \overline{8} \times 457$

iv. $\overline{16} \times \overline{2} \times \overline{48} \times \overline{137} \times 457 = \overline{1} \times \overline{2} \times \overline{8} \times 457 + \overline{1} \times \overline{2} \times \overline{8} \times \overline{3} \times \overline{6} \times 457$
(By using Boolean identities, $xy.\overline{xzw} = xy.\overline{yz}$ and $\overline{xy.yz} = \overline{xyz}$ respectively.)

v. $\overline{1} \times \overline{2} \times \overline{8} \times \overline{236} \times 457 + \overline{1} \times \overline{2} \times \overline{8} \times \overline{3} \times \overline{6} \times \overline{236} \times 457$

$= \overline{1} \times \overline{2} \times \overline{8} \times 457 + \overline{1} \times \overline{2} \times \overline{8} \times \overline{3} \times \overline{6} \times 457$
(By using Boolean $\overline{xy}.\overline{xz} = \overline{xy}$)

vi. $\overline{1}\times\overline{2}\times\overline{8}\times\overline{258}\times457+1\times\overline{2}\times8\times3\times6\times\overline{258}\times457$

$=\overline{1}\times\overline{2}\times\overline{8}\times457+1\times\overline{2}\times8\times3\times6\times457$

Hence, the reliability expression contributed by this path set to the overall 2TR expression would be:

$$\left(1-p_1\right)\left(1-p_2\right)\left(1-p_8\right)p_4p_5p_8+p_1(1-p_2)(1-p_8)(1-p_3)(1-p_6)p_4p_5p_7$$

We pursue similar steps for making a certain minimal cut set disjoint successively, if the cut sets were known a priori. For instance, if cut set number four i.e., {**1, 3, 7, 8**} is to be made disjoint then KDH88 would give rise to the following results:

$$\overline{2}\times\overline{6}\times1368+2\times\overline{5}\times\overline{6}\times\overline{4}\times1378,$$

The *unreliability* expression contribution turns out to be as:

$$p_2p_6q_1q_3q_7q_8+q_2p_5p_6p_4q_1q_3q_7q_8.$$

Example 5.3: Apply KDH88 on the network shown in Figure 5.1(b).

Solution: The 13 numbers of path sets and 9 numbers of cut sets of the system represented by this network graph are:

Path sets: {(**1, 4, 8**), (**2, 5, 8**), (**2, 6, 9**), (**1, 3, 5, 8**), (**1, 3, 6, 9**), (**1, 4, 7, 9**), (**2, 3, 4, 8**), (**2, 5, 7, 9**), (**2, 6, 7, 8**), (**1, 3, 5, 7, 9**), (**1, 3, 6, 7, 8**), (**1, 4, 5, 6, 9**), (**2, 3, 4, 7, 9**)}.
Cut sets: {(**1, 2**), (**8, 9**), (**2, 3, 4**), (**4, 5, 6**), (**6, 7, 8**), (**1, 3, 5, 6**), (**4, 5, 7, 9**), (**1, 3, 5, 7, 9**), (**2, 3, 5, 7, 8**)}.

By making path set number eight i.e., {**2, 5, 7, 9**} disjoint with path sets number 1, 2…7, we get:

$$\overline{14}\times\overline{6}\times\overline{8}\times2579=(1-p_1p_4)(1-p_6)(1-p_8)p_2p_5p_7p_9$$

It would be worth to note that how the terms *under bar* are interpreted once they emerge into multiples.

Similarly, by making cut sets number three i.e., {**2, 3, 4**}, for instance, would result into following form:

$$\overline{1}\times\overline{89}\times234=p_1(1-q_8q_9)q_2q_3q_4$$

$$=p_1(p_8+p_9-p_8p_9)q_2q_3q_4$$

5.3.2   Method 2: CAREL

The algorithm CAREL (Soh & Rai, 1991) uses the Boolean algebraic manipulation and advantages of (Rai & Aggarwal, 1978), PROB by (Grnarov et al., 1979) and SYSREL by (Hariri & Raghvendara, 1987) by proposing four operators viz. *COM*pare, *RED*uce, *CoMB*ine and *GEN*erate. The *COM* operator generates a set of conditional cubes, E_j, j = 1,2… (i-1) for a path identifier T_i and describes an event that T_i is operational while P_j for all j = 1,2… (i-1) fail. The *RED* operator removes the redundant conditional cubes i.e., cubes, which are superset of some cube(s), from the generated set E_j's to form non-redundant cubes called as minimal conditional cubes (MCC). These MCC are, in generals, not disjoint among themselves and are partitioned into two groups, viz., independent (IG) and dependent (DG). The independent group would have disjoint terms whereas dependent groups comprise of terms, which are made to be disjoint. If all MCC fall in IG category, then *CMB* generates a single term in a straightforward manner. However, for DG, the CMB operator is quite involved and differentiates CAREL from rest of the earlier methods. Finally, the *GEN* operator generates the exclusive and mutually disjoints (emd) events by combining each mutually disjoint term of DG with single term obtained from IG and path identifier T_i. The steps of the algorithm may be summarized as:

1. For all path sets T_i, i = 2, 3… m
   a. Obtain conditional cube (CC) sets by eliminating the common element(s) present in T_j, for all j = 1, 2… (i-1).
   b. Obtain minimal conditional cube sets (MCC) i.e., if a conditional cube set, say CC_k, is a sub set of another CC_l, then drop CC_l. Divide these MCC into two groups, viz. IG and DG.
   c. i. Combine IG to produce a single disjoint term, i.e., IG_n.
      ii. Combine DG to form sets of disjoint terms.
   d. Generate the emd by combing T_i and IG_n with each of the disjoint terms obtained in step c. (ii) of DG.
2. Compute R

To make the idea more clear about IG and DG, a brief explanation to segregate IG and DG along with the operations and results of CAREL four operators viz., *COM*, *RED*, *CMB*, and *GEN* is illustrated as example 5.4.

Example 5.4: Consider a network having following seven path sets:

(i) 2 6 9 or *bfi* (ii) 1 5 9 or *aei* (iii) 1 4 8 or *adh* (iv)2 3 8 or *bch* (v) 2 6 7 8 or *bfgh* (vi) 2 3 5 9 or *bcei* and (vii) 1 3 7 9 or *acgi*

Here, we represent a branch of the network graph either via an integer or an English alphabet, with a = 1 to i = 9. Explain the various possible scenarios in CAREL.

Solution: The following possible scenarios generally occur while applying the CAREL in disjointing process:

Case a: *dependent group*
Let path set, adh (number # 3) to be made disjoint with all earlier path sets.

S.No	Operator	Result	Comment
(i)	COM	$\overline{bfi}$ and $\overline{aei}$.	There is no link common with path set, adh.
(ii)	RED	$\overline{bfi}$ and $\overline{aei}$.	No set absorption. Also element i is common, DG is formed with these terms.
(iii)	CMB	$\overline{i}$ and $i\overline{bf}\ \overline{ae}$.	As $\overline{bfi}\ \overline{aei} \to \overline{i} + i\overline{bf}\ \overline{ae}$.
(iv)	GEN	$ad\overline{hi}$ and $adhi\overline{bf}\ \overline{ae}$.	Equivalent to reliability expression: $P_1 P_4 P_8 \{(1\text{-}p_9) + p_9 (1\text{-} P_2 P_6)(1\text{-}p_1 p_5)\}$.

Case b: *independent group*
Let path set, bcei (number # 6) to be made disjoint with all earlier path sets.

S.no	Operator	Result	Comment
(i)	COM	$\overline{f}, \overline{a}, \overline{adh}, \overline{h}$ and $\overline{fgh}$	Common elements (*bi*, *ei*, NIL, *bc*, *b*) have been removed from all previous path sets.
(ii)	RED	$\overline{f}, \overline{a}$ and $\overline{h}$.	$\overline{fgh}$ and $\overline{adh}$ have been absorbed by $\overline{h}$ being the supersets of $\overline{f}$ and/or $\overline{h}$. No further common element, so operator places them into IG.
(iii)	CMB	$\overline{a}\ \overline{f}\ \overline{h}$.	Single term of IG.
(iv)	GEN	$bcei\ \overline{a}\ \overline{f}\ \overline{h}$	Equivalent to reliability expression $P_2 P_3 P_5 P_9 (1\text{-}p_1)(1\text{-}p_6)(1\text{-}p_8)$.

Case c: *both independent and dependent group*

Let path set acgi (number #7) to be made disjoint with all prior path sets.

S.no	Operator	Result	Comment
(i)	COM	$\overline{bf}$, e, $\overline{dh}$, $\overline{bh}$, $\overline{bfh}$, and $\overline{be}$.	Common elements (I, ai, a, c, g, and ci) have been removed.
(ii)	RED	$\overline{bf}$, e, $\overline{dh}$ and $\overline{bh}$.	$\overline{bfh}$ and $\overline{be}$ have been absorbed by $\overline{bf}$ and e respectively. e forms IG and rest fall in DG.
(iii)	CMB	$\overline{b}\,\overline{dh}$, and $\overline{bf}\,\overline{h}$.	As $\overline{bf}_*\overline{dh}_*\overline{bh} \to \overline{b}\,\overline{dh} + \overline{bf}\,\overline{h}$.
(iv)	GEN	$acgie\,(\overline{b}\,\overline{dh} + \overline{bf}\,\overline{h}\,)$	Equivalent to reliability expression $P_1 P_3 P_7 P_9 (1\text{-}p_5)\,[(1\text{-}p_2)\,(1\text{-}p_4 p_8) + p_2 (1\text{-}p_6)(1\text{-}p_8)]$.

Let us once again consider the network graph of example 5.2 to demonstrate CAREL.

Example 5.5: Apply the CAREL on example 5.2.

Solution: For the path set number#7 CAREL would follow the steps on applying its operators as under:

    i. Applying COM operator

S. no.	Previous path set	Path set # 7	Remark
1.	1 6	4 5 7	Common links of Path # 7 have been removed from all earlier path sets.
2.	2 7̶		
3.	4̶ 8		
4.	1 3 7̶		
5.	2 3 6		
6.	2 5 8		

Note that the binary representation of the above terms becomes the conditional cubes in CAREL terminology.

    ii. Applying RED operator

S. no.	Path sets a priori	Path set number seven	Remark
1.	1 6	4 5 7	Being a subset, term
2.	2		number two absorbs
3.	8		terms five and six.
4.	1 3		
5.	236		
6.	258		

The operator RED is also responsible for placing the terms in independent and dependent groups' category. Thus, it places the second and third terms in IG, while the first and fourth terms belong to DG. The binary form of which are known as minimal conditional cubes (MCC).

iii. By applying CMB operator
On combining the IG terms would give a single term as:

$$\bar{2} \times \bar{8} \times 457$$

On combining DG terms,

$$\overline{16} \times \overline{13} \times 457 = \bar{1} \times 457 + \bar{1} \times \bar{3} \times \bar{6} \times 457$$

iv. By applying GEN operator
IG's single term is combined with each of the terms of DG to generate disjoint form for path set number seven as:

$$\bar{1} \times \bar{2} \times \bar{8} \times 457 + \bar{1} \times \bar{3} \times \bar{6} \times \bar{2} \times \bar{8} \times 457$$

Hence, the reliability expression contributed by this path set would be:

$$(1 - p_1)(1 - p_2)(1 - p_8)p_4 p_5 p_8 + p_1 (1 - p_2)(1 - p_8)(1 - p_3)(1-p_6)p_4 p_5 p_7$$

It is the same expression that we have obtained by applying KDH88 earlier.

Example 5.6: We apply the above process on the network graph of Figure 5.1(a) on knowing the minimal cut sets. Let it be the minimal cut set number four again.

The sequence of steps would be:

i. Operator COM

S. no	Earlier cut sets	Cut set number four	Remark
1	~~1~~ 2 4		Common links of
2	6 ~~7 8~~	1 3 7 8	cut set# 4 are removed from all
3	~~1~~ 2 ~~5 8~~		earlier cut sets.

ii. Operator RED

S. no	Cut sets a priori	Cut set number four	Remark
1	2 4	1 3 7 8	No absorption, but
2	6		Terms 1 and 3
3	2 5		are dependent.

iii. Operator CMB
The DG would give the following terms:

$$\bar{2}\times 1378 + 2\times\bar{4}\times\bar{5}\times 1378,$$

iv. Operator GEN
Combining with the IG would give the following expression contributed to TR:

$$\bar{2}\times\bar{6}\times 1378 + 2\times\bar{4}\times\bar{5}\times\bar{6}\times 1378 = p_2 p_6 q_1 q_3 q_7 q_8$$
$$+ q_2 p_4 p_5 p_6 q_1 q_3 q_7 q_8.$$

5.3.3   Comparison between KDH88 and CAREL

From the description of methodologies outlined in KDH88 and CAREL in the above examples/illustrations, we may make the following observations:

i. In KDH88, in order to obtain disjoint terms for a given path set or cut set, the process of comparison, checking and generation have to be carried out on all previous path sets with the path set under consideration. Consequently, it would require a large chunk of computer memory as the network complexity and size increase. However, it uses the simple notation of representing the disjoint terms, where an integer value in a term signifies the path index that has modified and generated the disjoint term. To get the reliability expression, equal integer values in a term are grouped together.

For instance, a final and arbitrary sequence code such as *011100220* represents that the branches **1, 5, 6** and **9** constitute a path set (corresponding to *0* entries in the sequence). In order to make it disjoint with all prior path sets, the positions 2, 3, 4 and 7, 8 in the sequence have been modified by the path set number#1 and #2, respectively. The reliability expression contributed by this path set would be: $p_1 p_5 p_6 p_9$ $(1\text{-}p_2 p_3 p_4) (1\text{-}p_7 p_8)$

ii. The CMB operator is the most time consuming and burdened operator among the four operators in CAREL. Additionally, CAREL uses a superscripted notation where variables indices are also to be tracked while formulating the disjoint terms in the final expression for a given path set. The notational complexity, its understanding and translating it into a computer program could be problematic.

For instance, the CAREL would characterize the same sequence exemplified in KDH88 as: $0 -3^4 -3^4 -3^4 \text{-}0\text{-}0 -2^5 -2^5$ *0;* the superscripted index *4* on inverted variables shows its belongingness to DG or IG number *four* with three terms in a cluster and superscripted index *5* to either DG or IG number *5* with two terms together, respectively. It is worth mentioning here that while doing such operations of combinations, not only the superscript but also the number over which they reside has to be tracked to interpret the final and resulting term accurately.

Consequently, the first two operators in CAREL could be implemented in bit form whereas for the other two, one has to resort some other means of coding it into a computer program.

The aforementioned points might be the reasons for exorbitant program execution time; memory requirements and even for system getting hung up. The type of warning message, which appeared after the *four hours* of patient waiting since the launch of the program, is shown in Figure 5.2 for the Figure 5.3 (16-Nodes, 30 links network graph, path sets = 499 and cut sets = 644) of the sample networks whose unreliability was tried to be evaluated using KDH88 in the year 2001 on a 200 MHz, 32 MB RAM, and 4.3 GB HDD personal computer running under win98 environment.

```
>>kdhRelTst3
Please enter pathSet(BranchWise)file with full dir path:fig9SrtRes.m
Branches in the Net:?30
unreliability of single branch:?0.1
FOR OUTPUT
Please enter Output file with full path:C:\Documents and
Settings\skc\Desktop\skc\ResDataHM1&2and KDH\kdh88Cuts\fig9Q1Res.m

??? Maximum recursion limit of 500 reached. Use set(0,'RecursionLimit',N)
to change the limit.  Be aware that exceeding your available stack space can
crash MATLAB and/or your computer.

Error in ==> C:\Documents and Settings\skc\Desktop\skc\KDH88\nextStepKdh3.m
On line 6  ==>   [disjoint,mask]=Mask(j,pro,minT);

Error in ==> C:\Documents and Settings\skc\Desktop\skc\KDH88\kdhRelTst3.m
On line 99  ==>   nextStepKdh3(n,1,k,pro,minT)

>>
```

Figure 5.2 The warning message for a large network on applying KDH88.

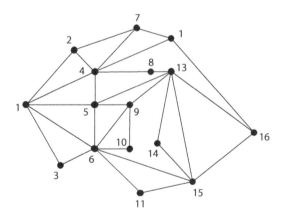

Figure 5.3 16-Node, 30 links network graph,

It may necessitate to code path or cut sets in some alternative way rather than in a string of 0/1/-1 but also some improvement in these existing methods to achieve the desired goal of obtaining reliability/unreliability expression and evaluation of complex systems (Chaturvedi, 2002).

5.4   Method 3: Hybrid Methods-HM

5.4.1   An Alternative Representation of Path or Cut Sets

Instead of representing path or cut sets in binary string as in CAREL, one can represent path or cut sets with their equivalent integer values to segregate the irredundant independent and dependent groups. This is achieved by the use of bit-wise OR/AND /XOR functions available in most of the computer language based application packages that operate on the integer representation. These integer values, as and when desired, can be expanded (compressed) using decimal to binary (binary to decimal) conversion, routine to the length of number of branches present in the network under consideration for their interpretation.

The path sets representation of network of 6-nodes,13 branches shown Figure 5.4, and operation responsible for generating and identifying independent and dependent groups on first two path sets are shown in Table 5.2

The combined operation, viz., $E_j = bitxor\ (bitor\ (P_i, P_j), P_j)$, for all i = 1, 2, …(j-1), describes an event that the path set P_j is operational while all path sets prior to P_j have failed. In other words, it generates a conditional integer set. The binary form of this integer sets generates conditional cubes (CC) of CAREL.

The *bitwise AND* operation among the integers in the reduced or minimal integer set forms two subsets viz., IG and DG. A zero result in the *AND* operation places that integer into independent integer group. One can easily substantiate it by expanding the integer values of IG or DG in binary form to see that in all binary vectors, none has a '1' at a common position while the DG would have such vector(s).

It is to be noted that all the operations described above are performed on integer representations. Once the irredundant groups (IG/DG) are

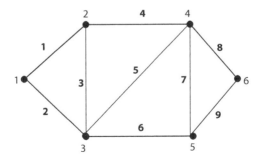

Figure 5.4 A 6 nodes, 9 links network.

Table 5.2 Path Sets Representation and Bit-Wise Operations

Path set no.	Path sets	Binary representation up to the length of network branches i.e. , of Figure 5.4: (6n9l)	Equivalent integer representation	Operation on e.g. for first two path sets and expanded result in binary form.
1.	1 4 8	100100010	290	*bitxor* (290,146) = 432
2.	2 5 8	010010010	146	*dec2bin* (432) =
3.	2 6 9	010001001	137	110110000
4.	1 3 5 8	101010010	338	
5.	1 3 6 9	101001001	329	*bitor* (290,146) = 434
6.	1 4 7 9	100100101	293	*dec2bin* (434) =
7.	2 3 4 8	011100010	226	110110010
8.	2 5 7 9	010010101	149	
9.	2 6 7 8	010001110	142	*bitand*(290,146) = 2
10.	1 3 5 7 9	101010101	341	*dec2bin* (2) =
11.	1 3 6 7 8	101001110	334	000000010
12.	1 4 5 6 9	100111001	313	
13.	2 3 4 7 9	011100101	229	

identified, we convert integer values to their equivalent binary representation by maintaining the length of each binary vector equal to the number of branches in the network. Subsequently, in the independent group, we replace each 0 entry by −1 and each nonzero entry by the path sets number to which they come from. This representation consequently would coincide with the representation used in KDH88.

For the dependent group, the index of the each path set is identified so that appropriate changes in the KDH88 generated disjoint terms can be made later, to identify that which path set has created the alteration, when the path sets in this group are made disjoint with respect to the path set under consideration.

On dependent group, we apply KDH88 recursively to generate mutually exclusive terms. Finally, each of these terms, generated by following KDH88, is combined with the single term obtained by combining the independent group elements to generate disjoint terms of path set P_i. In other words, we could conclude that KDH88 completely replaces CAREL CMB and GEN operator.

5.4.2   Hybrid Methods (HM)

The following two modifications in KDH88 or CAREL schemes can be done to speed up the process of obtaining disjoint terms (Chaturvedi & Misra, 2002)

5.4.2.1   HM-1

We can make the following improvements in the steps outlined in CAREL:

(c). ii   Identify the indexes of path sets in T_j, j= 1,2,..., (i-1), which forms the DG sets.

    iii   IApply KDH88 on these path sets, identified in the step above, to generate disjoint terms with respect to path set T_i.

(d).   Combine IG_n with each disjoint term obtained above.

  2. Compute TR.

5.4.2.2   HM-2

Alternatively, we can make the following improvements in KDH88:

1. Segregate path sets into two groups:
   i. Group-I shall have path sets T_k, $\forall$ k= 1, 2, 3... m_1, i.e., path sets of cardinality (n-1) and,
   ii. Rest of the path sets, i.e., a total of (m-m_1+1) into Group-II' Complement the variables not present in T_k, $\forall$ k = 1, 2...m_1.
   iii.Compute TR_1 for path set number one and TR_k, $\forall$ k= 1, 2...m_1.
2. For all path sets of Group-II, T_i, i = 2, 3... (m- m_1+1)
   a. Identify and obtain the indexes of path sets corresponding to MCCs (please refer CAREL 1 (b).
   b. Apply KDH88 on these path sets to obtain disjoint terms for T_i.
3. Compute $TR = TR_1 + TR_{m_1} + \sum_{i=2}^{m-m_1+1} TR_i$

The above schemes are explained in the ensuing sections/subsections:

5.5   Applying HM-1 and HM-2

In order to explain the intricacies of the schemes introduced in this chapter, let us apply them to determine the irredundant group for a path set, say, 142 (listed at ninth row) of Table 5.2. The corresponding conditional cubes (CC) are given in Table 5.3.

Table 5.3 MCC and CC for Path Sets Prior to Ninth Path Set i.e., (142)

S. no	All prior path sets to the 9th path set	CCs	CCs binary equivalent	MCCs (S. no. of CC)	Remark
1.	290	288	100100000	288 (1)	CC number:
2.	146	16	000010000	16 (2)	6 is contained in 1.
3.	137	1	000000001	1 (3)	4,8 are contained in 2
4.	338	336	101010000	96 (7)	5 is contained in 3.
5.	329	321	101000001		
6.	293	289	100100001		
7.	226	96	001100000		
8.	149	17	000010001		

ANDing operation puts MCC 2 and 3 in independent group whereas MCC 1 and 7 are placed under dependent group category.

We replace zeros by –1 meaning that these links are absent, and the nonzero entries by the path set number. Now we can solve it by applying the schemes outlined earlier as HM-1 and HM-2.

5.5.1   Applying HM-1

As we have become aware of that CC number 2 and 3 fall under the independent group category while 1 and 7 fall under dependent group category. They together form minimal conditional cubes (MCC) and remaining CC have been dropped as they are contained in one of these path sets, i.e., in 1, 2, 3 or 7. Hence,
IG =

> -1 -1 -1 -1 **2** -1 -1 -1 -1 -> generated due to MCC or path set number **2**
>
> -1 -1 -1 -1 -1 -1 -1 -1 **3** -> generated due to MCC or path set number **3**

Now path sets number 1 and 7 are to be made disjoint with path set number 9. From the dependent group index 1 and 7, path sets 1, 7 and 9 are converted into KDH88 notational format i.e.,

Min Terms =

>   0 -1 -1 0 -1 -1 -1 0 -1   (100100010; path set 1)
> -1 0 0 0 -1 -1 -1 0 -1   (011100010; path set 7)
> -1 0 -1 -1 -1 0 0 0 -1   (010001110; path set 9)

Applying KDH88, we obtain two terms, viz.,

TG =

-1 0 -1 *1* -1 0 0 0 -1
1 0 *7* 0 -1 0 0 0 -1

Combining independent terms provides us
IG_n =

-1 -1 -1 -1 *2* -1 -1 -1 *3*

The process of combining IG_n with each terms of TG, generates the exclusive and mutually disjoint terms for path set number 9 as:

TG =

$$-1\ 0\ -1\ \mathbf{1}\ 2\ 0\ 0\ 0\ 3 = \overline{4}\times\overline{5}\times\overline{9}\times 2678$$

$$\mathbf{1}\ 0\ \mathbf{7}\ \mathbf{0}\ 2\ 0\ 0\ 0\ 3 = \overline{1}\times\overline{3}\times\overline{5}\times\overline{9}\times 24678$$

Therefore, the contribution of this path set to the network reliability expression would be:

$$\left[\left(1-p_4\right)\left(1-p_5\right)\left(1-p_9\right)+(1-p_1)(1-p_3)(1-p_5)(1-p_9)p_4\right]\times p_2 p_6 p_7 p_8$$

5.5.2   Applying HM-2

We have seen that the path set numbered 1, 2, 3 and 7 would only generate MCC while others have been absorbed and hence dropped from the process of making them disjoint. In other words, to get the disjoint terms for path number 9, we are only concerned with these four path sets, which mean a reduction of four path sets out of the eight path sets that should have been compared had we used the scheme of KDH88. Now on these path sets, viz.,1, 2, 3 and 7, we apply KDH88 to obtain disjoint terms correspond to path set numbered 9. This results into the following disjoint terms:

$$-1\ 0\ -1\ \mathbf{1}\ 2\ 0\ 0\ 0\ \mathbf{3} \rightarrow \overline{4}\times\overline{5}\times\overline{9}\times 2678 \rightarrow (1-p_4)(1-p_5)(1-p_9)$$
$$\times p_2 p_6 p_7 p_8$$

$$\mathbf{1}\ 0\ \mathbf{4}\ \mathbf{0}\ 2\ 0\ 0\ 0\ 3 \rightarrow \overline{1}\times\overline{3}\times\overline{5}\times\overline{9}\times 24678 \rightarrow (1-p_1)(1-p_3)$$
$$(1-p_5)(1-p_9)p_4 \times p_2 p_6 p_7 p_8$$

This is the same expression what we have got using HM-1 earlier.

5.5.3   Complete Solution to Example 5.2

Having provided the adequate insight into the methodologies, we are now in a position to provide the complete solution for the network shown in Figure 5.1 (a) and (b). Over and above, both the methods provide the same expression and the only difference lies in the speed with which they provide the solution.

For Figure 5.1 (a), following the procedure (HM-1 or HM-2), we obtain the following terms of the reliability expression:

Using Path Sets

i.   <u>For Path set # 1</u>

$$p_1 p_6$$

ii.   <u>For Path set # 2</u>

$$(1 - p_1 p_6) p_2 p_7$$

iii.   <u>For Path set # 3</u>

$$(1 - p_1 p_6)(1 - p_2 p_7) p_4 p_8$$

iv.   <u>For Path set # 4</u>

$$(1 - p_2)(1 - p_4 p_8)(1 - p_6) p_1 p_3 p_7$$

v.   <u>For Path set # 5</u>

$$(1 - p_1)(1 - p_4 p_8)(1 - p_7) p_2 p_3 p_6$$

vi.   <u>For Path set # 6</u>

$$(1 - p_4)(1 - p_6)(1 - p_7) p_2 p_5 p_8$$

$$(1 - p_1)(1 - p_3)(1 - p_6)(1 - p_7) p_1 p_3 p_6 p_7$$

vii.   <u>For Path set # 7</u>

$$(1 - p_1)(1 - p_2)(1 - p_8) p_4 p_5 p_7$$

$$(1 - p_2)(1 - p_3)(1 - p_6)(1 - p_8) p_1 p_4 p_5 p_7$$

viii.   For Path set # 8

$$(1-p_2)(1-p_4)(1-p_6)(1-p_7)p_1p_3p_5p_8$$

ix.   For Path set # 9

$$(1-p_1)(1-p_2)(1-p_7)(1-p_8)p_3p_4p_5p_6$$

With the assumption of equal links reliabilities, p, above expressions would reduce to:

$$R(G) = 3p^2 + 4p^3 - 9p^4 - 10p^5 + 27p^6 - 18p^7 + 4p^8;$$

for $p = 0.9$, the system reliability would be 0.99763164000.
Executing the HM-1 program (available at www.scrivenerpublishing.com) on *Matlab®* prompt, for Figure 5.1(a) renders the following:

> >> carelKdhTst3
> Please enter pathSet(BranchWise)file with full dir
>   path:fig5.1aResPth.m
> Branches in the Net:?8
> Nodes in the Net:?5
> Reliability of single branch:?0.9
> FOR OUTPUT
> Please enter Output file with full path:fig5.1aResPthHM1.m
> t = 0.044625087941659
> SystemRel =0.99763164000, Total FunCall= 14
> total disjoint paths= 11

For detailed output, open the *fig5.1aResPthHM1.m* file.

Using Cut Sets

i.   For Cut set # 1

$$q_1q_2q_4$$

ii.   For Cut set # 2

$$(1-q_1q_2q_4)q_6q_7q_8$$

iii. <u>For Cut set # 3</u>

$$(1-q_4)(1-q_6q_7)q_1q_2q_5q_8$$

iv. <u>For Cut set# 4</u>

$$(1-q_2)(1-q_6)q_1q_3q_7q_8$$

$$(1-q_4)(1-q_5)(1-q_6)q_1q_2q_3q_7q_8$$

v. <u>For Cut set # 5</u>

$$(1-q_1)(1-q_7q_8)q_2q_3q_4q_6$$

vi. <u>For Cut set # 6</u>

$$(1-q_2)(1-q_8)q_4q_5q_6q_7$$

$$(1-q_1)(1-q_3)(1-q_8)q_2q_4q_5q_6q_7$$

vii. <u>For Cut set # 7</u>

$$(1-q_2)(1-q_6)(1-q_8)q_1q_3q_4q_5q_7$$

viii. <u>For Cut set # 8</u>

$$(1-q_1)(1-q_4)(1-q_7)q_2q_3q_5q_6q_8$$

On the assumption of equal unreliability (q) of links, the network unreliability expression would be:

$$Q(G) = 2q^3 + 4q^4 - 2q^5 - 13q^6 + 14q^7 - 4q^8 ;$$

For $q = 0.1$, $TQ\,(G) = 0.00236836000000$
or using minimal cutsets and executing the program renders:

>> *carelKdhTst3*
Please enter pathSet(BranchWise)file with full dir
   path:fig5.1aCuts.m
Branches in the Net:?8
Nodes in the Net:?5
Reliability of single branch:?0.1
FOR OUTPUT
Please enter Output file with full path:fig5.1aResCutsHM1.m
t = 0.039368435172284
SystemRel =0.00236836000, Total FunCall= 13
total disjoint paths= 10

Note that the input to reliability of single branch in the above is 0.1, which is unreliability of the links.

For detailed output, open the *fig5.1aResPthHM1.m* file.

Similarly, for Figure 5.1 (b)

Using Path Sets

i.   For Path set # 1

$$p_1 p_4 p_8$$

ii.   For Path set # 2

$$(1 - p_1 p_4) p_2 p_5 p_8$$

iii.   For Path set # 3

$$(1 - p_8) p_2 p_6 p_9$$

$$(1 - p_1 p_4)(1 - p_5) p_2 p_6 p_8 p_9$$

iv.   For Path set # 4

$$(1 - p_2)(1 - p_4) p_1 p_3 p_5 p_8$$

v.   For Path set # 5

$$(1 - p_2)(1 - p_8) p_1 p_3 p_6 p_9$$

$$(1 - p_2)(1 - p_4)(1 - p_8) p_1 p_3 p_6 p_8 p_9$$

vi.   For Path set # 6

$$(1 - p_6)(1 - p_8) p_1 p_4 p_7 p_9$$

$$(1 - p_2)(1 - p_3)(1 - p_8) p_1 p_4 p_6 p_7 p_9$$

vii.   For Path set # 7

$$(1 - p_1)(1 - p_5)(1 - p_6 p_9) p_2 p_3 p_4 p_8$$

viii.   For Path set # 8

$$(1 - p_1 p_4)(1 - p_6)(1 - p_8) p_2 p_5 p_7 p_9$$

ix. <u>For Path set # 9</u>

$$(1-p_4)(1-p_5)(1-p_9)p_2p_6p_7p_8$$

$$(1-p_1)(1-p_3)(1-p_5)(1-p_9)p_2p_6p_7p_8$$

x. <u>For Path set # 10</u>

$$(1-p_2)(1-p_4)(1-p_6)(1-p_8)p_1p_3p_5p_7p_9$$

xi. <u>For Path set # 11</u>

$$(1-p_2)(1-p_4)(1-p_5)(1-p_9)p_1p_3p_6p_7p_8$$

xii. <u>For Path set # 12</u>

$$(1-p_2)(1-p_3)(1-p_7)(1-p_8)p_1p_4p_5p_6p_9$$

xiii. <u>For Path set # 13</u>

$$(1-p_1)(1-p_5)(1-p_6)(1-p_8)p_2p_3p_4p_7p_9$$

On the assumption of equal links reliabilities, p, the network reliability expression would become:

$$R(G) = 3p^3 + 6p^4 - 8p^5 - 21p^6 + 40p^7 - 24p^8 + 5p^9$$

For $p = 0.9$, the network reliability would be 0.97718440500.

Using Cut Sets

i. <u>For Cut set # 1</u>

$$q_1q_2$$

ii. <u>For Cut set # 2</u>

$$(1-q_1q_2)q_8q_9$$

iii. <u>For Cut set # 3</u>

$$(1-q_1)(1-q_8q_9)q_2q_3q_4$$

iv. <u>For Cut set # 4</u>

$$(1-q_2)(1-q_8q_9)q_4q_5q_6$$

$$(1-q_1)(1-q_3)(1-q_8q_9)q_2q_4q_5q_6$$

v.   For Cut set # 5

$$(1-q_2)(1-q_4q_5)(1-q_9)q_6q_7q_8$$

$$(1-q_1)(1-q_4)(1-q_9)q_2q_6q_7q_8$$

$$\left(1-q_1\right)\left(1-q_3\right)\left(1-q_5\right)(1-q_9)q_2q_6q_7q_8q_9$$

vi.   For Cut set # 6

$$(1-q_2)(1-q_4)(1-q_8)q_1q_3q_5q_6$$

$$\left(1-q_2\right)\left(1-q_4\right)\left(1-q_7\right)(1-q_9)q_1q_3q_5q_6q_8$$

vii.   For Cut set # 7

$$(1-q_2)(1-q_6)(1-q_8)q_4q_5q_7q_9$$

$$\left(1-q_1\right)\left(1-q_3\right)\left(1-q_6\right)(1-q_8)q_2q_4q_5q_7q_9$$

viii.   For Cut set # 8

$$\left(1-q_2\right)\left(1-q_4\right)\left(1-q_6\right)(1-q_8)q_1q_3q_5q_7q_9$$

ix.   For Cut set # 9

$$\left(1-q_1\right)\left(1-q_4\right)\left(1-q_6\right)(1-q_9)q_2q_3q_5q_7q_8$$

On the assumption of equal links unreliability (q), the unreliability expression would be:

$$Q(G) = 2q^2 + 3q^3 - q^4 - 8q^5 - 7q^6 + 28q^7 - 21q^8 + 5q^9$$

For $q = 0.1$, $Q(G) = 0.02281559500000$

The Hybrid methods (Chaturvedi & Misra, 2002) are applied to a set of 13 test networks of small to large size shown in Figure 5.5, and the results have been compared on the basis of the following criterion:

i.   The numbers of disjoint terms generated.
ii.   Feasibility and CPU time taken on a low-end Desktop PC.

The branches reliability (unreliability), for the entire set of sample networks shown in Figure 5.5, has been chosen as 0.9 (0.1), nevertheless the program can accept the non-identical links (with different reliabilities as well). The results have also been compared in Table 5.4, Table 5.5 and Table 5.6, respectively, providing the number of total disjoint paths

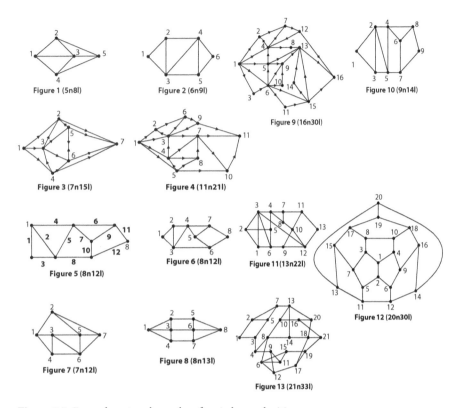

Figure 5.5 Example network graphs of varied complexities.

(DPATH) produced when KDH88 or CAREL alone has been used and CPU time taken by KDH88 and HM.

The CPU time taken by CAREL has not been compared as it has already been established in (Luo & Trivedi, 1998)vide *Table 2: comparison of I_VT, VT, KDH88 and CAREL* that KDH88 completely outperforms CAREL in all respects. The CPU time includes writing data to output file, which includes:

i.   path/cut set indexing,
ii.   creating disjoint terms for each path/cut set,
iii. computing reliability/unreliability contribution by each disjoint terms,
iv.   system reliability computation at each point,
v.   calling disjointing-function in KDH88 and HM at each point number of times recursively,
vi.   recording total number of recursions, and
vii. system reliability/ unreliability computation.

Table 5.4 Comparison of two terminal reliability evaluation with various methods (Path sets).

Figure no.	Path sets	DPATH			CPU time (sec)			Reliab ility
		KDH88	HM-I HM-II	CAREL	KDH88	HM-I	HM-II	
1.	9	11	11	11	0.22	0.16	0.16	0.9976
2.	13	17	17	16	0.77	0.27	0.22	0.9772
3.	14	23	23	23	0.44	0.44	0.44	0.9967
4.	18	83	83	94	2.86	2.75	1.60	0.9941
5.	20	30	30	30	1.15	0.55	0.54	0.9841
6.	24	38	38	39	0.93	0.77	0.60	0.9752
7.	25	53	53	50	1.37	1.05	0.94	0.9975
8.	29	77	77	76	2.80	2.91	1.49	0.9962
9.	36	528	*528*	*542*	35.92	17.47	18.18	0.9972
10.	44	82	*80*	87	5.17	2.47	1.82	0.9742
11.	281	2360	*2302*	2386	1009.36	152.75	133.69	0.9874
12.	780	!	*46707*	54032	!	2724.69	2226.25	0.9971
13.	1681	!	*90814*	-	!	11762.63	8781.71	0.9738

All test examples have been run on a 200 MHz, 32 MB RAM, and 4.3 GB HDD under win98 environment.

! Program got terminated due to stack overflow on the hardware and software platform used.

- Example not included in and solved by the method.

5.6 Global and k-terminal Reliability with SDP Approach

We have earlier mentioned about the advantage of SDP technique that it can be used with any given type of inputs, viz., path sets, cut sets, spanning trees or k-trees, and accordingly they would provide us reliability or unreliability expression for *TR*, *global* (or *all-terminal* reliability) and *k-terminal*

Table 5.5 Comparison of two terminal reliability evaluation with various methods (Cut sets).

Figure no.	Number of path/cut sets	Total number of disjoint paths				CPU time (seconds)			Unreliability (As calculated by KDH88, HM-1, HM-2 and tallied with CAREL)	Reliability (As calculated by KDH88, HM-1, HM-2 and tallied with CAREL)
		KDH88	CAREL	HM-1	HM-2	KDH88	HM-1	HM-2		
1. (5n8l)	9/8	10	10	10	10	0.030	0.08	0.06	0.0024	0.9976
2. (6n9l)	13/9	14	14	14	14	0.030	0.08	0.06	0.2282	0.9772
3. (7n14l)	52/26	74	-	74	74	0.321	0.27	0.28	0.0011	0.9989*
4. (11n21l)	151/133	840	-	830	830	30.253	5.458	5.528	0.0013	0.9987*
5. (8n12l)	20/20	39	40	39	39	0.190	0.150	0.140	0.0159	0.9841
6. (8n12l)	24/19	42	40	42	42	0.170	0.281	0.140	0.0249	0.9751
7. (7n13l)	25/20	43	39	43	43	0.150	0.150	0.581	0.0025	0.9975
8. (8n13l)	29/29	72	77	72	72	0.381	0.271	0.451	0.0038	0.9962
9. (16n30l)	499/644	!	-	14238	14230	!	206.597	176.704	0.0011	0.9989*
10. (9n14l)	44/25	80	79	80	80	0.381	0.340	0.360	0.0259	0.9741
11. (13n22l)	281/214	2000	2339	1996	1996	82.539	15.983	16.300	0.0126	0.9874
12. (20n30l)	780/7376	!	317978	225612	225612	!	32110.313	23467.715	0.0029	0.9971
13. (21n33l)	1681/3838	!	-	169673	169673	!	10987.219	8944.762	0.0262	0.9738

All test examples have been run on a *hp* Vectra, 866 MHz, 64 MB SDRAM, and 40 GB HDD under windows 2000 environment.

Treating Figure 3, 4, and 9 as undirected graph.

! Program got terminated due to stack overflow on the hardware and software platform used.

- Example not considered by the method.

Table 5.6 Recursive call to disjointing-function.

	Numbers of recursive call to disjointing-function by		
Figure no.	KDH88	HM-1	HM-2
1. (5n8l)	38	13	18
2. (6n9l)	54	23	31
3. (7n14l)	600	184	222
4. (11n21l)	54605	3253	4455
5. (8n12l)	325	79	133
6. (8n12l)	312	91	145
7. (7n13l)	321	96	130
8. (8n13l)	862	188	266
9. (16n30l)	!	74451	103139
10. (9n14l)	722	201	315
11. (13n22l)	126767	10451	13488
12. (20n30l)	!	2965149	3456764
13. (21n33l)	!	2419829	2828294

reliability for a given network. To emphasize and illustrate this point once again, let us consider the two networks (a) and (b) of Figure 5.1 again and determine their *g-reliability* and *k-terminal* reliabilities.

5.6.1   All-terminal Reliability Evaluation

The *spanning trees* for the Figure 5.1 (a) and (b), respectively are listed in Table 5.7. In order to assess the relative advantages of various SDP methods, we obtain results for these two networks by running the programs for Abraham, KDH88, and HM-1 methods and to verify relative advantages offered by SVI and MVI approaches. The results of the programs of computing *g-reliability* have been tabulated in Table 5.8. It is easy to verify that both the approaches, namely, SVI and MVI, provide the same g- reliability expression for the example. For example in case of network given in Figure 5.1(a), g-reliability is obtained as:

Table 5.7 Spanning trees for the networks graphs.

Figure 5.1(a)		Figure 5.1(b)			
1.	1 2 4 6	1.	1 2 4 6 8	46.	2 3 6 7 9
2.	1 2 4 7	2.	1 2 4 6 9	47.	2 3 6 8 9
3.	1 2 4 8	3.	1 2 4 7 8	48.	2 4 5 6 8
4.	1 2 5 6	4.	1 2 4 7 9	49.	2 4 5 6 9
5.	1 2 5 7	5.	1 2 4 8 9	50.	2 4 5 7 8
6.	1 2 5 8	6.	1 2 5 6 8	51.	2 4 5 7 9
7.	1 2 6 8	7.	1 2 5 6 9	52.	2 4 5 8 9
8.	1 2 7 8	8.	1 2 5 7 8	53.	2 4 6 7 8
9.	1 3 4 6	9.	1 2 5 7 9	54.	2 4 6 7 9
10.	1 3 4 7	10.	1 2 5 8 9	55.	2 4 6 8 9
11.	1 3 4 8	11.	1 2 6 7 8		
12.	1 3 5 6	12.	1 2 6 7 9		
13.	1 3 5 7	13.	1 2 6 8 9		
14.	1 3 5 8	14.	1 3 4 6 8		
15.	1 3 6 8	15.	1 3 4 6 9		
16.	1 3 7 8	16.	1 3 4 7 8		
17.	1 4 5 6	17.	1 3 4 7 9		
18.	1 4 5 7	18.	1 3 4 8 9		
19.	1 4 5 8	19.	1 3 5 6 8		
20.	1 4 6 7	20.	1 3 5 6 9		
21.	1 4 7 8	21.	1 3 5 7 8		
22.	1 5 6 7	22.	1 3 5 7 9		
23.	1 5 6 8	23.	1 3 5 8 9		
24.	1 6 7 8	24.	1 3 6 7 8		
25.	2 3 4 6	25.	1 3 6 7 9		
26.	2 3 4 7	26.	1 3 6 8 9		
27.	2 3 4 8	27.	1 4 5 6 8		
28.	2 3 5 6	28.	1 4 5 6 9		
29.	2 3 5 7	29.	1 4 5 7 8		
30.	2 3 5 8	30.	1 4 5 7 9		
31.	2 3 6 8	31.	1 4 5 8 9		
32.	2 3 7 8	32.	1 4 6 7 8		
33.	2 4 5 6	33.	1 4 6 7 9		
34.	2 4 5 7	34.	1 4 6 8 9		
35.	2 4 5 8	35.	2 3 4 6 8		
36.	2 4 6 8	36.	2 3 4 6 9		
37.	2 4 7 8	37.	2 3 4 7 8		
38.	3 4 6 7	38.	2 3 4 7 9		
39.	3 4 6 8	39.	2 3 4 8 9		
40.	3 5 6 7	40.	2 3 5 6 8		
41.	3 5 6 8	41.	2 3 5 6 9		
42.	3 6 7 8	42.	2 3 5 7 8		
43.	4 5 6 7	43.	2 3 5 7 9		
44.	4 5 6 8	44.	2 3 5 8 9		
45.	4 6 7 8	45.	2 3 6 7 8		

$$R_s = P_1 P_2 P_4 P_6 + P_1 P_2 P_4 P_7 (1-p_6) + P_1 P_2 P_4 P_8 (1-p_6)(1-p_7) + P_1 P_2 P_5 P_6 (1-p_4) +$$
$$P_1 P_2 P_5 P_7 (1-p_4)(1-p_6) + P_1 P_2 P_5 P_8 (1-p_4)(1-p_6)(1-p_7) + P_1 P_2 P_6 P_8 (1-p_4)(1-p_5)$$
$$+ P_1 P_2 P_7 P_8 (1-p_4)(1-p_5)(1-p_6) + P_1 P_3 P_4 P_6 (1-p_2) + P_1 P_3 P_4 P_7 (1-p_2)(1-p_6) + P_1$$
$$P_3 P_4 P_8 (1-p_2)(1-p_6)(1-p_7) + P_1 P_3 P_5 P_6 (1-p_2)(1-p_4) + P_1 P_3 P_5 P_7 (1-p_2)(1-p_4)$$
$$(1-p_6) + P_1 P_3 P_5 P_8 (1-p_2)(1-p_4)(1-p_6)(1-p_7) + P_1 P_3 P_6 P_8 (1-p_2)(1-p_4)(1-p_5)$$
$$+ P_1 P_3 P_7 P_8 (1-p_2)(1-p_4)(1-p_5)(1-p_6) + P_1 P_4 P_5 P_6 (1-p_2)(1-p_3) + P_1 P_4 P_5 P_7$$
$$(1-p_2)(1-p_3)(1-p_6) + P_1 P_4 P_5 P_8 (1-p_2)(1-p_3)(1-p_6)(1-p_7) + P_1 P_4 P_6 P_7 (1-p_2)$$
$$(1-p_3)(1-p_5) + P_1 P_4 P_7 P_8 (1-p_2)(1-p_3)(1-p_5)(1-p_6) + P_1 P_5 P_6 P_7 (1-p_2)(1-p_3)$$
$$(1-p_4) + P_1 P_5 P_6 P_8 (1-p_2)(1-p_3)(1-p_4)(1-p_7) + P_1 P_6 P_7 P_8 (1-p_2)(1-p_3)(1-p_4)$$
$$(1-p_5) + P_2 P_3 P_4 P_6 (1-p_1)$$
$$+ P_2 P_3 P_4 P_7 (1-p_1)(1-p_6) + P_2 P_3 P_4 P_8 (1-p_1)(1-p_6)(1-p_7) + P_2 P_3 P_5 P_6 (1-p_1)$$
$$(1-p_4) + P_2 P_3 P_5 P_7 (1-p_1)(1-p_4)(1-p_6) + P_2 P_3 P_5 P_8 (1-p_1)(1-p_4)(1-p_6)(1-p_7) +$$
$$P_2 P_3 P_6 P_8 (1-p_1)(1-p_4)(1-p_5) + P_2 P_3 P_7 P_8 (1-p_1)(1-p_4)(1-p_5)(1-p_6) + P_2 P_4 P_5$$
$$P_6 (1-p_1)(1-p_2) + P_2 P_4 P_5 P_7 (1-p_1)(1-p_3)(1-p_6) + P_2 P_4 P_5 P_8 (1-p_1)(1-p_3)(1-p_6)$$
$$(1-p_7) + P_2 P_4 P_6 P_8 (1-p_1)(1-p_3)(1-p_5) + P_2 P_4 P_7 P_8 (1-p_1)(1-p_3)(1-p_5)(1-p_6) +$$
$$P_3 P_4 P_6 P_7 (1-p_2)(1-p_3)(1-p_4) + P_3 P_4 P_6 P_8 (1-p_1)(1-p_2)(1-p_7) + P_3 P_5 P_6 P_7 (1-p_1)(1-p_2)$$
$$(1-p_4) + P_3 P_5 P_6 P_8 (1-p_1)(1-p_2)(1-p_4)(1-p_7) + P_3 P_6 P_7 P_8 (1-p_1)(1-p_2)(1-p_4)$$
$$(1-p_5) + P_4 P_5 P_6 P_7 (1-p_1)(1-p_2)$$
$$(1-p_3) + P_4 P_5 P_6 P_8 (1-p_1)(1-p_2)(1-p_3)(1-p_7) + P_4 P_6 P_7 P_8 (1-p_1)(1-p_2)(1-p_3)$$
$$(1-p_5).$$

Executing the HM-1 program (available at www.scrivenerpublishing.com) on *Matlab®* prompt, for Figure 5.1(a) renders the following:

>> *carelKdhTst3*
Please enter pathSet(BranchWise)file with full dir
path:fig5.1aSpanTree.m
Branches in the Net:?8
Nodes in the Net:?5
Reliability of single branch:?0.9
FOR OUTPUT
Please enter Output file with full path:fig5.1aSpanTreeHM1.m
t = 0.212887012623047
SystemRel =0.99556614000, Total FunCall= 44
total disjoint paths= 45

Table 5.8 g- Reliability evaluation and comparison with different methods (with all link reliabilities =0.9).

Example	Number of spanning-trees	Disjoint terms	Program execution time in seconds			g-Reliability
			Abraham	KDH88	HM-1	
Figure 5.1 (a)	45	45	0.99	1.76	0.77	0.995566140
Figure 5.1 (b)	55	55	1.31	3.29	0.99	0.975253204

On the assumption of equal links' reliabilities, p, we would obtain the following polynomial: $R_s = 45\,p^4 - 128\,p^5 + 142\,p^6 - 72\,p^7 + 14\,p^8$

5.6.2   Characteristics of a g-reliability Expression

There are certain facts, peculiar with g-reliability and not observed in other types of measures, worth to mention:

1. It can be observed from Table 5.8 that as far as *g-reliability* is concerned, both the SVI and MVI approaches result in the same number of disjoint terms equal to the number of spanning trees of the networks and there is no advantage of using MVI over the SVI method for obtaining SDP terms for *g-reliability* expression of the network. However, the HM-1 comes out faster than either SVI (such as Abraham's method) or any other MVI based methods such as KDH88 etc. This is evident from Table 5.8 and can be attributed mainly to less number of comparisons involved in HM-1 method.

2. The lowest degree term in the expression is (n-1) and coefficient of this term is equal to the number of spanning trees of the network graph under consideration.

3. The terms are alternatively positive and negative.

4. The sum of all the coefficient of the expression is unity. Also true for other reliability measures.

5. For a non-reducible network graph, if the expression is plotted against p would provide S-shaped curve implying that for *s*-coherent system when entire component attain sufficiently high reliability then only the network reliability would be greater than the reliability of a single link. It is also hold good for the other reliability measures.

5.6.3   k-terminal Reliability Evaluation

We can utilize the method of (Samad, 1987) or of (Rath & Soman, 1993) to enumerate *k-trees* (with specified *k-nodes*) by using the *spanning trees* enumerated earlier for the networks of Figure 5.1 to determine the *k-terminal reliability* in SDP form. The *k-trees* enumerated by the method of (Rath & Soman, 1993) and is discussed in Section 3.4 are listed in Table 5.9 and the results of the programs of computing *k-terminal* reliability are tabulated in Table 5.10.

Table 5.9 *k-trees* for the networks.

Figure 5.1 (a)k-nodes: {1, 3, 5}		Figure 5.1 (b) k-nodes: {1, 2, 4, 5}	
1.	3 7	1.	1 4 7
2.	1 2 6	2.	1 2 4 6
3.	1 2 7	3.	1 2 5 6
4.	1 3 6	4.	1 2 5 7
5.	1 6 7	5.	1 2 6 7
6.	2 3 6	6.	1 3 4 6
7.	3 4 8	7.	1 3 5 6
8.	3 5 8	8.	1 3 5 7
9.	4 5 7	9.	1 3 6 7
10.	4 5 8	10.	1 4 5 6
11.	4 7 8	11.	1 4 8 9
12.	1 2 4 8	12.	2 3 4 6
13.	1 2 5 8	13.	2 3 4 7
14.	1 4 5 6	14.	2 3 5 6
15.	1 5 6 8	15.	2 3 5 7
16.	2 4 5 6	16.	2 3 6 7
17.	2 4 6 8	17.	2 4 5 6
		18.	2 4 5 7
		19.	2 4 6 7
		20.	1 2 5 8 9
		21.	1 2 6 8 9
		22.	1 3 5 8 9
		23.	1 3 6 8 9
		24.	2 3 4 8 9
		25.	2 3 5 8 9
		26.	2 3 6 8 9
		27.	2 4 5 8 9
		28.	2 4 6 8 9

Table 5.10 *k- Terminal Reliability* Evaluation and Comparison with Different Methods (with all link reliabilities =0.9)

Example	k-nodes	Number of k-trees	Disjoint terms(Program execution time in seconds)			k-terminal reliability
			Abraham	KDH88	HM-1	
Figure 5.1 (a)	{1, 3, 5}	15	29 (0.28)	23 (0.27)	21 (0.22)	0.99752067000
Figure 5.1 (b)	{1, 2, 4, 5}	28	30 (0.49)	29 (0.67)	29 (0.44)	0.98509551300

The expression provided by the Abraham's method (SVI) and HM-1 (MVI) provide the following reliability expressions, respectively:

SVI:

$$P_3 P_7 + P_1 P_2 P_6 \{ (1-p_3) + p_3 (1-p_7)\} + p_1 p_2 p_7 (1-p_3)(1-p_6) + p_1 p_3 p_6$$
$$(1-p_2)(1-p_7) + p_1 p_6 p_7 (1-p_2)(1-p_3) + p_2 p_3 p_6 (1-p_1)(1-p_7) + p_3 p_4$$
$$p_8 \{ (1-p_1)(1-p_2)(1-p_7) + p_4 (1-p_1)(1-p_6)(1-p_7) + p_1 (1-p_2)(1-p_6)$$
$$(1-p_7) + p_1 p_2 (1-p_6)(1-p_7)\} + p_3 p_5 p_8 \{ (1-p_1)(1-p_2)(1-p_4)(1-p_7) +$$
$$p_2 (1-p_1)(1-p_4)(1-p_6)(1-p_7) + p_1 (1-p_2)(1-p_4)(1-p_6)(1-p_7) + p_1 p_2$$
$$(1-p_6)(1-p_7)\} + p_4 p_5 p_7 (1-p_1)(1-p_3) + p_1 (1-p_2)(1-p_3)(1-p_6) + p_4$$
$$p_5 p_8 \{1-p_1)(1-p_3)(1-p_7)+p_1(1-p_2)(1-p_3)(1-p_6)(1-p_7) + p_1 p_6 (1-p_2)(1-p_3)$$
$$(1-p_7) + p_1 p_2 (1-p_3)(1-p_6)(1-p_7)\} + p_4 p_7 p_8 \{(1-p_1)(1-p_3)(1-p_5)+p_1(1-p_2)$$
$$(1-p_3)(1-p_5)(1-p_6)\} + p_1 p_2 p_4 p_8 (1-p_3)(1-p_5)(1-p_6)(1-p_7) + p_1 p_2 p_5 p_8$$
$$(1-p_3)(1-p_4)(1-p_6)(1-p_7) + p_1 p_4 p_5 p_6 (1-p_2)(1-p_3)(1-p_7)(1-p_8) + p_1 p_5 p_6$$
$$p_8 (1-p_2)(1-p_3)(1-p_4)(1-p_7) + p_2 p_4 p_5 p_6 (1-p_1)(1-p_3)(1-p_7)(1-p_8) + p_2 p_4$$
$$p_6 p_8 (1-p_1)(1-p_3)(1-p_5)(1-p_7)$$

MVI

$$P_3 P_7 + P_1 P_2 P_6 (1-p_3 p_7) + p_1 p_2 p_7 (1-p_3)(1-p_6) + p_1 p_3 p_6 (1-p_2)(1-p_7)+$$
$$p_1 p_6 p_7 (1-p_2)(1-p_3)+ p_2 p_3 p_6 (1-p_1)(1-p_7) + p_3 p_4 p_8 \{(1-p_6)(1-p_7) +$$
$$(1-p_1)(1-p_2)(1-p_7)p_6\} + p_3 p_5 p_8 \{(1-p_4)(1-p_6)(1-p_7) + (1-p_1)(1-p_2)$$
$$(1-p_4)(1-p_7)p_6\} + p_4 p_5 p_7 \{(1-p_1)(1-p_3) + p_1(1-p_2)(1-p_3)(1-p_6)\} + p_4 p_5$$
$$p_8 (1-p_1 p_2 p_6)(1-p_3)(1-p_7) + p_4 p_7 p_8 \{(1-p_1)(1-p_3)(1-p_5) +p_1 (1-p_2)(1-p_3)$$
$$(1-p_5) (1-p_6)\} + p_1 p_2 p_4 p_8 (1-p_3)(1-p_5) (1-p_6) (1-p_7) + p_1 p_2 p_5 p_8 (1-p_3)$$
$$(1-p_4)(1-p_6)(1-p_7) + p_1 p_4 p_5 p_6 (1-p_2) (1-p_3)(1-p_7)(1-p_8) + p_1 p_5 p_6 p_8 (1-$$
$$p_2)(1-p_3)(1-p_4)(1-p_7) + p_2 p_4 p_5 p_6 (1-p_1)(1-p_3)(1-p_7)(1-p_8) + p_2 p_4 p_6$$
$$p_8 (1-p_1)(1-p_3)(1-p_5)(1-p_7)$$

For equal reliabilities of links, both the above *k-terminal reliability* expressions yield the following polynomial:

$$R_s = p^2 + 10p^3 - 10p^4 - 26p^5 + 51p^6 - 32p^7 + 7p^8$$

Similar expression can be obtained for the Figure 5.1(b) with the help of the program outputs given in Appendix 5A.1 , 5A.2 and 5A.3.

Executing the HM-1 program (available at www.scrivenerpublishing. com) on *Matlab*® prompt for Figure 5.1(b) renders the following:

>> *carelKdhTst3*
Please enter pathSet(BranchWise)file with full dir
path:fig5.1b1245KTree.m
Branches in the Net:?9
Nodes in the Net:?6

Reliability of single branch:?0.9
FOR OUTPUT
Please enter Output file with full path:fig5.1b1245KTreeHM1.m
t = 0.051977635829758
SystemRel =0.98509551300, Total FunCall= 32
total disjoint paths= 29

5.6.4 Number of k-trees

To observe how the number of *k-trees* varies for a given network, let us consider two criteria:

i. By taking the different *k-node* sets of same size, and
ii. By varying the size of *k-node* set by sequentially adding one node at a time in the set.

The variation that we get in the number of *k-trees* for a specified *k-node* set is shown in Table 5.11 for the Figure 5.1(a) and in Table 5.13 for the Figure 5.1(b). It can be observed that, a higher number for *k-trees* is obtained for that set, which contains the nodes that are distant-apart in the network.

The property of a network with respect to the number of *k-trees*, it would have, on varying the size of *k-node* set with the addition of one node at a time in the *k-node* set for the Figure 5.1(a) and (b) are shown in Table 5.12 and Table 5.14 respectively.

Table 5.11 Variation in the number of k-trees for different order of k-node set.

k-node sets of different order						
Example	2	k-trees	3	k-trees	4	k-trees
Figure 5.1 (a)	1 2	8	1 2 3	16	1 2 3 4	29
	1 3	7	1 2 4	19	1 2 3 5	29
	1 4	9	1 2 5	19	1 2 4 5	33
	1 5	9	1 3 4	16	1 3 4 5	29
	2 3	7	1 3 5	17	2 3 4 5	29
	2 4	9	1 4 5	19		
	2 5	9	2 3 4	17		
	3 4	7	2 3 5	16		
	3 5	7	2 4 5	19		
	4 5	8	3 4 5	16		

Table 5.12 Variation in number of k-trees with size of the k-node set.

Example	k-node set	Number of k-trees
Figure 5.1 (a)	1 2	8
	1 2 3	16
	1 2 3 4	29
	1 2 3 4 5	45

Table 5.13 Variation in the number of *k-trees* for different order of k-node set.

k-node sets of different order								
Example	2	k-trees	3	k-trees	4	k-trees	5	k-trees
Figure 5.1	1 2	11	1 2 3	15	1 2 3 4	18	1 2 3 4 5	34
(b)	1 3	10	1 2 4	14	1 2 3 5	25	1 2 3 4 6	39
	1 4	8	1 2 5	19	1 2 3 6	30	1 2 3 5 6	46
	1 5	12	1 2 6	23	1 2 4 5	28	1 2 4 5 6	46
	1 6	13	1 3 4	12	1 2 4 6	32	1 3 4 5 6	39
	2 3	9	1 3 5	18	1 2 5 6	37	2 3 4 5 6	34
	2 4	8	1 3 6	20	1 3 4 5	24		
	2 5	9	1 4 5	18	1 3 4 6	27		
	2 6	12	1 4 6	20	1 3 5 6	32		
	3 4	5	1 5 6	23	1 4 5 6	30		
	3 5	9	2 3 4	11	2 3 4 5	21		
	3 6	9	2 3 5	15	2 3 4 6	24		
	4 5	9	2 3 6	18	2 3 5 6	28		
	4 6	11	2 4 5	15	2 4 5 6	25		
	5 6	12	2 4 6	18	3 4 5 6	18		
			2 5 6	19				
			3 4 5	11				
			3 4 6	12				
			3 5 6	15				
			4 5 6	15				

Table 5.14 Variation in number of *k-trees* with size of the *k-node* set.

Example	k-node set	Number of k-trees
Figure 5.1 (b)	1 2	11
	1 2 3	15
	1 2 3 4	18
	1 2 3 4 5	34
	1 2 3 4 5 6	55

It can be observed that as we add nodes in the *k-node* set, the number of *k- trees* also increases. This increase in number of *k-trees* would continue till the *k-node* set becomes a set, which contains all the networks nodes. At this point, the number of *k-trees* coincides with the number of *spanning trees* of the network.

5.7   Unreliability with SDP Approach

We continue to apply the methods discussed in this Chapter to obtain unreliability measures by providing the necessary inputs to the algorithm described in this Chapter. This does not forbid readers to apply other methods referenced in this text or elsewhere.

Example 5.4: Considering the Figure 5.4, obtain its 2-terminal, global, k-terminal unreliability for the node set [2, 4, 5, 6] expressions and their respective values for each link unreliability of 0.1.

Solution: Referring example 4.6 in Chapter 4 and Figure 5.4,

- There are nine 2-terminal minimal cutsets between node $\{1, 6\}$: [$\{1\ 2\}$, $\{8\ 9\}$, $\{2\ 3\ 4\}$, $\{4\ 5\ 6\}$, $\{6\ 7\ 8\}$, $\{1\ 3\ 5\ 6\}$, $\{4\ 5\ 7\ 9\}$, $\{1\ 3\ 5\ 7\ 9\}$, $\{2\ 3\ 5\ 7\ 8\}$].

  $Q_{\{1, 6\}} = q_1q_2 + q_8q_9\ (1-q_1q_2) + q_2q_3q_4\ (1-q_1)(1-q_8q_9) + q_4q_5q_6$ $(1-q_8q_9)\ \{(1-q_2) + q_2\ (1-q_1)(1-q_3)\} + q_6q_7q_8\ (1-q_9)[(1-q_2)$ $(1-q_4q_5) + q_2\ (1-q_1)\{(1-q_4) + q_4\ (1-q_3)(1-q_5)\}] + q_1q_3q_5q_6(1-q_2)$ $(1-q_4)\{\ (1-q_8) + q_8\ (1-q_7)(1-q_9)\} + q_4q_5q_7q_9\ (1-q_6)(1-q_8)\{(1-q_2) + q_2\ (1-q_1)(1-q_3)\} + q_1q_3q_5q_7q_9\ (1-q_2)(1-q_4)(1-q_6)(1-q_8) + q_2q_3q_5q_7q_8\ (1-q_1)(1-q_4)(1-q_6)(1-q_9)$.

  For equal unreliability of links, i.e., $q_i = q = 0.1$, $\forall$ i = 1, 2, 3...9,

  $Q_{\{1, 6\}} = 2q^2 + 3q^3 - q^4 - 8q^5 - 7q^6 + 28q^7 - 21\ q^8 + 5q^9 = 0.0228$, and reliability = 0.9772

  Comment: Applying SDP approach on 13 pathsets of this network, the above result(Reliability) comes out to be the same with 17 disjoint terms (again reduction in number of disjoint terms, less number of efforts in disjoint process and thereby less round-off errors).

- The global minimal cutsets of the network turns out to be 15, i.e., : [$\{1\ 2\}$, $\{8\ 9\}$, $\{1\ 3\ 4\}$, $\{2\ 3\ 4\}$, $\{4\ 5\ 6\}$, $\{6\ 7\ 8\}$, $\{6\ 7\ 9\}$, $\{1\ 3$

5 6}, {2 3 5 6}, {4 5 7 8}, {4 5 7 9}, {1 3 5 7 8}, {1 3 5 7 9}, {2 3 5 7 8}, {2 3 5 7 9}], and

$Q_g = q_1q_2 + q_8q_9 (1-q_1q_2) + q_1q_3q_4 (1-q_2) (1-q_8q_9) + q_2q_3q_4$
$(1-q_1) (1-q_8q_9) + q_4q_5q_6 (1-q_8q_9) \{(1-q_1) (1-q_2q_3) + q_1 (1-q_2)$
$(1-q_3)\} + q_6q_7q_8 (1-q_9) [(1-q_1) \{ (1-q_4) + q_4 (1-q_5) (1-q_2q_3)\} +$
$q_1 (1-q_2) \{(1-q_4) + q_4 (1-q_3) (1-q_5) \}] + q_6q_7q_9 (1-q_8) [(1-q_1)$
$\{ (1-q_4) + q_4 (1-q_5) (1-q_2q_3) \} + q_1 (1-q_2) \{ (1-q_4) + q_4 (1-q_3)$
$(1-q_5) \}] + q_1q_3q_5q_6 (1-q_2) (1-q_4) \{ (1-q_8) (1-q_7q_9) + q_8 (1-q_7)$
$(1-q_9) \} + q_2q_3q_5q_6 (1-q_1) (1-q_4) \{ (1-q_8) (1-q_7q_9) + q_8 (1-q7)$
$(1-q_9) \} + q_4q_5q_7q_8 (1-q_6) (1-q_9) \{ (1-q_2q_3) (1- q_1) + q_1(1-q_2)$
$(1-q_3) \} + q_4q_5q_7q_9 (1-q_6) (1-q_8) \{ (1-q_1) (1-q_2q_3) + q_1 (1-q_2)$
$(1-q_3) \} + q_1q_3q_5q_7q_8 (1-q_2) (1-q_4) (1-q_6) (1-q_9) + q_1q_3q_5q_7q_9$
$(1-q_2) (1-q_4) (1-q_6) (1-q_8) + q_2q_3q_5q_7q_8 (1-q_1) (1-q_4) (1-q_6)$
$(1-q_9) + q_2q_3q_5q_7q_9 (1-q_1) (1-q_4) (1-q_6) (1-q_8)$. And R = 1-Q

For equal unreliability of links, i.e., $q_i = q = 0.1$, $\forall$ i = 1, 2, 3…9,

$Q_g = 2q^2 + 5q^3 - q^4 - 14q^5 - 20q^6 + 73q^7 - 60q^8 + 16q^9 = 0.0247$, and reliability = 0.9753

Comment: Applying SDP approach on 55 spanning trees of this network, the above result (Reliability) comes out to be the same with 55 disjoint terms (in comparison to 26 terms- an almost 50% reduction in number of disjoint terms, less number of efforts in disjoint process and thereby less round-off errors).

- The 13 *k*-terminal minimal cutsets are: [*{1 2}, {1 3 4}, {2 3 4 }, {4 5 6 }, {6 7 8}, {6 7 9}, {1 3 5 6 }, {4 5 7 8 }, {4 5 7 9}, {1 3 5 7 8 }, {1 3 5 7 9}, {2 3 5 7 8}, {2 3 5 7 9}]*, and

$Q_{\{2, 4, 5, 6\}} = q_1q_2 + q_1q_3q_4 (1-q_2) + q_2q_3q_4 (1-q_1) + q_4q_5q_6 \{(1-q_1)$
$(1-q_2q_3) + q_1 (1-q_2) (1-q_3)\} + q_6q_7q_8 \{ (1-q_1) (1-q_4) + q_4 (1-q_1)$
$(1-q_5) (1-q_2q_3) + q_1 (1-q_2) (1-q_4) + q_1q_4 (1-q_2) (1-q_3) (1-q_4) \} +$
$q_6q_7q_9 (1-q_8) \{ (1-q_1) (1-q_4) + q_4 (1-q_1) (1-q_2q_3) (1-q_5) + q_1(1-q_2) (1-q_4) + q_1q_4 (1-q_2) (1-q_3) (1-q_5)\} + q_1q_3q_5q_6 (1-q_2) (1-q_4)$
$\{(1-q_7)+ q_7 (1-q_8) (1-q_9)\} + q_4q_5q_7q_8 (1-q_6) \{ (1-q_1) (1-q_2q_3) +$
$q_1 (1- q_2) (1-q_3) \} + q_4q_5q_7q_9 (1-q_6) (1-q_8) \{ (1-q_1) (1-q_2q_3) +$
$q_1 (1-q_2) (1-q_3)\} + q_1q_3q_5q_7q_8 (1-q_2) (1-q_4) (1-q_6) + q_1q_3q_5q_7q_9$
$(1-q_2) (1-q_4) (1-q_6) (1-q_8) + q_2q_3q_5q_7q_8 (1-q_1) (1-q_4) (1-q_6) +$
$q_2q_3q_5q_7q_9 (1-q_1) (1-q_4) (1-q_6) (1-q_8)$.

For equal unreliability of links, i.e., $q_i = q = 0.1$, $\forall$ i = 1, 2, 3…nLink,

$Q_{\{2, 4, 5, 6\}} = q^2 + 5q^3 - 8q^5 - 20q^6 + 48q^7 - 32\,q^8 + 7q^9 = 0.014$
904 487, and reliability = 0.985 095 513

Executing the HM-1 program (available at www.scrivenerpublishing.com) on Matlab® prompt renders the following:

> >> carelKdhTst3
> Please enter pathSet(BranchWise)file with full dir
> path:fig5.4K2456Cuts.m
> Branches in the Net:?9
> Nodes in the Net:?6
> Reliability of single branch:?0.1
> FOR OUTPUT
> Please enter Output file with full path:fig5.4K2456CutsHM1.m
> t = 0.046603541735033
> SystemRel =0.01490448700, Total FunCall= 48
> total disjoint paths= 23
> >> 1-sysRel
> ans = 0.985095513000000

Comment: Applying SDP approach on 28 k-trees for same k-node set of this network, the above result(reliability) comes out to be the same with 29 disjoint terms (again reduction in number of disjoint terms, less number of efforts in disjoint process and thereby less round-off errors).

5.8   Some Suggested Guidelines

Based on their study, (Mishra, 2009), (Mishra et al., 2016) formulated some guidelines before proceeding to carry out the reliability analysis of a network system represented by a non-reducible network graph. Here are some suggestions for systems represented by a directed network:

i.   For most of the networks, the number of minimal pathsets is generally much less than the number of minimal cutsets. Number of terms in reliability expression also behaves in a similar manner for most of the networks. *Therefore, it is advisable to use minimal pathsets rather than in evaluating 2-terminal reliability for systems modelled through directed graphs.*

ii. The number of global cutsets is always less than the number of spanning trees for all cases. The difference between this gets widen as the network complexity further increases. Similar observations hold for number of terms in reliability expression. *Therefore, it is beneficial to use global cutsets rather than spanning trees (arborescence) in evaluating g-reliability for systems modelled through directed graphs.*

iii. The number of k-terminal cutsets or pathsets is depends on network configuration or topology. However, more investigations are yet to be done to reach the exact conclusion.

Appendix 5A.1: Program Output of g-reliability Expression for the Figure 5.1(b).

Results are provided by the program for method HM-1
**************DisjointSet***********SDPREL**********CUMSUMREL

    0   0   -1   0   -1   0   -1   0   -1   0.59049000000
For Path No#= 2.
----

    0   0   -1   0   -1   0   -1   1   0   0.05904900000   0.64953900000
For Path No#= 3.
----

    0   0   -1   0   -1   1   0   0   -1   0.05904900000   0.70858800000
For Path No#= 4.
----

    0   0   -1   0   -1   2   0   3   0   0.00590490000   0.71449290000
For Path No#= 5.
----

    0   0   -1   0   -1   2   4   0   0   0.00590490000   0.72039780000
For Path No#= 6.
----

    0   0   -1   1   0   0   -1   0   -1   0.05904900000   0.77944680000
For Path No#= 7.
----

    0   0   -1   2   0   0   -1   6   0   0.00590490000   0.78535170000
For Path No#= 8.
----

    0   0   -1   3   0   6   0   0   -1   0.00590490000   0.79125660000
For Path No#= 9.
----

    0   0   -1   4   0   7   0   8   0   0.00059049000   0.79184709000
For Path No#= 10.
----

    0   0   -1   5   0   7   9   0   0   0.00059049000   0.79243758000

For Path No#= 11.
----

  0   0 -1   3   8   0   0   0 -1 0.00590490000   0.79834248000

For Path No#= 12.
----

  0   0 -1   4   9   0   0 11   0 0.00059049000   0.79893297000

For Path No#= 13.
----

  0   0 -1   5 10   0 12   0   0 0.00059049000   0.79952346000

For Path No#= 14.
----

  0   1   0   0 -1   0 -1   0 -1 0.05904900000   0.85857246000

For Path No#= 15.
----

  0   2   0   0 -1   0 -1 14   0 0.00590490000   0.86447736000

For Path No#= 16.
----

  0   3   0   0 -1 14   0   0 -1 0.00590490000   0.87038226000

For Path No#= 17.
----

  0   4   0   0 -1 15   0 16   0 0.00059049000   0.87097275000

For Path No#= 18.
----

  0   5   0   0 -1 15 17   0   0 0.00059049000   0.87156324000

For Path No#= 19.
----

  0   6   0 14   0   0 -1   0 -1 0.00590490000   0.87746814000

For Path No#= 20.
----

  0   7   0 15   0   0 -1 19   0 0.00059049000   0.87805863000

For Path No#= 21.
----

  0   8   0 16   0 19   0   0 -1 0.00059049000   0.87864912000

For Path No#= 22.
----

  0 9   0 17   0 20   0 21   0   0.00005904900 0.87870816900

For Path No#= 23.
----

  0 10   0 18   0 20 22   0   0   0.00005904900 0.87876721800

For Path No#= 24.
----

  0 11   0 16 21   0   0   0 -1   0.00059049000 0.87935770800

For Path No#= 25.
----

  0 12   0 17 22   0   0 24   0   0.00005904900 0.87941675700

For Path No#= 26.
----

  0 13   0 18 23   0 25   0   0   0.00005904900 0.87947580600

For Path No#= 27.
----

  0 6 19   0   0   0 -1   0 -1   0.00590490000 0.88538070600

For Path No#= 28.
----

  0 7 20   0   0   0 -1 27   0   0.00059049000 0.88597119600

For Path No#= 29.
----

  0 8 21   0   0 27   0   0 -1   0.00059049000 0.88656168600

For Path No#= 30.
----

  0 9 22   0   0 28   0 29   0   0.00005904900 0.88662073500

For Path No#= 31.
----

  0 10 23   0   0 28 30   0   0 0.00005904900   0.88667978400

For Path No#= 32.
----

  0 11 24   0 29   0   0   0 -1 0.00059049000   0.88727027400

For Path No#= 33.

　0　12　25　0　30　0　　0　32　　0　0.00005904900　　0.88732932300

For Path No#= 34.

　0　13　26　0　31　0　33　0　　0　0.00005904900　　0.88738837200

For Path No#= 35.

　14　0　　0　　0　-1　0　-1　0　-1　0.05904900000　　0.94643737200

For Path No#= 36.

　15　0　　0　　0　-1　0　-1　35　0　0.00590490000　　0.95234227200

For Path No#= 37.

　16　0　　0　　0　-1　35　0　　0　-1　0.00590490000　　0.95824717200

For Path No#= 38.

　17　0　　0　　0　-1　36　0　37　0　0.00059049000　　0.95883766200

For Path No#= 39.

　18　0　　0　　0　-1　36　38　0　　0　0.00059049000　　0.95942815200

For Path No#= 40.

　19　0　　0　35　0　　0　-1　0　-1　0.00590490000　　0.96533305200

For Path No#= 41.

　20　0　　0　36　0　　0　-1　40　0　0.00059049000　　0.96592354200

For Path No#= 42.

　21　0　　0　37　0　40　0　　0　-1　0.00059049000　　0.96651403200

For Path No#= 43.

　22　0　　0　38　0　41　0　42　0　0.00005904900　　0.96657308100

For Path No#= 44.

| 23 | 0 | 0 | 39 | 0 | 41 | 43 | 0 | 0 | 0.00005904900 | 0.96663213000 |

For Path No#= 45.

| 24 | 0 | 0 | 37 | 42 | 0 | 0 | 0 | -1 | 0.00059049000 | 0.96722262000 |

For Path No#= 46.

| 25 | 0 | 0 | 38 | 43 | 0 | 0 | 45 | 0 | 0.00005904900 | 0.96728166900 |

For Path No#= 47.

| 26 | 0 | 0 | 39 | 44 | 0 | 46 | 0 | 0 | 0.00005904900 | 0.96734071800 |

For Path No#= 48.

| 27 | 0 | 40 | 0 | 0 | 0 | -1 | 0 | -1 | 0.00590490000 | 0.97324561800 |

For Path No#= 49.

| 28 | 0 | 41 | 0 | 0 | 0 | -1 | 48 | 0 | 0.00059049000 | 0.97383610800 |

For Path No#= 50.

| 29 | 0 | 42 | 0 | 0 | 48 | 0 | 0 | -1 | 0.00059049000 | 0.97442659800 |

For Path No#= 51.

| 30 | 0 | 43 | 0 | 0 | 49 | 0 | 50 | 0 | 0.00005904900 | 0.97448564700 |

For Path No#= 52.

| 31 | 0 | 44 | 0 | 0 | 49 | 51 | 0 | 0 | 0.00005904900 | 0.97454469600 |

For Path No#= 53.

| 32 | 0 | 45 | 0 | 50 | 0 | 0 | 0 | -1 | 0.00059049000 | 0.97513518600 |

For Path No#= 54.

| 33 | 0 | 46 | 0 | 51 | 0 | 0 | 53 | 0 | 0.00005904900 | 0.97519423500 |

For Path No#= 55.
----

 34 0 47 0 52 0 54 0   0   0.00005904900   0.97525328400
SystemRel =0.97525328400
total disjoint paths= 55
execution time =0.99000000000

Appendix 5A.2: Program Output of *k*-terminal *Reliability* Expression for Figure 5.1(b).

Results are provided by the program for the SVI method Abraham.
**************DisjointSet**********SDPREL***********CUMSUMREL

For Path No#= 1

								SDPREL	CUMSUMREL
-1	-1	0	-1	-1	-1	0	-1	0.81000000000	0.81000000000

For Path No#= 2

| 0 | 0 | 1 | -1 | -1 | 0 | -1 | -1 | 0.07290000000 | 0.88290000000 |
| 0 | 0 | 0 | -1 | -1 | 0 | 1 | -1 | 0.06561000000 | 0.94851000000 |

For Path No#= 3

| 0 | 0 | 1 | -1 | -1 | 1 | 0 | -1 | 0.00729000000 | 0.95580000000 |

For Path No#= 4

| 0 | 1 | 0 | -1 | -1 | 0 | 1 | -1 | 0.00729000000 | 0.96309000000 |

For Path No#= 5

| 0 | 1 | 1 | -1 | -1 | 0 | 0 | -1 | 0.00729000000 | 0.97038000000 |

For Path No#= 6

| 1 | 0 | 0 | -1 | -1 | 0 | 1 | -1 | 0.00729000000 | 0.97767000000 |

For Path No#= 7

1	1	0	0	-1	-1	1	0	0.00072900000	0.97839900000
1	0	0	0	-1	1	1	0	0.00065610000	0.97905510000
0	1	0	0	-1	1	1	0	0.00065610000	0.97971120000
0	0	0	0	-1	1	1	0	0.00590490000	0.98561610000

For Path No#= 8

1	1	0	1	0	-1	1	0	0.00007290000	0.98568900000
1	0	0	1	0	1	1	0	0.00006561000	0.98575461000
0	1	0	1	0	1	1	0	0.00006561000	0.98582022000
0	0	0	1	0	1	1	0	0.00059049000	0.98641071000

For Path No#= 9

1	-1	1	0	0	-1	0	-1	0.00729000000	0.99370071000
0	1	1	0	0	1	0	-1	0.00065610000	0.99435681000

For Path No#= 10

1	-1	1	0	0	-1	1	0	0.00072900000	0.99508581000
0	1	1	0	0	1	1	0	0.00006561000	0.99515142000
0	1	1	0	0	0	1	0	0.00059049000	0.99574191000
0	0	1	0	0	1	1	0	0.00059049000	0.99633240000

For Path No#= 11

1	-1	1	0	1	-1	0	0	0.00072900000	0.99706140000
0	1	1	0	1	1	0	0	0.00006561000	0.99712701000

For Path No#= 12

0	0	1	0	1	1	1	0	0.00006561000	0.99719262000

For Path No#= 13

0	0	1	1	0	1	1	0	0.00006561000	0.99725823000

For Path No#= 14

0	1	1	0	0	0	1	1	0.00006561000	0.99732384000

For Path No#= 15

0	1	1	1	0	0	1	0	0.00006561000	0.99738945000

For Path No#= 16

1	0	1	0	0	0	1	1	0.00006561000	0.99745506000

For Path No#= 17

1	0	1	0	1	0	1	0	0.00006561000	0.99752067000

SystemRel =0.99752067000, Total FunCall= 265

total disjoint paths= 29

execution time = 0.28000000000

Appendix 5A.3: Program Output of *k-terminal Reliability* Expression for Figure 5.1(b).

Results are provided by the program for the MVI method HM-1.

*****************DisjointSet*************SDPREL***********CUMSUMREL**********funNextStep called(times)****

```
 0  -1  -1   0  -1  -1   0  -1  -1   0.72900000000
```
For Path No#= 2.

```
 0   0  -1   0  -1   0   1  -1  -1   0.06561000000       0.79461000000
```
For Path No#= 3.

```
 0   0  -1   2   0   0  -1  -1  -1   0.06561000000       0.86022000000
```
For Path No#= 4.

```
 0   0  -1   1   0   3   0  -1  -1   0.00656100000       0.86678100000
```
For Path No#= 5.

```
 0   0  -1   2   4   0   0  -1  -1   0.00656100000       0.87334200000
```
For Path No#= 6.

```
 0   2   0   0  -1   0   1  -1  -1   0.00656100000       0.87990300000
```
For Path No#= 7.

```
 0   3   0   6   0   0  -1  -1  -1   0.00656100000       0.88646400000
```
For Path No#= 8.

```
 0   4   0   1   0   7   0  -1  -1   0.00065610000       0.88712010000
```
For Path No#= 9.

```
 0   5   0   6   8   0   0  -1  -1   0.00065610000       0.88777620000
```
For Path No#= 10.

```
 0   3   7   0   0   0   1  -1  -1   0.00065610000       0.88843230000
```

For Path No#= 11.

0	-1	-1	0	-1	2	1	0	0	0.00656100000	0.89499330000
0	2	6	0	10	0	1	0	0	0.00005904900	0.89505234900

For Path No#= 12.

6	0	0	0	-1	0	-1	-1	-1	0.06561000000	0.96066234900

For Path No#= 13.

1	0	0	0	-1	12	0	-1	-1	0.00656100000	0.96722334900

For Path No#= 14.

7	0	0	12	0	0	-1	-1	-1	0.00656100000	0.97378434900

For Path No#= 15.

8	0	0	13	0	14	0	-1	-1	0.00065610000	0.97444044900

For Path No#= 16.

9	0	0	13	15	0	0	-1	-1	0.00065610000	0.97509654900

For Path No#= 17.

10	0	14	0	0	0	-1	-1	-1	0.00656100000	0.98165754900

For Path No#= 18.

4	0	15	0	0	17	0	-1	-1	0.00065610000	0.98231364900

For Path No#= 19.

5	0	16	0	18	0	0	-1	-1	0.00065610000	0.98296974900

For Path No#= 20.

0	0	-1	11	0	3	4	0	0	0.00059049000	0.98356023900

For Path No#= 21.

0	0	-1	11	20	0	5	0	0	0.00059049000	0.98415072900

For Path No#= 22.

0	20	0	11	0	7	8	0	0	0.00005904900	0.98420977800

For Path No#= 23.

----

  0 21   0 11 22   0   9   0   0   0.00005904900   0.98426882700

For Path No#= 24.

----

  11   0   0   0   -1 12 13   0   0   0.00059049000   0.98485931700

For Path No#= 25.

----

  22   0   0 24   0 14 15   0   0   0.00005904900   0.98491836600

For Path No#= 26.

----

  23   0   0 24 25   0 16   0   0   0.00005904900   0.98497741500

For Path No#= 27.

----

  20   0 25   0   0 17 18   0   0   0.00005904900   0.98503646400

For Path No#= 28.

----

  21   0 26   0 27   0 19   0   0   0.00005904900   0.98509551300

SystemRel =0.98509551300

total disjoint paths= 29

execution time =0.44000000000

Exercises

5.1.   Given the probabilistic graph G shown in Figure Ex. 5.1, (nodes are perfectly reliable). Find the terminal pair (s, f) reliability expression.

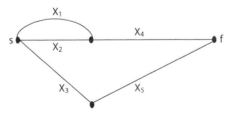

Figure Ex. 5.1 A network graph.

5.2.   Figure Ex. 5.2, shows the graph representing the ARPA network configuration in 1971. List all respective minimal paths for this network to obtain the terminal pair (S, T) and global reliability expression. Obtain the reliability (unreliability) of the network by assuming each link's reliability as 0.9.

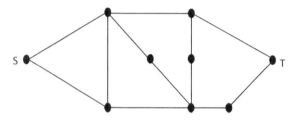

Figure Ex. 5.2 ARPA network configuration in 1971.

5.3.   Find minimal pathsets and minimal cutsets for the networks shown below, and obtain the terminal pair (S, T) reliability (unreliability) expression considering each link has equal probability of success equal to 0.9.

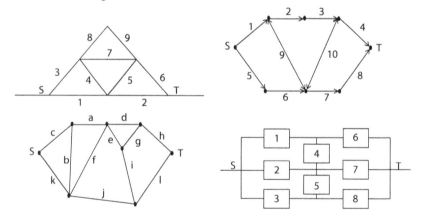

5.4.   Consider the directed graph G, shown in Figure Ex. 5.3, enumerate all minimal path sets, cutsets through visual inspection and obtain terminal reliability (unreliability) expression.

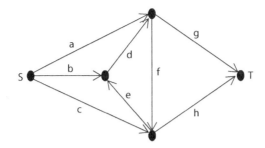

Figure Ex. 5.3 A directed graph G.

5.5.   For the network shown in Fig. Ex. 5.4, obtain the terminal reliability expression for (S,T) pair using Factoring theorem, verify the result using SDP approach using pathsets and cutsets.

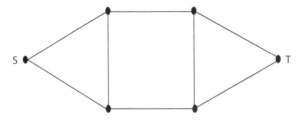

Figure Ex. 5.4 An example network.

5.6.   Plot the curve for p 0.1:0.99 for terminal and g-terminal reliability for the Figure 5.1 (a) and Figure 5.1 (b) and comment.

References

Abraham, J.A., 1979. An Improved Algorithm for Network Reliability. *IEEE Transaction on Reliability,* Vol. R-28(1), pp.58–61.

Aggarwal, K.K., Misra, K.B. & Gupta, J.S., 1975a. A fast Algorithm for Reliability Evaluation. *IEEE Transaction on Reliability,* Vol. R-24(1), pp.83–85.

Aggarwal, K.K., Misra, K.B. & Gupta, J.S., 1975b. A Simple Method for Reliability Evaluation of a Communication System. *IEEE Transactions on Communication,* Vol. COM 23(2), pp.563–566.

Chaturvedi, S.K., 2002. *Reliability Evaluation of Large and Complex System.* Ph.D. Thesis. India: IIT Kharagpur(WB).

Chaturvedi, S.K. & Misra, K.B., 2002. A Hybrid Method to Evaluate Reliability of Complex Networks. *International Journal of Quality and Reliability Management*, Vol. 19(8/9), pp.1098–1112.

Chaturvedi, S.K. & MIsra, K.B., 2002. An Efficient Multi-Variable Inversion Algorithm for Reliability Evaluation of Complex Systems using Path sets. *International Journal of Reliability, Quality and Safety Engineering*, Vol. 9(3), pp.237–259.

Grnarov, A., Kleinrock, L. & Gerla, M., 1979. A New Algorithm for Network Reliability Computation. *in Proc. of Computer Networking Symposium*, pp.17–20.

Hariri, S. & Raghvendara, C.S., 1987. SYREL: A symbolic Reliability Algorithm based on Path Cut Sets Method. *IEEE Transaction on Computers*, Vol C-36(10), pp.1224–1232.

Heidtmann, K. D., 1989. Smaller Sums of Disjoint Products by Sub Product Inversion. *IEEE Transaction on Reliability*, Vol. R-38(3), pp.305–311.

Luo, T. & Trivedi, K.S., 1998. An Improved Algorithm for Coherent Systems Reliability. *IEEE Transaction on Reliability*, Vol R-47(1), pp.73–78.

Mishra, R., 2009. *Minimal Cutset based Evaluation of Reliability Measures*. Ph.D. Thesis. India: IIT Kharagpur (WB).

Mishra, R., Saifi, M. A. & Chaturvedi, S. K., 2016. Enumeration of Minimal Cutsets for Directed Networks with Comparative Reliability Study for Paths and Cuts. *Quality and Reliability Engineering International*, Vol.32(2), pp.555–65. DOI: 10.1002/qre.1772.

Rai, S. & Aggarwal, K.K., 1978. An Efficient Method for Reliability Evaluation of General Networks. *IEEE Transactions on Reliability*, Vol R-27(3), pp.206–211.

Rath, D. & Soman, K.P., 1993. A simple Method for Generating k - Trees of a Network. *Microelectronics and Reliability*, Vol 33(9), pp.1241–1244.

Samad, M.A., 1987. An Efficient Method for Terminal and Multiterminal Path Set Enumeration. *Microelectronics & Reliability*, Vol 27(3), pp.443–446.

Soh, S. & Rai, S., 1991. CAREL: Computer Aided Reliability Evaluator for Distributed Computing Networks. *IEEE Transaction on parallel and Distributed Systems*, Vol.2(2), pp.199–213.

Veeraraghavan & Trivedi, K.S., Aug 1991. An Improved Algorithm for the Symbolic Reliability Analysis of Networks. *IEEE Transactions on Reliability*, Vol. 40(3), pp.347–358.

6

Unified Framework and Capacitated Network Reliability

In the design of communication networks, reliability has emerged as an important parameter due to the fact that failure of these networks affects its user adversely. The interest in the area of reliability evaluation is quite evident from numerous formulations of network reliability problems and articles appearing in the literature for the past couple of decades. This has resulted in the evaluation of various methodologies, techniques and algorithms to tackle these problems in an efficient and effective manner.

Briefly speaking, the *two*-terminal, *k*-terminal, and *g*-terminal reliability analysis techniques for general reliability structures include serial-reduction/parallel-combination, event-space enumeration, cutset/pathset unionizations, and pivotal decomposition using keystone components etcetera. Event-space enumeration is a sure-fire method but the enumerative efforts are excessive even for a small structure. An extensive work has been done for determining the network reliability measures, viz., *two*-, *g*-, and *k*-terminal reliability. This chapter provides a minimal cutset based unified framework to evaluate 2-,*g*-, and k-terminal reliability using MVI-SDP approach (Mishra & Chaturvedi, 2009).

6.1 The Unified Framework

In earlier Chapters, the methodology and usefulness of the MVI-SDP approach have been demonstrated to obtain reliability expression and its numerical value in a straight forward manner. However, the expression and inference rendered by the technique depends on the type of input provided to any SDP algorithm. Basically, the SDP technique is used to provide disjoint form of the terms (success or failure) appearing on its input. This is one of the biggest advantages that have been exploited to propose a common framework by using a suitable SDP algorithm with a single algorithm of enumerating different types of terms (already described in Chapter 4 and 5) suitable for a desired reliability measure. Summarily, Figure 5.1 depicts the majority of the methodologies adopted for applying the SDP techniques.

Clearly, the key issues in applying the approach are network representation (simple the better), enumeration of all possibilities of connectivity among a specified sets of nodes (depending on the reliability measures, viz., 2-, k-, or g- terminal) and making these possibilities disjoint with each other to form the reliability expression. Although, from spanning trees, one can generate pathsets or k-trees (Rath & Soman, 1993), but for a given network, processing of a large number of spanning trees to obtain pathsets and k-trees is so time consuming that researchers resorted to several specific algorithms rather than a single one.

The idea of the unified approach is depicted in Figure 6.2, where a single algorithm provides all types of minimal cutsets, which are used to evaluate respective reliability measures using MVI-SDP techniques. Note that

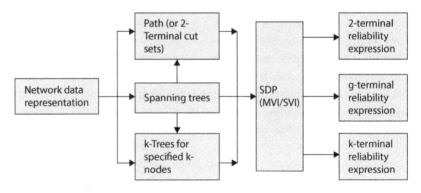

Figure 6.1 A scheme for evaluating reliability measures using SDP approach.

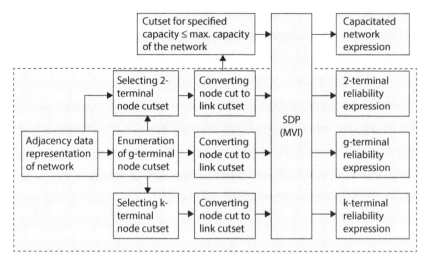

Figure 6.2 An alternative scheme for evaluating network reliability measures using SDP approach.

from the same framework 2-terminal capacitated reliability can also be obtained, which is discussed in next section of this Chapter.

6.2   Capacitated Reliability Measure: An Introduction

In earlier Chapters, it has been stated that a system can be modelled as a probabilistic graph G (V, E), which consists of a set of V nodes and a set E of links, directed or undirected depending upon the corresponding links being one-way (or two-way). Various measures for the reliability index for such networks have been proposed by (Colbourn, 1987). The most common quantitative index in reliability analysis of such system is 's-f reliability'. However, the assumption that the network can always carry the desired amount of information between (s, f) pairs of nodes whenever a connectivity exist (or the links capacities are large enough to sustain the transmission of any size) is unrealistic and economically unjustifiable in the design and analysis of such networks as the link capacity is a function of cost and definitely limited. Each link of the network can have different capacity and is required to transmit a specified amount of flow from source to the terminal node.

The reliability of such capacity constrained network can be defined as *the probability that the network has capable of carrying at least, a minimum* *specified capacity, (W_{min}), between (s, f) pair of nodes.* This definition can also be extended to other flow networks such as power distribution network, transportation network or a water supply network. Such performance index is also referred as *capacity related reliability* (CRR) (Soh & Rai, 1991).

The efficient methodologies in vogue use a priori information of either minimal path sets or cutsets of the network. The CRR computation is accomplished in two steps, *viz.*,

    i. Enumerate all the valid and irredundant sub-graphs (success or failure) of the networks, *i.e.* irredundant composite path (CP) from minimal pathsets or subset cut groups (SCG) from the minimal cutsets of the network. These sub-graphs formed due to a CP (or Removal of a SCG from the original graph) would either allow (or obstruct) the desired amount of information flow, say, $W_{min,}$ through the network.

    ii. Application of any technique such as sum of the disjoint product (SVI or MVI) to obtain the mutually exclusive terms of CP or SCG thereafter to obtain CRR or unreliability expression.

Efficient approaches do exist for the second step to obtain the mutually disjoint terms; however, the first step is still in open area of research and has attracted much attention in the recent past. The main thrusts in these methods have been on the efficient enumeration of success (or failure) sub networks in terms of the nodes and branches of the network for a desired capacity of flow. From this information, these methods obtain disjoint sets of these terms by employing well-established *Sum-of-Disjoint-Product* (SDP) techniques thereafter. The greatest advantage of this approach is that the disjoint terms so obtained would have a one-to-one correspondence with the reliability (unreliability) expression.

As noted in earlier Chapters that in most practical system, the number of minimal cutsets is much smaller than the number of minimal pathsets. It would be beneficial to address the CRR evaluation based on minimal cutsets rather than minimal pathsets with regards to computational efforts and memory requirements. Additionally, it is easier to handle a single minimal cutset at a time rather than handle two or more pathsets at a time to form a composite path (CP). Therefore, this Chapter focuses to enumerate irredundant subsets of minimal cutsets (SCG) of a communication network having heterogeneous link capacities, each of which is capable of blocking a flow of specified value, W_{min}, and is first step in CRR evaluation by using SDP techniques (Chaturvedi, 2007). The algorithm described in this Chapter generates the irredundant SCG that can be fed as input to any SDP based reliability evaluation algorithm discussed in earlier Chapters to obtain the CRR. The generation of such terms requires a priori knowledge of minimal cutsets arranged in order of increasing order of their flow blocking capacity and within the same value of blocking-capacity, a lexicographic ordering. The ordering scheme not only helps in reducing effort in enumerations but also help eliminates the internal/external redundancies through simple validity checks by proposing two equations. Besides, we describe a subset-generating scheme, starting from a certain order onwards to aid the generation of SCG process. This scheme is being used to generate next higher order subsets of a cut from the unqualified SCG, if any, to reduce the number of subsets enumerations.

The technique (Chaturvedi, 2007) explained in this Chapter is applied to several complex networks and a comparison with respect to the number of subsets generation, number of external/internal redundant subsets removal in obtaining irredundant SCG with recent algorithms are provided to show computational efforts and thus a better performance of the approach than the existing ones. Some of the definitions useful to understand the approach for flow networks for a specified W_{min} are provided here under:

6.2.1   Some Related Definitions

6.2.1.1   Minimal Cutset and Subset Cut Group

Minimal cutset for a flow network is a set of links of the network, which would obstruct the (s, f) connectivity and would not allow any amount of flow from source to destination whereas the minimal subset cut group (SCG) is a set of links of the network that would allow (s, f) connectivity of the network on the removal of links contained in it but the sub-network will not be able to transmit a specified amount of flow, *i.e.*, it would block the desired flow through the network despite the network being (s, f) connected.

6.2.1.2   External Redundant Subset Cut Group

A subset of a minimal cut is said to be external redundant SCG if has already been formed by some earlier minimal cutset (s) or its subset cut group.

6.2.1.3   Internal Redundant Subset Cut Group

A higher order subset of a minimal cutset is said to be internal redundant SCG if its lower order subsets would also capable of blocking a required amount of flow through the network.

6.2.1.4   Invalid Cut Set Cut Group

The SCG would be called as invalid one, if there exist some or no SCG of a minimal cutset that would be capable of obstructing the desired amount of flow through the network, those SCG would be called as invalid SCG.

6.2.1.5   Description of the Algorithm

The approach first constructs a cut-matrix from the minimal cut information from the minimal cutsets arranged in increasing order of their cut capacity. The number of rows of this matrix will be equal to the number of minimal cutsets and number of columns would be the total number of links present in the network under study. It then detects single-link SCG, if any, from this cut matrix. This single-link SCG is removed from further consideration as any supersets of single-link SCG will be a redundant SCG. Then, for remaining links contained in each cutset, it is determined that whether generation of subsets of the cut (SCG) is required? If so, then what order onwards to block the specified amount of flow, W_{min}?

To answer the above questions, an enumeration scheme that enumerates a particular order of subsets from a given set is provided. And two simple equations, which operate on the cut-matrix to check the validity of a cutset (as SCG (as a whole) or it needs subsets enumerations and of what order onwards?) are devised. These two equations are further applied to validate the irredundant SCG, redundant SCG or invalid SCG. The end product of algorithm is irredundant SCG devoid of any redundancy check overheads by which most of the existing algorithm suffer. In the next section, entire approach has been presented with an example.

6.3   Algorithm Description

In the following section, we present some of the preliminaries forming the building blocks of the approach by utilizing the following information on the network system, *viz.*, 's-f' minimal cutsets, link-capacities, minimum specified carrying capacity of the network; and cut capacities and maximum carrying capacity of the network from the cut information. Let the cutset-matrix, be A and its cut-capacity vector (as a sum of each link capacity contained in a particular cut) for each cutset be, CA.

6.3.1 Equations: The idea

For a specified flow, W_{min}, a minimal cut of the network may itself be a SCG or its subsets would form SCG. There could be three possibilities for a SCG *i.e.*, (i) it can block the desired flow, W_{min} or (ii) it can be a redundant one (external/internal) or (iii) it cannot block the flow at all (invalid). The equation to compute the capacity of the network on removal of some links contained in a SCG (or cutset as whole) with a capability of removing external redundancy is based on the following idea:

For any i^{th} minimal cut set, ordered in their respective flow-capacity and lexicography, a SCG of this cutset would either keep the maximum carrying capacity of the network intact or it would decrease the capacity to a certain lower level less than the maximum carrying capacity of the network, *i.e.,* to the current flow-capacity of the network, N_s, on removal of such links in SCG from the network can be computed by,

$$N_s = \min[CX] \tag{6.1}$$

Where,

$CX = CA_j - f_k \ \forall j \leq i$
CA_j = Capacity of jth element of CA
f_k = Sum of capacities of links contained in k^{th} SCG (or cut) of certain order.

Equation (6.1) not only provides the exact network flow capacity on removing a set of links from the network whose capacity-sum is in f_k but also helps in identifying external or both external/internal redundant SCG. However, working on several examples, it does fail to locate the existence of SCG that would be only internally redundant.

The following equation solves the problem:

A SCG is said to be internally redundant, if any link contained in it has its,

$$Capacity\ value < \Delta,\ where\ \Delta = W_{min} - N_s \tag{6.2}$$

The value of Δ provides the margin by which the network capacity can be improved through the reinsertions of link(s) from a SCG (*note that the SCG is nothing but link(s) taken out from the network under consideration*). And if any reinsertion of link(s) of this set cannot improve the capacity of the network up to, W_{min}, implying that this link(s) in this set is redundant and the SCG under consideration is an internally redundant SCG.

6.3.2 Is Cut itself a SCG or does it need its Subsets Enumeration?

Equations (6.1) and (6.2) are utilized to ascertain whether a cut itself is a SCG or its subsets would form SCG. Obviously, any i^{th} minimal cut would produce a current network flow capacity, N_s, equal to zero occurring only at i^{th} position in Equation (6.1). Thus, $\Delta = W_{min}$. Now, if no link in the cut has a capacity $< \Delta$ would imply that the cut itself is a SCG. However, if the cut has some link(s) capacities $\leq \Delta$, then there could be a certain sets of links of this cut, which are capable of blocking a flow of W_{min}. Thus, subsets of this cut will have to be formed to determine those SCG.

Other possibilities, which will force to enumerate subsets of a cut, could be:

i. *When $N_s \neq 0$ ($< W_{min}$) but occur only at i^{th} position.*
This situation occurs when the first order SCG from a cut have already been identified and removed. However, this situation can be dealt with, in a similar manner as is done for the cut itself and is explained in the beginning of this section.

ii. *When $N_s \neq 0$ ($< W_{min}$) occurs at i^{th} and at j^{th} position or only at j^{th} position(s)($j < i$)*
This situation occurs when the first order SCG from a cut i ($i > 1$) and/or some of
the SCG have already been identified and removed, however, these SCG are externally redundant. Besides, $N_s < W_{min}$, may occur at more than one positions.

6.3.3 What Initial Order?

Once it is established that the subsets of a minimal cutset are to be formed, the next task is to determine from what order of subsets to be enumerated initially to reduce the number of enumerations and validity checks? The situation arises when a minimal cutset has some link(s) capacity $\leq \Delta$ or situation (ii) as stated above. This is dealt with, in the following manner:

For an ith cut:

   i. Arrange the capacities of links contained in the cut in decreasing order.
  ii. Calculate, $M = CA_i - W_{min}$
 iii. Determine the minimum number of links needed to provide capacity value $> M$, by summing their individual capacities.

The number of links so determined would be the initial order of SCG to be enumerated, which would be checked for valid/invalid/redundant SCG. The remaining SCG, if any, are then carried over for next higher order SCG enumerations.

The following examples are used to explain the above points. Consider a network shown in Figure 6.3 with its minimal cutsets and cut capacities as given in Table 6.1. The link capacities are shown in brackets along with their respective link number. Note that the minimal cutsets are arranged in order of their capacity and lexicography.

Example 6.1: Consider the 3rd cut with its link capacities shown in brackets, {1 (10), 2(9)}, CA3 = 19. Let Wmin = 6. Applying Equation (6.1), Ns = min [15, 18, 0] = 0, occurs at position, i = 3. From Equation (6.2), $\Delta = 6$. Since there is no link with capacity $\leq \Delta$, {1, 2} is itself an irredundant SCG.

Consider 4th cut, {9(9), 10(5), 11(6)}, CA_4 = 20. Applying Equation (6.1) and (6.2); it is seen that provide, $N_s = min$ [15, 12, 19, 0] = 0 occurs at position $i = 4$ and $\Delta = 6$. Since there are links with capacity $\leq \Delta$, SCG will have to be formed.

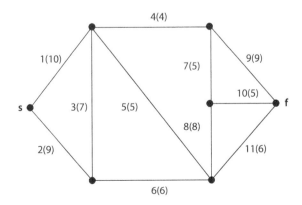

Figure 6.3 Network of 6 Nodes and 11 Links with C_{max} = 15 units.

Table 6.1 Minimal cutsets for the network of Figure 6.3.

Minimal cutset	Cut capacity (Σ)
$C_1 = \{4, 5, 6\}$	15
$C_2 = \{4, 8, 11\}$	18
$C_3 = \{1, 2\}$	19
$C_4 = \{9, 10, 11\}$	20
$C_5 = \{4, 7, 10, 11\}$	20
$C_6 = \{1, 3, 6\}$	23
$C_7 = \{2, 3, 4, 5\}$	25
$C_8 = \{5, 6, 7, 9\}$	25
$C_9 = \{7, 8, 9, 11\}$	28
$C_{10} = \{5, 6, 8, 9, 10\}$	33
$C_{11} = \{2, 3, 5, 7, 9\}$	35
$C_{12} = \{1, 3, 5, 8, 11\}$	36
$C_{13} = \{1, 3, 5, 7, 10, 11\}$	38
$C_{14} = \{2, 3, 5, 8, 9, 10\}$	43

Example 6.2 case (i): Consider the 8th cut $\{5\ (5), 6\ (6), 7\ (5), 9(9)\}$, $CA_8 = 25$. Let $W_{min} = 10$. This cut had a first order SCG $\{6\}$. The remaining links in the cut are $\{5, 7, 9\}$. Applying Equation (5.1), *i.e.*, $N_s = min\ \{10, 18, 19, 11, 15, 23, 20, 6\} = 6$ at position $i = 8$. From Equation (5.2), $\Delta = 4$. Since there is no link $\leq \Delta$, $\{5, 7, 9\}$ is itself a SCG.

Example 6.3 case (ii): Consider 12th cut, which had a first order SCG $\{1\}$, i.e., $\{3(7), 5(5), 8(8), 11(6)\}$, $CA_{12} = 36$ and $W_{min} = 10$. Applying Equation (6.1) yields, $N_s = 4$ occurs at $i = 2\ (\neq 12)$. So, $M = 26$ and link capacity are arranged in decreasing order as $\{8, 7, 6, 5\}$. All four links are failed to provide capacity > 26 and so no SCG generation is performed.

Consider 5th cut, $\{4(4), 7\ (5), 10(5), 11(6)\}$. For $W_{min} = 10$, $N_s = min\ \{11, 8, 19, 9, 0\} = 0$ and $N_s < W_{min}$ occurs at three positions, viz., at $\{2, 4, 5\}$. Therefore, after calculating $M = 10$ and arranging the capacities in decreasing order $\{6, 5, 5, 4\}$, we find that the SCG of minimum order two are to be generated and if required, then higher order.

For $W_{min} = 6$, there is a single position at which $N_s < W_{min}$ and $M = 14$. Thus, SCG of third order only are to be generated.

Clearly, this method greatly reduces the number of subsets generation. The following example illustrates and proves points.

Example 6.4: Consider $i = 11^{th}$ minimal cutset $\{2\ (9), 3\ (7), 5\ (5), 7\ (5), 9\ (9)\}$ of the network. For, $W_{min} = 10$ units, Equation (5.1) and (5.2) yields $Ns < W_{min}$ at three positions, viz., at $\{7, 8, 11\}$ with $M = 25$. By arranging the capacities of links in decreasing order as {9, 9, 7, 5, 5}, the minimum number of links needed to get capacity $> M$ is four. It entails the SCGs to be generated of order four from this 5th order cutset, *viz.*, {2, 3, 5, 7}, {2, 3, 5, 9}, {2, 3, 7, 9}, (2, 5, 7, 9 and {3, 5, 7, 9}, respectively. Consider first SCG, {2, 3, 5, 7} for which, $N_s = 4$ occurs at 7th position ($< i$). This clearly implies that the SCG is redundant. Validating other SCG in this manner, it is found that all SCG are redundant.

In the above examples, the number of SCG of order two and higher would be 26, *i.e.*, (2^5-6), had we started generating SCG of second order onwards. However, only five SCG are generated. Obviously, the number of SCG and their order would further reduce if the valid SCG were obtained at the initial stages. In fact, this happens as the desired capacity, W_{min}, increases from some minimum value to the maximum carrying capacity of the network.

6.3.4   Efficient Enumeration of Particular Order SCG of a Minimal Cut

Once we establish the order of enumeration, we can generate SCG of a particular order in the following manner. Let us represent a 6th order cut with a set of ordered numbers, $S_6 = \{1, 2, 3, 4, 5, 6\}$ to represent the position of a link in the cut. Let order of subsets generation required turns out to be the third order. Taking the last three terms of S_6 (equal to the order of enumeration needed) provides a term = {4, 5, 6}. From this term, all other terms are generated by decreasing each term in a logical manner by noting that the first term in this set could decrease up to 1, second up to 2 and third up to 3. In other words, the last term of third order in the list would be {1, 2, 3}. Table 6.2 explains the enumeration scheme with remarks (a) and (b) at relevant points to write a computer program.

It may be noted that by following steps (a) and (b), SCG of any order can be generated. In implementation, a mapping is done, *i.e.*, a minimal cutsets say {1, 5, 7, 8, 13, 14} is mapped with a set {1, 2, 3, 4, 5, 6} Note that a term {2, 3, 4}, for example for a cut {1, 5, 7, 8, 13, 14}, should be interpreted a SCG {5, 7, 8}.

6.3.5   External or Both External/ Internal Redundancy Removal

In Equation (6.1) for the ith cutset, $N_s < W_{min}$, may occur at position(s) lesser than i^{th}. It implies that some SCG have already been encountered in the SCG of some other and already processed (such as SCG generation and

Table 6.2 Enumerating SCGs of a particular order from a set of numbers.

S. No.	SCGs	Remark
1.	{4, 5, 6}	(a) Decrease first digit up to 1
2.	{3, 5, 6}	
3.	{2, 5, 6}	
4.	{1, 5, 6}	(b) First digit cannot be decreased further. Decrease the next digit by one and replace all previous digit one less than this value keeping all other digits as they were.
5.	{3, 4, 6}	Repeat (a)
6.	{2, 4, 6}	
7.	{1, 4, 6}	Repeat (b)
8.	{2, 3, 6}	Repeat (a)
9.	{1, 3, 6}	Repeat (b)
10.	{1, 2, 6}	Repeat (b). Only third digit can be reduced.
11.	{3, 4, 5}	Repeat (a)
12.	{2, 4, 5}	
13.	{1, 4, 5}	Repeat (b)
14.	{2, 3, 5}	Repeat (a)
15.	{1, 3, 5}	Repeat (b)
16.	{1, 2, 5}	Repeat (b). Only third digit can be reduced.
17.	{2, 3, 4}	Repeat (a)
18.	{1, 3, 4}	Repeat (b)
19.	{1, 2, 4}	Repeat (b). Only third digit can be reduced.
20.	{1, 2, 3}	No digit can be reduced. Stop.

external or internal redundant check etc…) cut ($< i$). Thus, the SCG of a particular order of this i^{th} cut is generated. On these each SCG, we reapply Equation (6.1) and check, if $N_s < W_{min}$, occurs at a position(s) lesser than i^{th}, if it happens then the SCG would be externally redundant.

Example 6.5: Reconsidering $i = 11^{th}$ minimal cutset {2, 3, 5, 7, 9} of the network shown in Figure 6.3 and consider the following cases:

Case (i): Let us consider one of its SCG {2, 3, 5, 7} for $W_{min} = 10$. Equation (6.1) for this combination would be: $N_s = min$ {10, 18, 10, 20, 15, 16, 4, 15, 23, 28, 9} = 4 units and $N_s < W_{min}$ occurs at 7th and 11th positions rather than only at 11th position, $(< i, i.e., 7 < 11)$. This implies that although {2, 3, 5 7} is a SCG but it is a superset of SCG {2, 3} generated by 7th minimal cutset, {2, 3, 4, 5}, processed earlier and is therefore externally redundant. In fact, for the 7th minimal cutset, Equation (6.1) for the subset {2, 3} is min [15, 18, 10, 20, 20, 16, 9] = 9, and minimum occurs at 7th position, which provides {2, 3} as a valid SCG and this SCG is not used further to generate its third order SCG. Likewise, {2, 5, 7, 9} would be detected as a superset of a valid SCG {5, 7, 9} produced by 8th cut set earlier.

Case (ii): Consider 5th minimal cutset, {4, 7, 10, 11}, of the same network wherein after the test on this cut, it is found that SCG of order two onwards are required to be generated.

Let us consider the subset (SCG), {4, 7}, for which Equation (6.1) yields, min [11, 14, 19, 20, 11] = 11 > W_{min} (Not a valid SCG but possibly adding one or more link of the cut to this SCG might give a valid SCG. Thus it is be taken to generate next higher order combination). However, for its next order combination, {4, 7, 10} and {4, 7, 11}, Equation (6.1) yields:

min [11, 15, 19, 15, 6] = 6 (a valid SCG), and

min [11, 8, 19, 14, 5] = 5 (A redundant SCG).

In this case the current network flow capacity on removing links {4, 7, 11} would be 5 units (can be verified visually). However, $N_s < W_{min}$ has occurred at two positions. Therefore, this SCG is redundant. Basically, {4, 7, 11}⊇ {4, 11} or {7, 11}, which are valid and non-redundant SCG. In fact, it is a case of both external for {4, 11} and internal redundant for {7, 11} SCG detected by Equation (6.1) but can also be removed using Equation (6.2).

Similar, situation can occur on a tie between the minimums, *i.e.,* for a SCG, {10, 11}, min [15, 12, 19, 9, 9] = 9. Here again, the current network flow capacity would be 9 units. However, the set is not a valid SCG as $N_s < W_{min}$ has occurred at 4th position as well.

6.3.6   Internal Redundancy Removal

Let us again illustrate it through a suitable example by extending the cases.

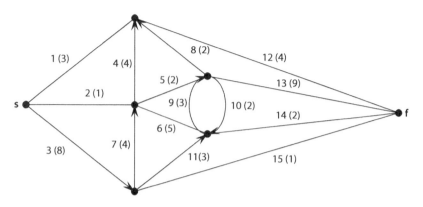

Figure 6.4 Network of 7 Nodes and 15 Links.

Case (iii): Consider the example in Figure 6.4 of (Example and Figure 2 in (Soh & Rai, 2005). Only, the network is reproduced for the sake of brevity. The maximum network flow capacity is 10 units and let the desired network capacity (W_{min}) be 4 units.

Consider SCG, {1, 2, 7, 11} of the third minimal cutset, {1, 2, 7, 11, 15} in the order of its blocking capacity with respective capacities of links as {3, 1, 4, 3, 1}. Applying Equation (6.1) yields, $N_s = min$ {10, 8, 1} = 1 < 4 units, which appears to be a non-redundant SCG.

However, capacity of link '2' < Δ (= 3) and even if link '2' is reinserted in the network could only raise the network capacity to 2 units, still less than W_{min}. So link 2's presence or absence does not matter for a specified W_{min} = 4. In fact, {1, 2, 7, 11}⊇ {1, 7, 11}, and {1, 7, 11} has already been detected as an irredundant SCG in an earlier iteration implying {1, 2, 7, 11} is an internally redundant SCG.

The foregoing paragraphs have explained the building blocks of the approach. Using the above observations and cases, one can easily write the various algorithmic steps to follow. The program available at www. scrivenerpublishing.com contains the implementation of the algorithm in Matlab(R).

6.4   The CRR Evaluation Algorithm

Steps:

1. *Cut Matrix:* Formulate cut matrix, *A* (of order *nC* by *L*), wherein rows corresponds to the various minimal cutsets

and columns indicate the links contained in that particular cutset. Besides, all the non-zero entries in a particular row (indicating the presence of links in that cutset) are replaced by the capacities of the individual links contained in the cutset, *i.e.*,

$$A_{ij} = \begin{cases} C_j; & \text{if } j^{th} \text{ branch having capacity } C_j \text{ contained in } i^{th} \text{ cutsets.} \\ 0; & \text{otherwise.} \end{cases}$$

2. *Cut-Capacity Vector*: Generate a column vector, *CA* (of order *nC*), which has it i^{th} element as the sum of all the non-zero entries in the ith row of cut matrix, *A*, *i.e.*,

$$CA_i = \sum_j C_{ij} \forall i = 1,2 \ldots nC$$

3. *Generating and Validating SCG*

   a. *First Order Minimal SCG*

   Scan the cut matrix column-wise. Locate the first non-zero entries, $C_{ij} \forall j = 1,2 \ldots L$, in each column and compute, $N_s = \min [CA_i - C_{ij}]$.
   If $N_s < W_{min}$ then link l_{ij} is a valid SCG. Make all column entries zero corresponding to link, l_{ij}.
   The next step generates higher order SCG and removes external/internal redundancies, if any, through validity check using Equations (6.1) & (6.2).

   b. *Higher Order Minimal SCG Generation and Redundancy Elimination*

   Select the rows sequentially ($i = 1, 2 \ldots nC$), which have more than one non-zero entries. Find the corresponding links to form a SCG$_i$. Apply Equations (6.1) on this SCG$_i$ to determine N_s and $N_s < W_{min}$ at how many position(s).

      i. $N_s < W_{min}$ occurs only at ith position. Determine if any link capacity in SCG$_i < \Delta$. If No, store SCG$_i$ and go to (b) to process next cut.
      If yes then go to (iii).
      ii. If $N_s < W_{min}$ occurs at less than at i^{th} position only or more than one positions. Go to (iii).

iii. Determine the order of SCG to enumerate and generate SCG of this order. If no order of SCG can be found valid, go to (b) to process next cut. Otherwise,

iv. For each SCG, compute N_s as,

$N_s = min [CX], nPos = [CX] < W_{min}$

$\Delta = W_{min} - N_s$

Where,

$$CX = CA_j - C_K \forall j \leq i$$

CA_j = Capacity of jth element of CA
C_k = Sum of capacities of links contained in k^{th} SCG of certain order.

v. External and Internal Redundancy Check

External

If $N_s < W_{min}$ and occurred at position i, check for internal redundancy.

If N_s has occurred at position (s) < i, then remove it from the list of combinations from further consideration.

Internal

If any link capacity in SCG < Δ, then it is an internal redundant SCG; remove it from further consideration.

Store and remove the qualified and redundant SCG.

For remaining SCG, if any, check

If order of SCG < order of the cut, then generate next higher order SCG and repeat the step from 3 b (iv). Else, repeat from step 3(b) for next cut.

6.5 A Complete Example

Consider the network shown in Figure 6.3. Obviously, the capacity of the network, C_{max}, is 15 units. Let W_{min} = 10 units, we apply each step of the algorithm on this network. The Cut-matrix, A, Cut-capacity vector and steps involved are shown side-by-side in Table 6.3.

Therefore, for specified minimum flow requirement, W_{min} = 10 units, the 14 non-redundant valid SCG are: {{1}, {6}, {4, 5}, {4, 8}, {4,11}, {8, 11},

Table 6.3 Algorithmic steps to solve illustrative example.

Step #1.	Step #2.

$$
A =
\begin{bmatrix}
0 & 0 & 0 & 4 & 5 & 6 & 0 & 0 & 0 & 0 \\
0 & 0 & 0 & 4 & 0 & 0 & 0 & 8 & 0 & 6 \\
10 & 9 & 0 & 0 & 0 & 0 & 0 & 0 & 0 & 0 \\
0 & 0 & 0 & 0 & 0 & 0 & 0 & 0 & 9 & 6 \\
0 & 0 & 4 & 0 & 0 & 0 & 5 & 0 & 5 & 6 \\
10 & 0 & 7 & 0 & 6 & 0 & 0 & 0 & 0 & 0 \\
0 & 9 & 7 & 4 & 5 & 0 & 0 & 0 & 0 & 0 \\
0 & 0 & 0 & 5 & 6 & 0 & 0 & 9 & 0 & 6 \\
0 & 0 & 0 & 0 & 0 & 5 & 8 & 9 & 0 & 0 \\
0 & 0 & 0 & 5 & 6 & 0 & 0 & 9 & 0 & 0 \\
0 & 9 & 7 & 5 & 0 & 5 & 8 & 0 & 0 & 0 \\
10 & 0 & 7 & 0 & 0 & 0 & 0 & 0 & 0 & 6 \\
10 & 0 & 7 & 5 & 0 & 0 & 0 & 5 & 5 & 6 \\
0 & 9 & 7 & 5 & 0 & 8 & 9 & 5 & 5 & 0
\end{bmatrix}
$$

$$
CA =
\begin{bmatrix}
15 \\
18 \\
19 \\
20 \\
20 \\
23 \\
25 \\
25 \\
28 \\
33 \\
35 \\
36 \\
38 \\
43
\end{bmatrix}
$$

(Continued)

Table 6.3 Cont.

Step #3. a
Only links, 1 and 6, gives network-flow-capacity = 9, *i.e.*, less than W_{min}. Thus, these two links form single order SCG, viz.,

$$A = \begin{bmatrix}
0 & 0 & 0 & 4 & 5 & 0 & 0 & 0 & 0 & 0 & 0 & 0 \\
0 & 0 & 0 & 4 & 0 & 0 & 0 & 0 & 8 & 0 & 0 & 6 \\
0 & 9 & 0 & 0 & 0 & 0 & 0 & 0 & 0 & 0 & 0 & 0 \\
0 & 0 & 0 & 0 & 0 & 0 & 0 & 0 & 0 & 9 & 5 & 6 \\
0 & 0 & 4 & 0 & 0 & 5 & 0 & 0 & 0 & 0 & 5 & 6 \\
0 & 7 & 0 & 0 & 0 & 0 & 0 & 0 & 0 & 0 & 0 & 0 \\
9 & 7 & 4 & 5 & 0 & 5 & 0 & 9 & 0 & 0 & 0 & 0 \\
0 & 0 & 0 & 0 & 5 & 0 & 5 & 0 & 9 & 0 & 0 & 0 \\
0 & 0 & 0 & 0 & 0 & 0 & 0 & 5 & 8 & 9 & 0 & 6 \\
0 & 0 & 0 & 5 & 0 & 5 & 0 & 0 & 8 & 9 & 5 & 0 \\
0 & 9 & 7 & 0 & 0 & 5 & 0 & 9 & 0 & 9 & 0 & 0 \\
0 & 0 & 0 & 0 & 5 & 0 & 5 & 0 & 8 & 0 & 0 & 6 \\
\end{bmatrix}$$

Step #3. b
Row #1: SCG {4, 5}
$N_s = Min [6] = 6 < 10 \rightarrow \{4, 5\}$ at position 1. (Entire SCG check).
$\Delta = 4$, No link capacity $< \Delta \rightarrow$ a valid SCG.
Row #2: SCG {4, 8, 11}
$N_s = Min [11, 0]$ at position 2. $\Delta = 10$. *Link(s) have capacity $< \Delta$ and M = 8, so second order SCG to be generated.*
SCG {{4, 8}, {4, 11}, {8, 11}}
$Min [11, 6] = 6 < 10 \rightarrow \{4, 8\}$ valid SCG.
$Min [11, 8] = 8 < 10 \rightarrow \{4, 11\}$ valid SCG.
$Min [15, 4] = 4 < 10 \rightarrow \{8, 11\}$ valid SCG. No further SCG.

Row #3: No SCG.
Row #4: Similar to Row 2, {{9, 10}, {9, 11}, {10, 11}} → all valid SCG
Row #5: SCG {4, 7, 10, 11}
$N_s = Min$ [11, **8**, 19, **9**, **0**] = 0, and $Ns < W_{min}$ occurs at three position, [2, 4, 5]. M =10, Second order SCG are to be generated.
SCG are {{**4, 7**}, {**4, 10**}, {**4, 11**}, {**7, 10**}, {**7, 11**}, {**10, 11**}}
{4, 11}→ min [11, **8**, 19, 14, 10} (redundant)
{7, 11}→ min [15, 12, 19, 14, **9**] (valid)
{10, 11}→ min [15, 12, 19, **9**, **9**] (redundant)
SCG {{**4, 7**}, {4, 10}, {**7, 10**}} used to form next order. {4, 7, 10}
→ min [11, 14, 19, 15, **6**], Δ=4. No link capacity < Δ a valid SCG.

{4, 7, 11} → min [15, 11, **8**, 19, 14, **5**] (redundant). Similarly, {4, 10, 11} and {7, 10, 11} (redundant)
Row #6: No combinations.
Proceeding in the similar manner and using Equations (6.1) & (6.2) the following non-redundant cut group are obtained:
Row #7: {2, 3} (second and third order SCG
Row # 8: {5, 7, 9} (No SCG generation)
Row # 9: {7, 8, 9} (Third order generation)
Row #10–11: Generates all redundant 4th order SCG. **Row 12–13:** None. **Row 14:** Generates all redundant 5th order SCG.

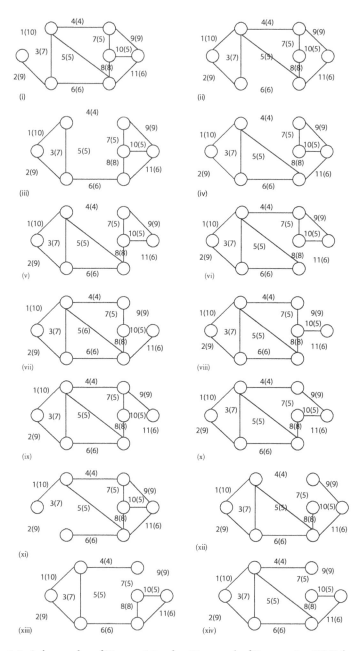

Figure 6.5 Sub-graphs of Figure 6.3 after Removal of Respective SCG for $W_{min} = 10$ units

{9, 10}, {9, 11}, {10, 11}, {7, 11}, {2, 3}, {4, 7, 10}, {5, 7, 9}, {7, 8, 9} out of 39 SCG generated by the algorithm. The resultant SCG of the network of Figure 6.3 have been shown in Figure 6.5 to show that removal of links contained in any SCG would render the network that cannot carry a load of 10 units, despite being *(s, t)* connected.

The valid SCG so obtained are used to evaluate the CRR expression and its value for the network using any of SDP approaches (Single or Multi variable), as mentioned earlier. The program available at www.scriven-erpublishing.com contains the *Matlab®* code from SCG enumeration to reliability.

The program can be executed as:

>> flwprg
minmalCutDataFile(withpath)?:fig6.3TCutData.m
Output Data File:fig6.3SCG10Units.m

The SCG generated and stored in the file *fig6.3SCG10Units.m* can be fed to MVI/SVI programs to evaluate the capacitated reliability of the flow constrained network graph.

6.6   Experimental Results, Comparison and Discussion

Since, the key issue in CRR problem lying in generation of valid SCG from subsets of cuts, author makes the performance comparison with reference to this with the recent approaches of (Soh & Rai, 2005) (Soh et al., 2006) based on-how the valid SCG are generated and from how many subsets. To make a comparison among the approaches, the following comparative statements can be made:

1. The approach takes an entire cut and tests whether it is a valid SCG or its subsets of a particular order onwards to be enumerated. However, A1 and SCE proposed by Soh and Rai generate the subsets from the links (defined as *small links* in their paper), if any. The difference between the generation schemes used in (Soh & Rai, 2005) (Soh et al., 2006) lies in generating subsets from lower to higher (A1) and higher to lower orders (SCE). Both the schemes thus suffer from overheads of extracting small links from a cut, a test for

generating/not generating higher (lower) order SC, super-sets extraction and removal of redundant subsets.

2. In the proposed approach, obtaining subsets is a single-step process utilizing Equations (6.1) and (6.2), respectively. The subsets themselves are SCG containing valid/invalid/redundant SCG. In their approach SCG are obtained by the *set-theoretic difference* operation performed on the cut by each of its subsets. In the process many internal/external redundant terms gets generated.

3. The proposed approach obtains valid SCG using Equations (6.1) , (6.2) and cut matrix, which removes external/internal redundancies and redundant cuts of the network in a straightforward manner. In their approach the internal redundancies are removed from SC (SCG) to obtain minimal subset cut (MSC) at the time of processing i^{th} cut. When MSC for all cuts have been generated, the external redundancies are removed to obtain network minimal subset cut (NMSC or valid SCG).

4. Algorithms proposed by (Soh & Rai, 2005) (Soh et al., 2006) employed a theorem (T3) to remove the redundant cutsets and to reduce the number of subsets generations. It means that whenever a cut is taken for processing, it has to be compared with all NMSC obtained from earlier processing of cuts or a valid NMSC will have to be compared for such cuts that have satisfied T3 earlier. Besides, there are situations where T3 does not provide any benefits, e.g., Network of Figure 7 and Network of Figure 9 for various values of W_{min} of (Soh & Rai, 2005). There is no way a priori to ascertain whether T3 would provide benefits or not, thus there remain overheads of applying T3.

To compare the performance of the algorithm, we provide a comparison of some networks, which are treated as complex in (Soh & Rai, 2005) (Soh et al., 2006) . The complex networks are shown in Figure 6.6 and Figure 6.7, respectively. The cutsets of these networks are 214 and 7376, respectively. The results for various W_{min} are also tabulated in Table 6.4 and Table 6.5 respectively Column#4 of the Tables shows whether T3 provides the benefits or not. A graphical representation of experimental results of the number of subsets enumerated by various algorithms (Columns#2,3 and 5 of Table 6.4 and Table 6.5) with varying W_{min} is also shown in Figure 6.8 and Figure 6.9 respectively, for visualizing the efficiency of the algorithm.

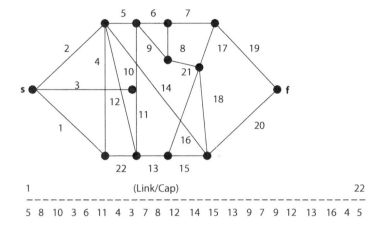

Figure 6.6 Network of 13 Nodes and 22 Links.

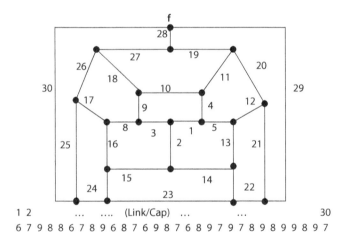

Figure 6.7 Network of 20 Nodes and 30 Links.

From the results provided (in bold) in Table 6.4 and Table 6.5, it can be well-observed that:

1. If the desired flow remaining less than the minimum capacity branch in the network, all the minimal cut sets would be valid cut groups. For these cases, there would not be any necessity of generating any subsets. It is the same conclusion that has been drawn by in (Soh & Rai, 2005) (Soh et al., 2006). However, the proposed algorithm outperforms both

Table 6.4 Results and comparison for the network in Figure 6.6.

W_{min}	Subsets by				Valid SCG
	A1	SCE	T3/Benefit?	By (Chaturvedi, 2007)	
1–3	0	0	–	0	214
4	213	175	Y/Y	1 246	230
5	388	245	Y/Y	1 480	218
6	731	390	Y/Y	1 637	294
7	1 085	620	Y/Y	3 127	298
8	1 842	1 044	Y/Y	4 753	287
9	2 986	1 555	Y/Y	2 411	190
10	5 971	2 756	Y/Y	2 667	246
11	7 880	3 900	Y/Y	1 359	171
12	10 060	5 039	Y/Y	1 707	143
13	17 354	8 462	Y/Y	2 201	173

Table 6.5 Results and comparison for the network in Figure 6.7.

W_{min}	Subsets by				Valid SCG
	A1	SCE	T3/ Benefit?	By (Chaturvedi, 2007)	
1–6	0	0	–	0	7 376
7	16 925	10 196	Y/Y	62 381	7 644
8	68 978	25 395	Y/Y	70 226	8 855
9	198 032	48 906	Y/Y	70 374	7 067
10–12	378 642	70 374	Y/Y	70 374	4 962
13	864 170	244 292	Y/N	223 371	4 675
14	1 114 879	331 881	Y/N	214 568	5 278
15	1 185 575	346 776	Y/N	222 601	4 794
16	1 197 592	3337 25	Y/N	131 241	2 184
17	1 198 806	321 063	Y/N	71 647	1 199
18	1 198 816	311 826	Y/N	51 634	782
19	1 513 832	474 411	Y/N	65 367	624
20	2 075 477	769 937	Y/N	96 971	647
21	2 466 397	967 941	Y/N	124 814	773
22	2 599 331	1 003 599	Y/N	71 171	479

A1 and SCE as the W_{min} approaches closer to the maximum capacity of the network.

2. At certain points onwards, algorithms A1 and SCE both generate more subsets of cuts even after taking the benefits of T3 in comparison to the proposed algorithm. Thus, T3 become overheads after a certain value of capacity requirement onwards.

3. Wherever T3 starts providing no benefit, the proposed algorithm generates much less number of subsets in comparison to both the algorithms A1 and SCE with T3 application becoming redundant.

4. As the network complexity increases, T3 does not provide much benefit. The proposed algorithm starts outperforming both A1 and SCE at an earlier stage and in a greater way.

5. From the foregoing points (3) and (4), it can be concluded that whenever network complexity increases or wherever T3 is not applicable, the proposed algorithm expected to perform better than algorithms of in (Soh & Rai, 2005) (Soh *et al.*, 2006).

Summarily, the method definitely efficient as it substantially reduces the number of subsets generations, removes the internal/external redundancies simultaneously rather than its removal after generating all cut groups. Equation (6.1) can also be used to provide the network capacity on removal of certain links from a cut set. Further, as the desired capacity approaches closer to the maximum capacity of the network, the number of subsets generation drastically decreases in comparison to A1 and SCE wherein there are polynomial rise in number of generated subsets.

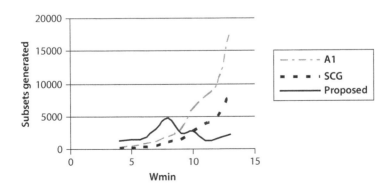

Figure 6.8 Comparison of subsets generated for Figure 6.4.

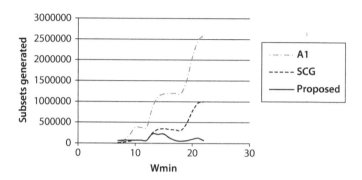

Figure 6.9 Comparison of subsets generated for Figure 6.5.

The exercises of this chapter is deliberately left blank to the ingenuity of the readers to formulate by taking the several network graphs discussed in earlier Chapters of this text.

References

Chaturvedi, S.K., 2007. Irredundant Subset Cut Genaeration to Compute Capacity Related Reliability. *International Journal of Performability Engineering*, Vol. 3(2), pp. 243–256.

Colbourn, C.J., 1987. *The combinatorics of Network Reliability*. New York: Oxford University Press.

Mishra, R. & Chaturvedi, S.K., 2009. A Cutsets based Unified Framework to Evaluate Network Reliability Measures. *IEEE Transaction on Reliability*, Vol. 56(4), pp. 658–666.

Rath, D. & Soman, K.P., 1993. A simple Method for Generating k - Trees of a Network. *Microelectronics and Reliability*, Vol 33(9), pp. 1241–1244.

Soh, S., Lim, K.Y. & Rai, S., 2006. Evaluating Communication Network Reliability with Heterogenous Link Capacities using Subset Enumeration. *International Journal of Performability Engineering*, Vol. 2(1), pp. 3–17.

Soh, S. & Rai, S., 1991. CAREL: Computer Aided Reliability Evaluator for Distributed Computing Networks. *IEEE Transaction on parallel and Distributed Systems*, Vol.2(2), pp. 199–213.

Soh, S. & Rai, S., 2005. An Efficient Cutset Approach for Evaluating Communication-Network Reliability with Heterogenous Link-Capacities. *IEEE Transactions on Reliability*, Vol. 54(1), pp. 133–144.

7

A LAN and Water Distribution Network: Case Studies

This chapter presents two case studies; viz., (i) a Local Area Network catering the research and social needs of IIT Kharagpur community at various levels and network existed during 2000–2006. Since then due to rapidly changing technology, both in terms of software and hardware in this area, several advancements have been made to this network. (ii) Water Distribution Networks taken from the literature and studied by (Kansal & Devi, 2007) (Mishra & Chaturvedi, 2009). Note that the analyses of these cases have been conducted based on the text presented in this book; therefore, we have omitted much of the details of analyses.

7.1   Case Study-I: IIT Kharagpur LAN Network

The modelling approach is applied on a segment IIT Kharagpur LAN (IIT-KGP-LAN) layout to evaluate reliability expressions for all node pairs. A brief introduction to the LAN layout taken from (Goyal, 2006) is presented below.

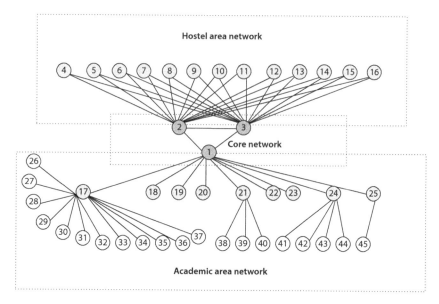

Figure 7.1 A Segment of IIT Kharagpur LAN Layout existed in the Year 2006.

IIT Kharagpur campus is spread over a large area of about 2100 acres. It can broadly be divided into three areas: a) Academic, b) Hostels and c) Faculty/ Staff residential area. The first two areas were very well connected by the LAN. Connectivity to rest of the part was available only through dial up connections to different servers. A segment of the IIT LAN, acting as backbone for connecting academic area and hostels, is taken in the present analysis.

As shown in Figure 7.1, the network segment taken in this analysis consists of 45 nodes. There are basically three types of nodes in this layout and are named as: a) *Foundation Core Switches* (FCSW), b) Distribution Switches (DSW) and c) *Access Switches* (ASW). The network has three foundation cores, N1, N2 and N3, respectively (nodes 1, 2 and 3 in the Figure 7.1). These foundation cores are connected with each other using full mesh topology. The foundation core node N1 acts as the centre node of the network and is connected to different applications servers, emails servers, and different internet connections through firewall. However, these servers/ connections are not considered in present analysis. The distribution switches in academic area (node 17 to 25) are located in different departments of the institute. These are directly connected to node N1 using tree topology. Remaining two foundation cores are called Hostel cores as both of the nodes are connected to each distribution switch (node 4 to 16) located in hostels. All the distribution switches are further connected to access switches (node 26 to 45), located at different laboratories in the academic area and different sections of the hostels, using tree topology. These access switches are then connected to hubs, which are further connected to computers. This whole network provides connectivity to nearly 10,000 computers.

Only foundation cores, distribution/access switches provided for different departments, distribution switches provided for hostels are considered in present analysis. A brief description of this IIT-KGP-LAN is given in Table 7.1. Rest of the network is connected to this network using tree topology and it can be included in the analysis without much effort, which is discussed later. Further, the reliability of each link was assumed as 0.9, otherwise, it entails an exhaustive reliability data analysis to ascertain the reliability of each link, which is not the notion of this case study.

7.1.1   k-Terminal and Global Reliability Evaluation for Hostel Area of IIT Kharagpur LAN

The k-and g-terminal reliability expressions for Figure 7.2 have been evaluated using the k-trees (k- cutsets), and spanning trees (g- cutsets) as an input to (Chaturvedi & Misra, 2002) method. The final results of the k-, and g-terminal reliability for hostel area of IIT-KGP-LAN are shown in Table 7.2 on the basis of number of terms. A comparison of results of the number of k-nodes with k-trees (k-cutsets) is shown in Figure 7.3, which clearly indicatess that the number of k-trees exponentially increase as the number of k-nodes are increased, whereas the number of k-cutsets are increasing very slightly with increase in number of k-nodes and it appears to be constant for the network having large number of k-nodes. The resultant all terminal reliability for hostel area of IIT-KGP-LAN was estimated to = 0.868 745 813.

7.1.2   All Terminal Reliability Evaluation for Academic Area of LAN

The Academic area network is a *star* connected network, therefore its all terminal reliability is equal to multiplication of reliability of its links. With 29 links, its reliability becomes $0.9^{29} = 0.047\ 101\ 287$.

7.1.3   All Terminal Reliability Evaluation for IIT Kharagpur LAN Network

The two networks for Hostel and Academic area do not have any common link therefore ATR expressions of these two networks are independent of each other and multiplying the two all terminal reliability values gives complete network as shown in Figure 7.1 and its all terminal reliability = 0.040 919 046.

Table 7.1 Description of nodes in Figure 7.1.

Node#	Name	Node#	Name
1	Academic Core	24	Library DSW
2	Hostel Core – 1	25	Biotechnology ASW
3	Hostel Core – 2	26	Physics & Meteorology Dept. ASW
4	JCB Hall DSW	27	Chemistry ASW
5	LLR Hall DSW	28	Geology & Geophysics ASW
6	VS Hall DSW	29	Humanities & Social Sciences ASW
7	HB Hall DSW	30	Materials Science ASW
8	BCR Hall DSW	31	Mathematics ASW
9	RK Hall DSW	32	Medical Science & Technology ASW
10	RP Hall DSW	33	Metallurgical & Materials ASW
11	Nehru Hall DSW	34	Mining ASW
12	Azad Hall DSW	35	Rubber Technology Center ASW
13	Patel Hall DSW	36	Architecture & Regional Planning ASW
14	MBM/SN Hall DSW	37	Industrial Engg. & Management ASW
15	IG/MT Hall DSW	38	Civil Dept. ASW
16	MS Hall DSW	39	V G School of Management ASW
17	Academic DSW	40	Information Technology ASW
18	Computer Science Dept. DSW	41	Reliability Engineering Center ASW
19	Electronics and Comm. Dept. DSW	42	Ocean Engg. & Naval Dept. ASW
20	Electrical Dept. DSW	43	Aerospace Engineering ASW
21	Mechanical Dept. DSW	44	Cryogenic Dept. ASW
22	Chemical Dept. DSW	45	Rural Development Center ASW
23	Agriculture and Food Dept. ASW		

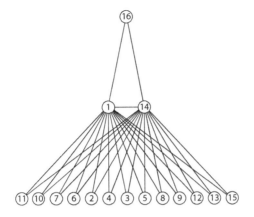

Figure 7.2 Layout of hostel area of IIT Kharagpur LAN.

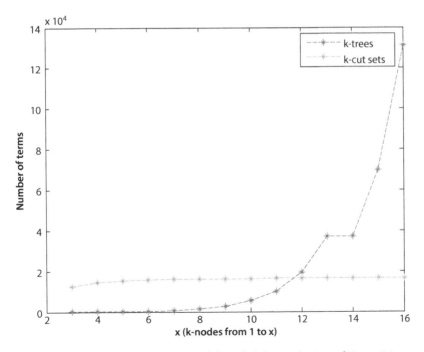

Figure 7.3 Plot of number of terms required for Reliability Evaluation of Figure 7.1.

Table 7.2 Computational results for k-, and g-terminal reliability of hostel area IIT-KGP-LAN network shown in Figure 7.2.

Fig. #	Set of k nodes	Number of k-trees	Number of k-terminal cutsets	Reliability for p = 0.9
1	{1, 2, 3}	42	12 290	0.980100 000
2	{1, 2, 3, 4}	94	14 339	0.970299 000
3	{1, 2, 3, 4, 5}	194	15 364	0.960596 010
4	{1, 2, 3, 4, 5, 6}	386	15 877	0.950990 050
5	{1, 2, 3, 4, 5, 6, 7}	754	16 134	0.941480 149
6	{1, 2, 3, 4, 5, 6, 7, 8}	1 458	16 263	0.932065 348
7	{1, 2, 3, 4, 5, 6, 7, 8, 9}	2 802	16 328	0.922744 694
8	{1, 2, 3, 4, 5, 6, 7, 8, 9, 10}	5 362	16 361	0.913517 247
9	{1, 2, 3, 4, 5, 6, 7, 8, 9, 10, 11}	10 226	16 378	0.904382 075
10	{1, 2, 3, 4, 5, 6, 7, 8, 9, 10, 11, 12}	19 442	16 387	0.895338 254
11	{1, 2, 3, 4, 5, 6, 7, 8, 9, 10, 11, 12,13}	36 850	16 392	0.886384 872
12	{1, 2, 3, 4, 5, 6, 7, 8, 9, 10, 11, 12, 13, 14}	36 864	16 396	0.886384 872
13	{1, 2, 3, 4, 5, 6, 7, 8, 9, 10, 11, 12, 13, 14, 15}	69 632	16 397	0.877521 023
14	{1, 2, 3, 4, 5, 6, 7, 8, 9, 10, 11, 12, 13, 14, 15, 16}	131 072	16 398	0.868745 813

7.2   Case Study-II: Real-Type of Large Size Unsaturated Water Distribution Networks

The computation of reliability of a water distribution network requires enumerating various combinations of pipelines linking the source with all the demand nodes. Consider, a typical case network of 17-node 21-link (Figure 7.4 (a) (Kansal & Devi, 2007)), (Mishra & Chaturvedi, 2009) unsaturated real-type water distribution network (WDN) represented in Figure 7.4. In this network, node '1' is a supply and all others are demand nodes. The nodes are connected through '21' links. All nodes in this network are important as these represent either supply or demand nodes. For the system to be reliable, no node should remain to be isolated. Table 7.3 represents the connection (node-links) matrix of the network. Here the objective is to determine the reliability in terms of connectivity.

In order to find the system reliability, first step is to identify all the minimal global cutsets of the network. For this purpose, the network is analyzed by the procedure for the generation of *g*-minimal cutsets, which for this WDN comes out to be 400. It may be noticed that the number of all spanning trees generated (Kansal & Kumar, 2000) for the same network was 3381, which is very large as compare to minimal global cutsets. After the enumeration of all the minimal global cutsets, if the probability of success for each link is assumed to be 0.9 (or probability of failure of each link is 0.1), then the exact reliability of the network is found to be 0.836 104 945 452.

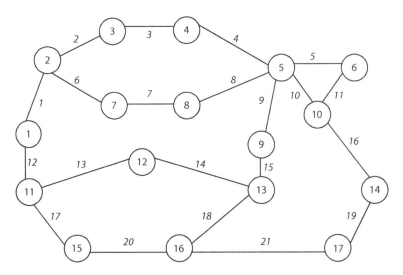

Figure 7.4 A case network of 17 Node 21 Link WDN.

Table 7.3 Node link matrix of seventeen nodes unsaturated network.

From node	To Node																
	1	2	3	4	5	6	7	8	9	10	11	12	13	14	15	16	17
1	-	1	-	-	-	-	-	-	-	-	12	-	-	-	-	-	-
2	1	-	2	-	-	-	6	-	-	-	-	-	-	-	-	-	-
3	-	2	-	3	-	-	-	-	-	-	-	-	-	-	-	-	-
4	-	-	3	-	4	-	-	-	-	-	-	-	-	-	-	-	-
5	-	-	-	-	-	5	-	8	9	10	-	-	-	-	-	-	-
6	-	-	-	-	5	-	-	-	-	11	-	-	-	-	-	-	-
7	-	6	-	-	-	-	-	7	-	-	-	-	-	-	-	-	-
8	-	-	-	-	8	-	7	-	-	-	-	-	-	-	-	-	-
9	-	-	-	-	9	-	-	-	-	-	-	-	15	-	-	-	-
10	-	-	-	-	10	11	-	-	-	-	-	-	-	16	-	-	-
11	12	-	-	-	-	-	-	-	-	-	-	13	-	-	17	-	-
12	-	-	-	-	-	-	-	-	-	-	13	-	14	-	-	-	-
13	-	-	-	-	-	-	-	-	15	-	-	14	-	-	-	18	-
14	-	-	-	-	-	-	-	-	-	16	-	-	-	-	-	-	19
15	-	-	-	-	-	-	-	-	-	-	17	-	-	-	-	20	-
16	-	-	-	-	-	-	-	-	-	-	-	-	18	-	20	-	21
17	-	-	-	-	-	-	-	-	-	-	-	-	-	19	-	21	-

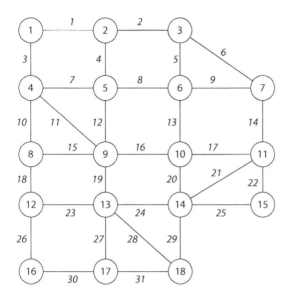

Figure 7.5 A case network of 18 Node 31 Link WDN.

As a second case we consider a large size WDN of a planned city. The network presented in Figure 7.5 consists of 18 nodes connected via 31 links (Figure 7.4 (b) (Kansal & Devi, 2007)). The number of minimal global cutsets for this WDN comes out to be 1237, which is still very less as compare to the number of all spanning trees and the exact reliability of the network is found to be 0.959 441 084 191.

The global minimal cuts are obtained using the program and reliability of the network is obtained by using HM-2 (i.e., nmTst3.m). Following are the steps to run the program for Figure 7.5:

```
>> genCutset
adjMatdataFile(withpath)?:18N31La.m
SourceNode No.? (Assign Highest Number):18
TotalBranch :?:31
FOR OUTPUT
Please enter Output file with full path:18N31La_Out.m
Evaluating Cuts for g-Terminal Reliability
>> nmTst3
Please enter pathSet(BranchWise)file with full dir path:18N31La_out.m
Branches in the Net:?31
Nodes in the Net:?18
Reliability of single branch:?0.1
FOR OUTPUT
```

Please enter Output file with full path:18N31La_outHM2.m
t = 1.003797559706168e+03
SystemRel =0.04055891581, Total FunCall=10080129
total disjoint paths= 449794
>> 1-sysRel
ans = 0.959441084191438

References

Chaturvedi, S.K. & Misra, K.B., 2002. A Hybrid Method to Evaluate Reliability of Complex Networks. *International Journal of Quality and Reliability Management*, Vol. 19(8/9), pp.1098–1112.

Goyal, N.K., 2006. *On Some Aspects of Reliability Analysis and Design of Communication Networks*. Ph.D. Thesis. IIT, Kharagpur (India).

Kansal, M.L. & Devi, S., 2007. An Improved Algorithm for Connectivity Analysis of Distribution Networks. *Reliability Engineering and System Safety*, Vol. 92(10), pp.1295–1302.

Kansal, M.L. & Kumar, A., 2000. Computer Aided Reliability Analysis of Water Distribution Networks. *International Journal of Modellimg & Simulation*, 20(3), pp.264–273.

Mishra, R. & Chaturvedi, S.K., 2009. A Cutsets based Unified Framework to Evaluate Network Reliability Measures. *IEEE Transaction on Reliability*, Vol. 56(4), pp.658–666.

Mishra, R. & Chaturvedi, S.K., 2009. Comments on "An Improved Algorithm for Connectivity Analysis of Distribution Networks" [Reliability Engg System Safety 2007;92(10):1295–1302]. *Reliability Engineering & System Safety*, 94(3), p.783.

Epilogue

The present text was aimed at providing modelling and analysis techniques for the evaluation of reliability measures (2-terminal, all-terminal, k-terminal reliability) for systems whose structure can be described in the form of a probabilistic graph. The techniques described in this text are used to look at networks of tens or hundreds of nodes and could said to be based on the exhaustive search algorithms intended to provide information on the network connectivity, dependability, and vulnerability-qualitatively or quantitatively, and are precursor to furthering the area of network reliability. The challenge is to make such algorithms to cope up with networks of larger dimensions, by exploiting new and more compact data structures and their handing thereof, or even to explore the possibility of approximations (Bounds on network reliability).

Many complex physical, technological, social, biological, and economical systems of today's real world or even the ubiquitous internet can be represented in the form of a gigantic network graph and can be characterized by a set of nodes connected by directed or undirected arcs. The nodes then represent the entities of the system and the arcs represent the relational links among the entities. The node entities are homogeneous/heterogeneous, static/dynamic, and unpredictable whereas the edges manifolds to be wired/wireless, and fixed/arbitrary. In some networks (e.g., mobile networks), the nodes are constantly in motion and/or operate on limited power, and links can be obstructed by intervening objects resulting into an intermittent connectivity. The complexity of such systems can reach millions or even billions of vertices. With the appearance of networks of such colossal orders and characteristics, a completely new field of research has emerged to study the statistical properties of these huge networks, together with the study of their robustness to random failures, errors and attacks.

These changes of scale necessitate and force the corresponding changes in modelling and analysis approaches. Besides, the growing dependence of our modern society on technological systems and information networks also demand a high degree of reliability of such networks. For example, the majority of communication applications from mobile conversations to credit card transactions assume the high level of reliability/availability. Therefore, the degree to which the system is capable of providing the required operation needs to be quantitatively assessed by defining proper measurable quantities. Additionally, the quantitative assessment of such measures becomes essential in their design, planning, implementation, validation, manufacturing, and field operations. In this context, simply scaling-up of the approaches dealt in this book and many of the questions answered would not be feasible.

To tackle new scenarios in this area, the focus is directed towards to understand and use of the large-scale statistical properties of a system graph with the aim of predicting the behaviour of network on the basis of measured structural properties and the local rules governing individual nodes. For instance, if we consider Internet as a very large social connection network, then one of its amazing properties is so-called small world property, i.e., the shortest path length leading from one node to another would be, on the average, very small, about 5-6. This is provided by the fact that the network node in-degrees (measured by the number of edges incident to them) have so-called heavy tail distribution. Simply speaking, there are a relatively small number of very heavy "popular" nodes with large number of edges and majority of nodes with relative small weight.

Ad hoc networking is another emerging technology, which allow devices to establish communication anytime and anywhere without the aid of a centralized infrastructure, due to its flexibility of rapid deployment in a given geographical region and malleable dynamic topology with multi-hop. Apart from the characteristics like ever changing topology, scalability, mobility, routing protocols, power management, heterogeneity, bandwidth management, interoperability etc. posing challenges to analysts and designers, it is yet to be seen that what other types of reliability metric, modelling, and analysis approach would be appropriate.

Quite recently, it has become clear for many of the real networks of present era (e.g., wireless networks) that their complex structure is a natural consequence of the principles of their evolution and of their growth where random graph models of *Erdős-Rényi* (Erdős & Rényi , 1959) and graph theory results based on this would not be feasible at all. The alternative could be Geometric Random Graph (GRG) (Penrose, 2003) or Waxman (Waxman, 1988) model or evolving graph models as they are capable of capturing the information on topology of the present day's dynamic networks (Albert & Barabasi, Jan 2002), (Hekemat & Mieghem, 2003), (Pellegrini et al., 2007)

Apart from the modelling and analysis issues, there is another area wide open is-Design of such networks with some chosen performance(s) criteria-which is affected by various factors such as reliability, cost, choices of link, network capacity, available technologies et. Last but not the least, field of network reliability is still wide open for novel researches and this quest of excellence is continued...

References

Albert, R. & Barabasi, A.L., Jan 2002. Statistical Mechanics of Complex Networks. *Review of Modern Physics*, Vol. 74.

Erdős , P. & Rényi , A., 1959. On Random Graphs. I. *Publicationes Mathematicae*, 6, pp.290–297.

Hekemat, R. & Mieghem, P.V., 2003. Degree Distribution and Hopcount in Wireless Adhoc Networks. In *Proceedings of IEEE ICON 2003.*, 2003.

Pellegrini, F.D., MIorandi, D., Carreras, I. & Imirich, C., 2007. A graph based model for Disconnected Adhoc Networks. In *International Conference on Computer Communication,IEEE.*, 2007.

Penrose, M., 2003. *Random Geometric Graphs (Oxford Studies in Probability, 5).* New York: Oxford University Press.

Waxman, B.M., 1988. Routing of multipoint connections. *IEEE Journal on Selected Areas in Communications*, 6(9), pp.1617–1622.

Bibliography

Inclusion Exclusion(2-Terminal)

Buzacott, J. A. (1987). Node Partition Formula for Directed Graph Reliability. *Networks, 17*, pp.227–240.

Buzacott, J. A., & Chang, J. S. K. (Dec 1984). Cut- Set Intersections and Node Partitions. *IEEE Transactions on Reliability, R-33*(5), pp.385–389.

Kim, Y. H., Case, K. E., & Ghare, P. M. (1972). A Method for Computing Complex System Reliability. *IEEE Transactions on Reliability, R-21*, pp.215–219.

Lin, P. M., Leon, B. J., & Huang, T. C. (1976). A New Algorithm for Symbolic System Reliability Analysis. *IEEE Transactions of Reliability, R-25*.

Locks, M. O. (Dec 1985). Recent Developments in Computing of System Reliability. *IEEE Transactions on Reliability, R-34*(N5), pp.425–435.

Inclusion Exclusion(g-Terminal)

Buzacott, J. A. (1987). Node Partition Formula for Directed Graph Reliability. *Networks, 17*, pp. 227–240.

Buzacott, J. A., & Chang, J. S. K. (Dec 1984). Cut- Set Intersections and Node Partitions. *IEEE Transactions on Reliability, R-33*(5), pp.385–389.

Calculation of Bounds(2-Terminal)

Beichelt, F., & Spross, L. (1989). Bounds on the Reliability of Binary Coherent Systems. *IEEE Transactions on Reliability, Vol. 38*(4), pp.425–427.

Brecht, T. B., & Colbourn, C. J. (1986). Improving Reliability Bounds in Computer Networks. *Networks, Vol.16*, pp.369–380.

Hsieh, Y. C. (Sep 2003). New Reliability Bounds for Coherent Systems. *Journal of the Operational Research Society, Vol. 54*(9, Part Special Issue: Modelling Organizational Knowledge), pp. 995–1001.

Sebastio, S., Trivedi, K. S., Wang, D., & Yin, X. (Nov 2014). Fast Computation of Bounds for Two Terminal Network Reliability. *European Journal of Operational Research, Vol. 238*(3), pp.810–823.

Calculation of Bounds(k-Terminal)

Brecht, T. B., & Colbourn, C. J. (1986). Improving Reliability Bounds in Computer Networks. *Networks, Vol.16*, pp.369–380.

Calculation of Bounds(g-Terminal)

Brecht, T. B., & Colbourn, C. J. (1986). Improving Reliability Bounds in Computer Networks. *Networks, Vol.16*, pp.369–380.

Provan, J. S. (1986). Bounds on the Reliability of Networks. *IEEE Transactions on Reliability, Vol. 35*(3), pp.260–268.

Monte Carlo(2-Terminal)

Botev, Z. I., L'Ecuyer, P., Rubino, G., Simard, R., & Tuffin, B. (2013). Static Network Reliability Estimation via Generalized Splitting. *INFORMS Journal on Computing, Vol. 25*, pp.56–71.

Cancela, H., L'Ecuyer, P., Lee, M., Rubino, G., & Tuffin, B. (2010). *Analysis and Improvements of Path- Based methods for Monte Carlo Reliability Evaluation of Static Models.* Paper presented at the Simulation methods for reliability and availability of complex systems.

Easton, M. C., & Wong, C. K. (1980). Sequential Destruction Method for Monte Carlo Evaluation of System Reliability. *IEEE Transactions on Reliability, R - 29,* pp. 27–32.

Hui, K. P., Bean, N. G., Kraetzl, M., & Kroese, D. (2003). *Network Reliability Estimation using the Tree Cut and Merge Algorithm with Importance Sampling.* Paper presented at the Proceedings of the Fourth International Workshop on Design of Reliable Communication Networks (DRCN 2003).

Lin, J. Y., & Donaghev, C. E. (1993). *Monte Carlo Simulation to Determine Minimal Cut Sets and System Reliability.* Paper presented at the Proceedings of the 1993 Annual Reliability and Maintainability Symposium, Atlanta, GA, USA.

Sanseverino, C. M. R., & Moreno, J. A. (2002). Reliability evaluation using Monte Carlo simulation and support vector machine. *Computational Science- ICCS 2002*, pp.147–155.

Zenklusen, R., & Laumanns, M. (2011). High Confidence Estimation of Small S-T Reliabilities in Directed Acyclic Networks. *Networks, Vol. 57*, pp.376–388.

Monte Carlo(k-Terminal)

Adjabi, S., & Bouchama, K. (2011). K- Terminal Reliability evaluation of a tele-communications network represented by a discrete and dynamic model. *International Journal of Operations Research(IJOR), Vol. 8*(3), pp. 34–43.

Cancela, H., & Khadiri, M. E. (1998). Series- parallel reductions in Monte Carlo network- reliability evaluation. *IEEE Transactions on Reliability, Vol. 47*(2), pp.159–164.

Cancela, H., & Khadiri, M. E. (2003). The Recursive Variance-Reduction Simulation Algorithm for Network Reliability Evaluation. *IEEE Transactions on Reliability, Vol. 52*, pp.207–212.

Elperin, T., Gertsbakh, I., & Lemonosov, M. (1991). Estimation of Network Reliability using Graph Evolution Models. *IEEE Transactions on Reliability, Vol. 40*, pp.572–581.

Hui, K. P., Bean, N. G., Kraetzl, M., & Kroese, D. (2003). *Network Reliability Estimation using the Tree Cut and Merge Algorithm with Importance Sampling.* Paper presented at the Proceedings of the Fourth International Workshop on Design of Reliable Communication Networks (DRCN 2003).

Monte Carlo(g-Terminal)

Hui, K. P., Bean, N. G., Kraetzl, M., & Kroese, D. (2003). *Network Reliability Estimation using the Tree Cut and Merge Algorithm with Importance Sampling.* Paper presented at the Proceedings of the Fourth International Workshop on Design of Reliable Communication Networks (DRCN 2003).

Domination Theory(2-Terminal)

Locks, M. O. (Dec 1985). Recent Developments in Computing of System Reliability. *IEEE Transactions on Reliability, R-34*(N5), pp. 425–435.

Willie, R. R. (1980). A Theorem Concerning Cyclic Directed Graphs with Applications to Network Reliability. *Networks, Vol. 10*, pp. 71–78.

SDP(2-Terminal)

Abraham, J. A. (1979). An Improved Algorithm for Network Reliability. *IEEE Transaction on Reliability,, Vol. R-28*(1),pp. 58–61.

Beichelt, F., & Spross, L. (Apr 1987). An Improved Abraham - Method for Generating Disjoint Sums. *IEEE Transactions on Reliability, R- 36*(1), pp.70-74.

Chatelet, E., Dutuit, Y., Rauzy, A., & Bouhoufani, T. (1999). An optimized procedure to generate sums of disjoint products. *Reliability Engineering & System Safety, Vol. 65*(3), pp.289–294.

Chaturvedi, S. K., & Misra, K. B. (2002a). An Efficient Multi-Variable Inversion Algorithm for Reliability Evaluation of Complex Systems using Path sets. *International Journal of Reliability, Quality and Safety Engineering, Vol. 9*(3), pp. 237–259.

Chaturvedi, S. K., & Misra, K. B. (2002b). A Hybrid Method to Evaluate Reliability of Complex Networks. *International Journal of Quality and Reliability Management, Vol. 19*(8/9), pp.1098–1112.

Heidtmann, K. D. (1989). Smaller Sums of Disjoint Products by Sub Product Inversion. *IEEE Transaction on Reliability, Vol. R-38*(3), pp.305–311.

Jane, C. C., & Yuan, J. (2001). A Sum of Disjoint Products Algorithm for Reliability Evaluation of Flow Networks. *European Journal of Operational Research, Vol. 131*, pp.664–675.

Locks, M. O. (Dec 1985). Recent Developments in Computing of System Reliability. *IEEE Transactions on Reliability, R-34*(N5), pp.425–435.

Locks, M. O. (Oct 1987). A Minimizing Algorithm for Sum of Disjoint Products. *IEEE Transactions on Reliability, R- 36*(4), pp. 445–453.

Luo, T., & Trivedi, K. S. (1998a). An Improved Algorithm for Coherent Systems Reliability. *IEEE Transaction on Reliability, Vol R-47*(1), pp 73–78.

Luo, T., & Trivedi, K. S. (1998b). *An Improved Multiple Variable Inversion Algorithm for Reliability Calculation.* Paper presented at the 10th Intern. Conf. Tools, Palma de Mallorca, Spain, Sept 1998 in: Puigjaner R., Savino N.N., Serra B. (eds.), Computer Performance Evaluation, Modelling Techniques and Tools.

Misra, R., & Chaturvedi, S. K. (2009). A Cutsets based Unified Framework to Evaluate Network Reliability Measures. *IEEE Transaction on Reliability, Vol. 58*(4), pp.658–666.

Rai, S., Veeraraghavan, M., & Trivedi, K. S. (1995). A Survey of Efficient Reliability Computation using Disjoint Products Approaach. *Networks, Vol. 25*, pp. 147–163.

Soh, S., & Rai, S. (1991). CAREL: Computer Aided Reliability Evaluator for Distributed Computing Networks,. *IEEE Transaction on parallel and Distributed Systems, Vol.2*(2), pp.199–213.

Veeraraghavan, & Trivedi, K. S. (Aug 1991). An Improved Algorithm for the Symbolic Reliability Analysis of Networks. *IEEE Transactions on Reliability, Vol. 40*(3), pp. 347–358.

Xing, J., Feng, C., Qian, X., & Dai, P. (2012). *A Simple Algorithm for Sum of Disjoint Products*. Paper presented at the Reliability and Maintainability Symposium (RAMS), Proceedings- Annual. IEEE.

Yeh, W. C. (2015). An Improved Sum-of-Disjoint products Technique for Symbolic Multi State Flow Network Reliability. *IEEE Transactions on Reliability, Vol. 64*(4), pp.1185–1193.

Yeh, W. C. (Feb2007). An improved sum-of-disjoint-products technique for the symbolic network reliability analysis with known minimal paths. *Reliability Engineering & System Safety, Vol. 92*(2), pp.260–268.

Zhao, Lian-Chang, & Jun-Chen, X. (1995). An Efficient Minimizing Algorithm for sum of disjoint products. *Microelectronics Reliability, Vol. 35*(8), pp.1157–1162.

Zuo, M. J., Tian, Z., & Huang, H. Z. (2007). An efficient method for reliability evaluation of multistate networks given all minimal path vectors. *IIE Transactions, Vol.39*(8),pp. 811–817.

SDP(k-Terminal)

Chaturvedi, S. K., & Misra, K. B. (2002). A Hybrid Method to Evaluate Reliability of Complex Networks. *International Journal of Quality and Reliability Management, Vol. 19*(8/9), pp.1098–1112.

Misra, R., & Chaturvedi, S. K. (2009). A Cutsets based Unified Framework to Evaluate Network Reliability Measures. *IEEE Transaction on Reliability, Vol. 58*(4), pp.658–666.

SDP(g-Terminal)

Chaturvedi, S. K., & Misra, K. B. (2002). A Hybrid Method to Evaluate Reliability of Complex Networks. *International Journal of Quality and Reliability Management, Vol. 19*(8/9), pp.1098–1112.

Misra, R., & Chaturvedi, S. K. (2009). A Cutsets based Unified Framework to Evaluate Network Reliability Measures. *IEEE Transaction on Reliability, Vol. 58*(4), pp.658–666.

State Enumeration(2-Terminal)

Corinne, L., & Manouvrier, J. F. (1999). Exact Methods to Compute Network Reliability. *Statistical and Probabilistic Models in Reliability*, pp.279–294.

Factoring(2-Terminal)

Choi, M. S., & Jun, C. H. (1995). Some Variants of Polygon- to- Chain Reductions in evaluating Reliability of Undirected Network. *Microelectronics and Reliability, Vol. 35*(1), pp.1–11.

Moskowitz, F. (1958). The Analysis of Redundancy Networks. *AIEE Transactions on Communication Electronics, Vol. 39*, pp.627–632.

Nakazawa, H. (1976). Bayesian Decomposition Method for Computing Reliability of an Oriented Network. *IEEE Transactions on Reliability, R- 25*, pp.77–80.

Rebaiaia, M. L., & Daoud, A. K. (2013). A new Algorithm for Generating Minimal Cutsets in Non Trivial Network. *AASRI Procedia, Science Direct, Elsevier, Vol. 5*, pp.67–76.

Rebaiaia, M. L., Daoud, A. K., & Merlano, A. (November 2009). A Practical Algorithm for Network Reliability evaluation based on the Factoring Theorem- A Case study of a Generic Radio Communication Network. *Journal of Quality, Vol. 16*(5), pp.23–32.

Rosenthal, A. (1977). Computing the Reliability of Complex Networks. *SIAMJ. Appl.Math., Vol. 32*, pp.384–393.

Theolougou, O. R., & Carlier, J. G. (1991). Factoring and Reduction for Networks with Imperfect Vertices. *IEEE Transactions on Reliability, Vol. 40*(2), pp.210–217.

Wang, W., & Zhang, H. (1997). The methods of Reduction in Networks Reliability Computing. *Microelectron Relioability, Vol. 37*(3), pp.461–465.

Factoring(k-Terminal)

Satyanarayana, A. (1982). A Unified formula for Analysis of some Network Reliability problems. *IEEE Transactions on Reliability, R-31*, pp.23–32.

Wood, R. K. (1985). A Factoring Algorithm using Polygon - to- Chain Reductions for computing K- terminal Network Reliability. *Networks, Vol. 15*, pp.173–190.

Factoring(g-Terminal)

Choi, M. S., & Jun, C. H. (1995). Some Variants of Polygon- to- Chain Reductions in evaluating Reliability of Undirected Network. *Microelectronics and Reliability, Vol. 35*(1), pp.1–11.

Satyanarayana, A., & Chang, M. (1983). Network Reliability and the Factoring Theorem. *Networks, Vol. 13*, pp.107–120.

Theolougou, O. R., & Carlier, J. G. (1991). Factoring and Reduction for Networks with Imperfect Vertices. *IEEE Transactions on Reliability, Vol. 40*(2), pp.210–217.

Wang, W., & Zhang, H. (1997). The methods of Reduction in Networks Reliability Computing. *Microelectron Relioability, Vol. 37*(3), pp.461–465.

Transformation Method(2-Terminal)

Gadani, J. P. (1981). System Effectiveness Evaluation Using Star and Delta Transformations. *IEEE Transactions on Reliability, Vol. 30*(1), pp.43–47.

Gadani, J. P., & Misra, K. B. (1982). Quadrilateral Star Transformation: an Aid for Reliability Evaluation of Large Complex Systems. *IEEE Transaction on Reliability, Vol. R-31*(1), pp.49–59.

Ramamoorty, M., & Balgopal. (May 1970). Block Diagram Approach to Power System Reliability, Power Apparatus and Systems. *IEEE Transactions on Power Apparatus and Systems, Vol. PAS- 89*(5), pp.802–811.

Rosenthal, A., & Frisque, A. D. (1977). Transformations for Simplifying Network Reliability Calculations. *Networks, Vol. 7*, pp. 97–111.

Wang, S. D., & Sun, C. H. (1996). Transformations of star-delta and delta-star reliability networks. *IEEE Transactions on Reliability, Vol. 45*(1), pp.120–126.

Topological Method(2-Terminal)

Aggarwal, A., & Satyanarayan, A. (1984). An (O/E) Time Algorithm for Computing the Reliability of a Class of Directed Networks *Operations Research,, Vol. 32*, pp.493–517.

Misra, K. B. (1970). An Algorithm for Reliability Evaluation of Redundant Networks. *IEEE Transaction on Reliability,, Vol. R-19*(4), pp.146–151.

Misra, K. B., & Rao, T. S. M. (1970). Reliability Analysis of Redundant Networks Using Flow Graphs. *IEEE Transaction on Reliability, Vol. R-19*(1), pp.19–24.

Resende, L. I. P. (Dec 1988). Implementation of a Factoring Algorithm for Reliability Evaluation of Undirected Networks. *IEEE Transactions on Reliability, Vol. R- 37*(5), pp.462–468.

Satyanarayan, A., & Prabhakar, A. (1978). New Topological Formula and Rapid Algorithm for Reliability Analysis of Complex Networks. *IEEE Transaction on Reliability, Vol. R-27*(2), pp.82–100.

Topological Method(k-Terminal)

Satyanarayana, A. (1982). A Unified formula for Analysis of some Network Reliability problems. *IEEE Transactions on Reliability, R-31*, pp.23–32.

BDD/OBDD/ROBDD(2-Terminal)

Chang, Y. R., Amari, S. V., & Kuo, S. Y. (2004). Computing System Failure Frequencies and Reliability Importance Measures using OBDD. *IEEE Transactions on Computers, Vol. 53*(1), pp.54–68.

Kuo, S., Lu, S. K., & Yeh, F. M. (1999). Determining Terminal Pair Reliability based on Edge Expansion Diagrams using OBDD. *IEEE Transactions on Reliability, Vol. 48*(3), pp.234–246.

Rauzy, A. (2003). A New Methodology to Handle Boolean Models with Loops. *IEEE Transactions on Reliability, Vol. 52*, pp.96–105.

Rebaiaia, M. L., & Daoud, A. K. (2013). Network Reliability Evaluation and Optimization Methods, Algorithms and Software Tools. *CIRRELT*.

Yeh, F. M., Lu, S. K., & Kuo, S. Y. (2002). OBDD Based evaluation of K- Terminal Network Reliability. *IEEE Transactions on Reliability, Vol. 51*, pp.443–451.

BDD/OBDD/ROBDD(k-Terminal)

Rebaiaia, M. L., & Daoud, A. K. (2012). *A Contribution for computing the Reliability of Networks using Reduced Binary Decision Diagrams.* Paper presented at the the 9th International Conference on Modeling, Optimization and Simulation (MOSIM2012), Bordeaux, France.

Yeh, F. M., Lin, H. Y., & Kuo, S. Y. (2002). *Analysing Network Reliability with Imperfect Nodes using OBDD.* Paper presented at the Proceedings of the 2002 Pacific Rim International Symposium on Dependable Computing (PRDC'02).

Index

Also of Interest

Check out these published and forthcoming titles in the Performability Engineering Series

Machine Tool Reliability
By Bhupesh Kumar Lad, Divya Shrivastava and Makarand S. Kulkarni
Published 2016. ISBN 978-1-119-03860-3

Binary Decision Diagrams and Extensions for Systems Reliability Analysis
By Suprasad Amari and Liudong Xing
Published 2015. ISBN 978-1-118-54937-7

Quantitative Assessments of Distributed Systems
Methodologies and Techniques
By Dario Bruneo and Salvatore Distefano
Published 2015. ISBN 978-1-118-59521-3

Fundamentals of Reliability Engineering
By Indra Gunawan
Published 2014. ISBN 978-1-118-54956-8

Building Dependable Distributed Systems
By Wenbing Zhao
Published 2014. ISBN 978-1-118-54943-8